# Muslim Europe or Euro-Islam

# TRANSNATIONAL PERSPECTIVES
## The Middle East and "Others"

*Series Editor*: Nezar AlSayyad

Transnational Perspectives is a joint publication series of the Center for Middle Eastern Studies at the University of California at Berkeley and Lexington Books. It contains edited volumes based on conferences and symposia which were organized by the center as part of its transnational research initiative. Unlike comparative research which focuses on similarities and differences between regions, transnational research examines the socio-spatial connections through which global cartographies are constituted and transformed. It is also an epistemological technique which pays attention to how concepts and discourses are produced within specific geopolitical regions and histories, and which allows knowledge of one region to be used to interrogate another.

Nezar AlSayyad and Manuel Castells, editors
*Muslim Europe or Euro-Islam:*
*Politics, Culture, and Citizenship in the Age of Globalization*, 2002

Ananya Roy and Nezar AlSayyad, editors
*Urban Informality: The Middle East, South Asia, and Latin America in an Era of Liberalization*
(expected 2003)

Irene Bierman and Nasser Rabbat, editors
*Cairo: Making the City Medieval*
(expected 2004)

# Muslim Europe or Euro-Islam

## Politics, Culture, and Citizenship in the Age of Globalization

Edited by

Nezar AlSayyad and Manuel Castells

LEXINGTON BOOKS

A division of
ROWMAN & LITTLEFIELD PUBLISHERS, INC.
*Lanham • Boulder • New York • Toronto • Plymouth, UK*

*To Europe's Muslims.*

LEXINGTON BOOKS

A division of Rowman & Littlefield Publishers, Inc.
A wholly owned subsidiary of The Rowman & Littlefield Publishing Group, Inc.
4501 Forbes Boulevard, Suite 200
Lanham, MD 20706

Estover Road
Plymouth PL6 7PY
United Kingdom

Copublished with the
Center for Middle Eastern Studies (CMES)
University of California at Berkeley
Berkeley, California 94720

British Library Cataloguing in Publication Information Available

**Library of Congress Cataloging-in-Publication Data**

Muslim Europe or Euro-Islam : politics, culture, and citizenship in the age of globalization / edited by Nezar AlSayyad & Manuel Castells.
    p. cm.
  Includes bibliographical references and index.
  ISBN 0-7391-0338-5 (alk. paper)—ISBN 0-7391-0339-3 (pbk. : alk. paper)
    1. Muslims—Europe. 2. Europe—Ethnic relations. 3. Islamic
countries—Relations—Europe. 4. Europe—Relations—Islamic countries.
5. Islam—Europe. I. AlSayyad, Nezar. II. Castells, Manuel.

D1056.2.A7 M87 2001
305.6'97104—dc21

2001050240

Printed in the United States of America

♾️™ The paper used in this publication meets the minimum requirements of American National Standard for Information Sciences—Permanence of Paper for Printed Library Materials, NSI/NISO Z39.48–1992.

# CONTENTS

# PREFACE

This book owes its initial idea to a discussion that Manuel Castells and I had in 1997. As chairs of two research centers that focus on different area studies, the Middle East and Western Europe, we were both interested in the new work that was being done in a variety of disciplines on issues of identity and citizenship. We observed that while issues of identity and citizenship remained at the forefront of concern in our respective areas, the research produced by scholars on these subjects was neither being fully disseminated nor discussed beyond the specialists in each area. This disturbing situation, we concluded, was a by-product of the often-insular nature of area-studies research.

A few months later, the Ford Foundation announced a major initiative entitled "Crossing Borders," designed to encourage collaborative projects by faculty members who were working on similar research questions but in different geographical regions. The Ford Foundation's intent was to redefine the face and scope of area studies for a new century. The Institute of International Studies (IIS) was the designated administrative unit of the Ford initiative in our home institution, the University of California at Berkeley. The IIS grant provided us with the initial funds to convene the symposium "Islam and the Changing Identity of Europe" in late 1998.

We organized the event into three panels that dealt with the themes of Islam in Europe, globalization and citizenship, and the changing nation-state. We asked a distinguished group of scholars from all over the world to give invited papers. The success of the symposium, the many requests we received for drafts of the papers presented, and the willingness of the speakers to revise their papers were our main impetus in putting this book together.

We are very glad that Lexington Books proposed the copublication of a new series entitled "Transnational Perspectives: The Middle East and 'Others'" with the

Center for Middle Eastern Studies at Berkeley. We hope that this book will live up to the premise of the series—the belief that what happens over "here" is always shaped, and hence can only be fully understood, by what happens over "there." However, we recognize that no work on the subject of this book can claim to be either comprehensive or representative. We are not concerned with presenting an exhaustive view, nor with advancing any particular new paradigm. Instead, the contributors to this volume focus on individual case studies or themes. In individual chapters, they ask unfamiliar questions in very familiar sites and vice versa.

There are several institutions and individuals that should be acknowledged. First, we would like to thank the Ford Foundation for taking the initiative to question the future of area studies. We would like to acknowledge the leading roles played by Michael Watts and David Szanton in articulating the Ford Foundation's Crossing Borders Initiative on the Berkeley campus and for funding the symposium. We would also like to thank Jane Turbiner at the Center for Middle Eastern Studies for her able management of the event. At a later stage, Casondra Sobieralski, Madhuri Nandgaonkar, and Sara Saedi all helped with the book project.

Our research assistants, Julie Eakin, Mrinalini Rajagopalan, and earlier in the process, Preeti Chopra, played a very important role in checking out references, finding relevant information, communicating with the authors, and managing the papers. Along with David Moffat, Julie and Mrinalini in particular deserve special credit for the final handling of the manuscript. Thanks are also due to Larry Michalak for helping with the book proposal. At Lexington Books, executive editor Serena Leigh initiated the idea of the series and handled the book in its final stages. We are grateful for both her patience and persistence. Finally, Annabelle Ison and Stuart Chan of Ison Design produced the elegant format of this book. We are grateful for their effort. We hope that our students and colleagues at Berkeley and elsewhere will find this collection intellectually stimulating as well as of use in further research and teaching endeavors.

Nezar AlSayyad
Berkeley, May 2001

# Introduction: Islam and the Changing Identity of Europe

## Nezar AlSayyad and Manuel Castells

Europe has been undergoing profound ideational changes in the era of globalization. This is partially due to the substantial Muslim minority populations which have sprung up in different countries. Five centuries after the expulsion of Muslims and Jews from Spain, Europe is once again becoming a land of Islam—albeit for a minority of the European population. Unstoppable waves of immigrants from Africa, the Middle East, and Asia, attempting to escape poverty and, sometimes, persecution for the promise of a better life for their children—often at the price of losing their own lives—cross the treacherous waters of the Gibraltar strait every day, the Rio Grande of Europe. Within the European context itself there are factors which are beginning to change the way Europe is feeling and thinking about itself and about Islam. These factors range from the changing meaning of state sovereignty to the larger pressures of globalization, and they must be analyzed in the larger context of state and civil society relations in an era of global change.

First, state sovereignty in Europe is now exercised within the broader framework of the European Union (EU) and economic globalization. States historically constituted in the modern age have been characterized, on the one hand, by the control of money and, on the other, by the control of violence. This is starting to change as the European Central Bank redefines economic sovereignty. We also need to consider that one of the fastest-growing European economies at the turn of the century is Turkey. The obvious arguments for its EU membership may overcome the reluctance of European countries in the future, particularly if the Turkish political system cleans up its democratic act. The Muslim populations of the former Yugoslavia may also find their way into an integrated Europe—either by their countries joining it in the long term or by the people joining it through migrant labor in the short term.

Of course, we have to emphasize the control of violence, meaning the army, defense pacts, and the North Atlantic Treaty Organization (NATO). Such arrangements have played a very important role in European history. Without considering this factor, we cannot make serious claims, even with a French ideology, for instance, that France still remains different, because even France obeys the same rules as everyone else in NATO. If we add to this the parallel and related decentralization of responsibilities to local and regional authorities, we can see how the nation-state in Europe today has lost considerable importance. (For example, in Spain only about 75 percent of legislation today comes from the national government; what is left needs some form of approval from or compatibility with Brussels-based legislation.)

Second, Europe is increasingly becoming a multiethnic society. This trend is fundamental and irreversible. For example, the German elections of 1997 brought the potential for great change. About three million out of the seven million foreigners who currently live in Germany may now hope to become citizens under the revised legislation that has been agreed upon by the Green Party and the Social Democrats. This new legislation could completely change the political and social landscape of Germany.

The growth of Muslim population is also, and mainly, the result of differential birth rates. In Europe, the native-born population's fertility rate is about one and a half, while the rate for most ethnic populations ranges from two and a half to nearly three, depending upon the country. These rates in fact belong to an already settled population of immigrants whose children, for example, comprise a growing proportion of the British and French population in the last quarter century. More recently they have been joined by generations of citizens of other European countries. And if millions of Muslim Turks, many of them born in Germany, are not German citizens, this is due to the curious German nationality law under which people of German ancestry born in Kazakhstan, with no knowledge of the German language, can have their citizenship recognized more easily than children born in Germany of foreign parents. In demographic terms, the next generation will most likely adopt the patterns of behavior of the population at large. However, Germany, like other European countries, is set to completely change its demographic structure in the next twenty years. Despite those changes, the problem with Europe today is not that it is not multiethnic, but that it does not consider itself multiethnic.

Third, in the midst of the growing uncertainty that Europeans feel about their national identity, there has been an explosion of debates about identities and multinationalities within European society. The growing diversity of the ethnic composition of the European states is the main factor behind these debates. The most typical case here is Spain, which witnessed the end of local terrorism at the end of the century, enhancing the possibility of a vast state achieved through peaceful means. Spanish social peace is evident, and democracy is stable. But suddenly the big question being debated in Spain is: Is there such a thing as Spain? For example, most Catalans feel Spanish and European and Catalan—in various sequential orders, depending on personal history. And the understanding of Basque feelings is a complex subject beyond the scope of analysis here.

Opinion polls indicate that, in principle, people feel French, Spanish, or British—and then European—with different levels of intensity. However, in many countries, national or cultural identities are more complicated. Thus in Scotland, many people feel more Scottish than British, but not necessarily in the same way the English feel British. As for feeling European, most British feel that the continent is still a separate domain regardless of the existence of the Channel Tunnel. The United Kingdom remains special; but even in this case one must recognize the Scottish National Party, which recently won an election with a program for the independence of Scotland that followed exactly the same arguments as Catalonia and Spain. Even the self-proclaimed capital of Europe, Brussels, is built on the shaky ground of identity compromise between Flemish and Walloons. The basic premise of the new European society is to be independent and yet to act in common on many fronts.

If we are to switch to less serious intellectual and political debates and more instrumental ones such as the notion of Padania in Italy, the fragility of national construction becomes even more apparent. At the moment of Italian unification, more than a hundred years ago, only a small portion of the country's population spoke proper Italian as its first language. Although it was not truly Italian, it was decided that Fiorentino (the dialect of Florence, because of its great Renaissance history) should set the standard for Italian. It is this construction that lies at the heart of national identity discourse.

Fourth, national identities are also becoming increasingly amorphous because of the increasing decoupling between the instrumentality of the state (i.e., citizenship) and the ethnic, cultural, and historical roots of identity. And while the French Revolution (and the school of the Third Republic) did an efficient job of creating *le Petit Francais* by quasi-exterminating cultures and languages alien to the Île de France, there has been enough of a resurgence of sub-French identities to provoke the resignation of the extreme nationalist members of the French Socialist government.

However, it is important to realize that the construction of European institutions will remain unstable as long as there is no shared European identity. Until now, European integration has brought considerable economic benefit to most countries. But in case of a major economic crisis (a likely event at some point) it is not clear that, in a democratic political system, demagogic parties or leaders would not convince the majority of citizens in a given country to pull out from major integration. In fact, polls indicate that, given the choice, most German citizens would have kept their beloved Deutschmark, instead of giving it up in exchange for a Euro tainted by Liras and other currencies of lesser values. If and when the whole story of the so-called secret deal between François Mitterrand and Helmut Kohl concerning European unification is revealed, the German public may well react in unpredictable ways. This shows that there is a limit to institutional and economic integration without a culture of sharing in a society that is still without some kind of a common identity. In the long term, the emergence of a European network state and a fully integrated Europe an economy without a European identity (over-layered on national and regional identities) seems to be an unsustainable situation.

Fifth and most important, for those of us who are interested in the study of societies and space in the era of globalization there are some important positions of which we must be mindful. We must be aware that even if there is a "Global culture," an "Islamic culture," or a "European culture," these are cultures that are marked by the control and management of diversity. They are also essentially cultures of dominant groups in which the persistent diversity of the constituent or local subcultures is often a product of globalization itself.[1]

Historically, European identity, as Josep Fontana has shown, was created in opposition to others—who were named "infidels" or "barbarians." In fact, in many cases it was the defense of Christian identity against Islam that set the ground for the existence of so-called European culture.[2] In recent years, the European unification was marked by a reaction against the hegemony of the United States and, for a brief but decisive period, against Japanese and Asian economic competition. Europeans know that they are not American or Asian, and the majority of them seem to not want to be so. Nevertheless, they become confused when asked to define what their "Europeanness" is. The identification with Europe correlates with social class and education: the lower the social status, the less trust people have in the institution.

In this context, multiculturalism and multiethnicity from supposedly non-European origin may become disturbing to many Europeans. When one's identity becomes blurred, it is more difficult to accept the other. And when one's identity feels threatened, it becomes hardened in nonnegotiable ways. Thus, precisely at the time that Europe has had to adapt to the growing presence of Islam among its people, national identities are being deconstructed and reconstructed, both from below and from above.

Another issue involves the connection between this so-called global culture, or universal culture, and space. This is important, for we seem to be heading toward a placeless culture that is created through the increasing interconnectedness of local and national communities, and this coincides with the globalization of images via media networks and the Internet. Here we need to consider the rise of the space of flows as opposed to the space of places, in which organizations, international or otherwise, are connected by flows of information whose logic is largely uncontrolled by any specific local society, but whose impact is likely to shape the lives of these local societies and subcultures. The presumption of cultural and ethnic homogeneity underlying civic, educational, and political institutions cannot be sustained any longer. This is true of Europe as much as it is of the countries of the Muslim world. It follows that this new social landscape has to be explored through research rather than be asserted through ideology. Research is essential because the answers to the many dilemmas raised by these observations appear different for each country, and in some cases for various regions within a given country.

Islam and Europe are two different concepts, one whose origin is seemingly geographic while the other appears religious or cultural in nature. What is it, then, that allows us to engage in their pairing? Although both Europe and Islam are seen as living, historical civilizations with universal intentions, we must ask ourselves if we are being too reductionist when we accept this essentialization. While political reality is often reductionist itself, we have to be careful as we embark on our intellectual endeavor. We must not be synecdochic, as we must not mistake the part for the whole.

The study of Islam has often been the territory of so-called Islamic or Middle Eastern experts. As a field, Middle Eastern studies owes its genesis to the work of Orientalist scholars, many of whom came from Europe. The work of these scholars can be traced back to colonial times, when much of the research was actually driven by the foreign service concerns of the European empires. Today, in Middle Eastern studies there are generally two related schools of thought regarding Islam. One is that of Bernard Lewis and Sam Huntington, who seem to view Islam as a totalizing force. The other is that of John Esposito, who seems to view Islam as involving personal pietism rather than activism.[3] In this regard, we have to be cautious about attributing causality to Islam, or approaching Muslims or Islam as monolithic or even timeless. To begin, therefore, we posed a few questions to the contributors of this book. Does Islam offer a special case for citizenship? How powerful is Islam as a force in the making of identity? How do migrations and citizenship issues affect the relations between the Muslim countries of migrant origin and the European countries of resident destination? How do the practices of assimilation and multiculturalism relate to Islam or to minority populations in Europe?

The contributors to this book had a challenging task, for we live in an era of global communication where all forms of tradition and traditional parameters are changing very rapidly. We have seen how political conflict has given rise to the practices of local subcultures resorting to ethnic, racial, and religious allegiances to keep themselves from being swallowed by the majority culture. Indeed, in the United States, the common struggles of multiculturalism (and in California, bilingualism) and gender politics are examples of attempts to embrace difference as a fundamental constituent of national or even community identity. It is ironic that as the identity of the former colonizers—in this case the former European empires—is undergoing major transformation, often attempting to be more inclusive, the national identity of the formerly colonized—the Third World peoples whose citizens have constituted the bulk of the new migrants to Europe—is moving in a seemingly opposite direction, sometimes becoming more exclusive and more linked to ethnic or religious association. Despite our academic preoccupation with globalization as a discourse, the world continues to demonstrate a movement toward cultural differentiation and not homogenization, in which each individual belongs to many cultures and in which people have multiple cultural identities.

The topics in this book are among the most important that we can discuss in today's world, both intellectually and politically. Topics that refer to the relationship between the two themes—that is, the dialectic between globalization and identity—are conditioning much of our current debates. This is the project underlying this book: to chart a terrain of inquiry and analysis concerning one fundamental dimension of the transformation of European societies at the onset of the twenty-first century and to learn from this European observation to reconceptualize the relationship between culture and institutions in the era of globalization.

## NOTES

1. N. AlSayyad, "Cuture, Identity, and Urbanism in a Changing World," in M. Cohen, ed., *Preparing for the Urban Future* (Baltimore, Md.: Johns Hopkins University Press, 1996).

2. J. Fontana, *The Distorted Past: A Reinterpretation of Europe*, trans. C. Smith (Oxford, U.K.: Blackwell, 1995).

3. S. Huntington, *The Clash of Civilizations and the Remaking of World Order* (New York: Simon & Schuster, 1996); B. Lewis, *Islam and the West* (New York: Oxford University Press, 1993); and J. Esposito, *The Islamic Threat: Myth or Reality* (New York: Oxford University Press, 1995).

# PART I

## ISLAM, EUROPE, AND THE IDENTITY OF THE CHANGING NATION-STATE

# I

# Muslim Europe or Euro-Islam: On the Discourses of Identity and Culture

## Nezar AlSayyad

Few things seem to scare the French as much as the sight of Muslim school-girls wearing head scarves.[1]

Scores of angry [Turkish Parliament] members rose to their feet, clapped rhythmically and chanted "Out! Out!" as the newly elected member Merve Kavakci entered the chamber wearing a blue head scarf.[2]

It may be surprising that at the turn of the millennium, the scarf—an unintended symbol of Islam—can elicit such strong reactions within nations at the far eastern and western sides of the European continent. But Europe in fact has been undergoing profound ideational changes in the era of globalization, due in part to the new Muslim populations which have sprung up in the United Kingdom, France, Germany, and elsewhere. The essays included in this book explore political and cultural aspects of the emerging identities of these new citizens: how they see themselves, how they are seen by non-Muslim Europeans, and how the conflicting views on these questions are influencing collective identities in contemporary Europe.

The globalization process has been characterized by the large-scale movement of people from former colonies to the countries of the former colonizers, sometimes leading to confrontations over identity issues. Muslims in Europe resist being treated as "outsiders," but at the same time many of them also resist—and face barriers to—assimilation as traditional European citizens. In the process, not only are these new citizens negotiating new identities, but the relatively indigenous populations of Europe are being forced to rethink their own collective identities, both as Europeans and as citizens of specific countries.

Such conflicts are no longer about migration in the traditional sense, because so many Muslims in Europe are no longer migrants. Although they are still viewed by some as recent arrivals, Muslim populations have in fact been present in Europe for a long time. Several generations of Arab, Indian, black African, North African, and Turkish Muslims have been born in France, Britain, Germany, and elsewhere. The view that Muslims in Europe are guest workers who will eventually go home has long been untenable, but many Europeans have been slow to recognize the corollaries: that there are now large, permanent, indigenous Muslim populations in most of the countries of Europe; that they will not assimilate in the same way as previous waves of migration; and that Islam is now a European religion.[3]

Europe may have new citizens, but is there a new concept of citizenship? Theoretically, since there is no separation of religion and state in Islam, some Muslims tend to reject secular society, demanding considerable autonomy to conduct affairs within their communities in accordance with Islamic principles. According to this view, Islam is a totalizing force which dictates every aspect of a Muslim's life—or at least a more powerful force in public life than is generally the case for Christianity and Judaism, Europe's other major religions.

Then does Islam offer a special case of citizenship? While many Muslims resist Euro-American postindustrial culture on moral grounds, they often thrive in the infrastructure of globalization, which is the product of capitalism. There are also indications that Muslims in Europe are devising a liberal form of Islam which is accommodating of European ideas of citizenship.

It is important to note that there are significant differences among Muslims in Europe, especially between Islamists and secular Muslims. Many secular Muslims favor political integration while rejecting assimilation. There are also important differences among Islamists, who espouse different political ideologies of Islam. Some Western observers may speak of a monolithic Islam, or at least a monolithic Islamic fundamentalism, but Islam has always been an ambiguous ethos from which different Muslims have drawn different meanings and contradictory inspirations. Some find Islam to be socialist in intent, while others focus on its capitalist spirit; some read an ethos of democratic participation into Islam, while others assign justification for the imposition of authority to specialists in Islamic theology. In any case, political Islam offers a powerful alternative discourse to ideologies of secularism of both the capitalist right and the socialist left. For both Muslim and non-Muslim Europeans, new citizenships and new ethnicities are being articulated through this continuing dialectic.

Another significant issue in this debate recently has been the emergence of conflict between assimilationist and multicultural views. Assimilationists argue that Muslims in Europe are gradually becoming more and more like other Europeans. For example, the birth rates of Arab women from North Africa tend to decline in Europe. And although the first generation of immigrants tend to retain elements of their culture of origin, subsequent generations tend to assimilate much of the dominant culture over the course of time. Multiculturalists, on the other hand, argue both the inevitability and the desirability of multiple ethnic heritages and cultural diversity. These two positions overlap in some areas. For example, education is important to both; but for assimilationists, the function of education is to transform foreigners (or the children of foreigners) into citizens, while for multiculturalists education is about helping new citizens value and maintain their languages and cultures of origin. How powerful a force is Islam in determining identity? Some suggest that other factors—such as ethnic, national, regional, tribal, or class origins—can be stronger than religion. Clearly, the identities of Europe's Muslim populations are not fixed but vary across time and place. In the short term, identity appears to be situational, whereas in the long term, some aspects of identity are maintained while their content changes.

Because generalizing theories about Islam are impossible to verify or disprove and may be of limited value, it is probably more useful to turn from theories about Islam to what Muslims themselves think and do in specific settings. It is equally important to examine the range of perspectives of non-Muslims toward the Muslim populations in their midsts. Here, attitudes from the colonial past persist, and examples of such attitudes from political, academic, and media discourses are easy to find. Sometimes concealed but often openly expressed, the idea that Europe is by definition a Christian continent is also common. While not all non-Muslims see Islam as a threat, formal professions of the value of diversity by governments or political groups do not necessarily translate into acceptance of Muslim communities as respected entities in Europe.

The scarf epigraphs that begin this chapter clearly indicate that the reactions to the symbols that mark the presence of Islam in Europe, and within its eastern and western parts, reveal deeper cultural and political positions. Clifford Geertz, in *Islam Observed*, offered a relevant seminal comparison of Islam in Indonesia with Islam in Morocco—the eastern and western "antipodes" of the Islamic world.[4] With the acceleration of the movement of Muslims beyond Morocco and Indonesia, many would argue that there are no Islamic antipodes anymore—that, like the British Empire at one time, the sun never sets on the Islamic world. Like Geertz, the contributors to this volume are interested in manifestations of Islam in different settings. Yet where Geertz looked at Islam in settings in which Muslims were a majority, we look at settings in which Muslims are a minority, and at some of the special circumstances that result from that condition. Like Geertz's earlier study, this volume emphasizes the diversity, historicity, and adaptability of Islam. With this purpose in mind, it would seem appropriate, therefore, before discussing the collective and individual arguments of the book, to engage in a brief exercise at the antipodes of Europe—France and Turkey—bracketing Islam in two secularist settings, with attention to what may seem a minor detail, an item of clothing of some Muslim women.

## THE HEAD SCARF OBSERVED: FRAMING EUROPEAN ISLAM

In 1990, in the United Kingdom, a two-year-old dispute over the wearing of head scarves by two Muslim sisters was resolved in a compromise acceptable to both parties. The banning of flowing head scarves during class for Doris Delides, headmistress of Altrincham Grammar School, near Manchester, was a matter of common sense. However, for the Pakistani sisters Fatima and Aisha Alvi, who were students at the school, wearing the scarves was a matter of religious faith. In 1988, the Altrincham governors decided that head scarves were a hazard when worn in school laboratories or gym and ordered that they be banned in all classes. Letters were exchanged between the authorities and some angry parents; however, the ban persisted. On December 21, 1989, the two sisters wearing the traditional white head scarves came to school. They were told to remove them or to go home. The sisters went home. This occurrence continued every school day for a month. Fatima Alvi, the elder sister, began giving interviews to reporters. She told the reporters that there were three male teachers at the school and Islam taught that girls should cover their hair in front of men. "We want to show the strength of our religious feelings," Fatima said.[5]

Altrincham's sixteen governors met on January 23, 1990, to discuss the matter, and their deliberations took two hours. The governors felt that by enforcing the ban they were unnecessarily giving rise to religious tensions. After the meeting, Chairman Gilbert Thompson said, "I know we are setting a precedent, but we have to take account of changes in our society." It was decided that female students would be allowed to wear dark blue scarves, the school's colors; however, they were still banned from wearing scarves in the labs and gym. Muslim leaders in Great Britain responded favorably to the decision, and when Fatima heard the news she said, "I'm looking forward to going to school without being thrown out."[6]

In 1989, Ernest Chenieres, principal of a high school in Creil, a working-class suburb of Paris, told three teenagers that they could not attend school if they continued to wear the head scarf associated with conservative Muslim societies. This showdown, the beginning of a lengthy controversy, led to a vigorous debate in French society over civil rights and the separation of church and state in France, a country with a century-old tradition of secularism in public schools. The teenaged girls at the heart of this controversy were fourteen-year-old Leila and thirteen-year-old Fatima Achaboun, the daughters of a religiously observant Moroccan immigrant employed at an automobile body shop, and fourteen-year-old Samira Aaeedani, of Tunisian descent, whose father was a former municipal employee, but now, unemployed, spent his time teaching Islam in his neighborhood.

Lionel Jospin, France's Education Minister at that time, decided that the Muslim girls should be "persuaded" to remove their veils in class, but if they refused to do so, they should still be allowed to attend class. He believed that the denial of this right would be a form of religious discrimination. However, French teachers, whose union threatened a strike over the issue, and many members of the Socialist Party, to which Jospin belonged, rejected his decision. Finding his cabinet divided over the issue, Prime Minister Michel Rocard referred the matter to the Council of State, the highest council of government, for a decision.[7]

Temporarily laid to rest, the scarf controversy in France did not go away. In 1992 the Council of State overturned its original ruling, which had been to allow each school to settle the issue as it saw fit, by ordering a school to reintegrate three girls who had been disallowed from attending class because they refused to remove the veil.[8] Then, when the wearing of scarves, or *hijab*, further increased in popularity in 1994, it came to be viewed by the French as a political statement in sympathy with the Islamic fundamentalist movement, which was then challenging Algeria's military-backed government. In areas with a large concentration of Arab and Turkish immigrants the practice spread from school to school, and by September an estimated 700 girls were wearing head scarves across France.[9] This new surge in head scarf popularity caused the French government on September 10 to declare that it would ban the wearing of head scarves in public schools, since the practice violated the tradition of secular education in France. In a published interview, Education Minister Francois Bayrou said that he was going to deliver instructions to principals of all public schools to enforce the ban immediately. The wearing of scarves by Muslim girls, he said, divided Muslims from non-Muslims in schools, thereby circumventing the principle of the separation of church and state. In an interview published in the weekly *Le Point*, the Education Minister said, "The national will cannot be ignored." His instructions to the heads of schools would be clear: "We will continue to accept discreet religious signs, as has always been the case. But we cannot accept ostentatious signs that divide our youth."[10]

It was this statement, among others, that caused a *Christian Science Monitor* writer to comment, "Few things seem to scare the French as much as the sight of Muslim schoolgirls wearing head scarves."[11] At the time, popular opinion polls showed that 86 percent of the French population was opposed to the wearing of scarves in schools. Of these, some viewed the scarves as a symbol of the oppression of women. For others the scarves symbolized a more general fear that fundamentalists would prevent the integration of the country's five million Muslims. Many others, including Interior Minister Charles Pasqua, read signs of a deeper threat in the extreme Islamist movement.

The Bayrou directive, popular with the teachers' union and the general French public, met with some opposition. Some criticized the directive as discriminatory. They argued that while the directive effectively banned scarves, it still allowed more discreet religious symbols such as crucifixes and Stars of David to be carried by students. France's Muslim community was obviously uneasy about the directive, and on October 3, 1994, police were called in to prevent twenty-two Muslim girls wearing scarves from entering Faidherbe High School in the northern industrial city of Lille. Supporters of the students led a 100-person-strong demonstration, some carrying banners saying "Stop the aggression against Islam." In September of the same year, 1,200 students at the Romain-Rolland de Goussainville School north of Paris called a one-day strike after the principal prevented four veiled students, who refused to remove their veils, from attending class. The principal said that he was simply following the directive. Other critics, including the newspaper *Le Monde*, argued that the government's directive could have the effect of encouraging the wearing of the veil, a phenomena that was, until then, restricted to only a few schools. Furthermore, it risked the removal of many girls from the educational system, which might be their only avenue toward emancipation.[12]

By 1996, the "Muslim scarf affair" was still an unresolved issue in France, puzzling British visitors who were accustomed to turbaned Sikh youngsters in their country. At the height of the affair in 1994, pupils were expelled for wearing scarves at the same time there was a sweep of suspected Islamic extremists in Algeria. Since then there had been little change in the situation, as Mr. Barreau, a former Catholic priest, has continued to advise the new Interior Minister on the subject. The French Constitutional Council ruled in October 2000 that even though the Education Ministry had banned "ostentatious religious signs," schools were not to suspend students who wore scarves if no obvious religious proselytizing was involved.[13]

Significant differences mark the reactions of the British and French to the wearing of head scarves in schools. Indeed, not all scarf stories mean the same thing or lead to the same conclusion. On May 2, 1999, the newly elected Turkish Parliament erupted in fury and prevented one of its female members from taking her oath of office while wearing a head scarf. Scores of angry members rose to their feet, clapped rhythmically, and chanted "Out! Out!" as the newly elected member Merve Kavakci entered the chamber with a navy blue scarf. After a recess caused by the uproar, Kavakci did not return to take her oath with other members of Parliament and was thus not qualified to take part in deliberations.

The clash in Parliament reflected a profound debate that is spreading through Turkish society. Three-quarters of a century ago, the founder of the Turkish Republic, Mustafa Kemal Ataturk, decreed reforms that shattered centuries-old traditions. He abolished the sultanate, banned religious brotherhoods, adopted Latin script to replace Arabic, and banned the fez, the veil, and the head scarf. Today, most members of the political elite believe that restrictions on free expression are necessary to prevent the rise of religious fundamentalism, separatism, and other causes they consider hostile to Western values. Kavakci was a member of the religious-oriented Virtue Party, which secularists have denounced as subversive. In fact, the party had to be restructured in the wake of these accusations to survive in the Turkish political landscape; so although Kavakci had emphasized that her scarf simply reflected her private commitment to Islam, Prime Minister Bulent Ecevit said, in the speech addressing the scarf issue, "No one may interfere with the private life of individuals, but this is not a private space. This is the supreme foundation of the state. It is not a place in which to challenge the state."[14]

These scarf stories tell another intricate and complex story of history and geography; of colonialism and postcolonialism; and of citizenship and nationhood in the era of globalization. On the surface it may appear that all European and aspiring-to-be European citizens and nations have come to reject the scarf—and, indeed, its blunter sister, the veil—as a symbol of the intrusion of Islam on public and even political life. A deeper read would reveal that these rejections stem from fundamentally different experiences, standpoints, and rationales.

If one were to step back a hundred years or so in time, no one could have imagined a group of distinguished Turkish men jumping up and down in a stately house booing a woman simply because she is wearing a scarf or a veil. Similarly, it would have been unusual in a liberalizing France of the late nineteenth century to ban a conservative form of dress, one which was common in many parts of the religious rural hinterland, simply because it accentuated national or religious differences. In fact, such an attire, as we know from the many accounts of Orientals who traveled in Europe in the late nineteenth century, would have mainly aroused interest and curiosity. So why is it that in less than a century we get this dramatic change, and how can we explain its wide occurrence among such diverse nations and peoples? The answer to this question lies of course in the history of colonialism and its two offshoots, colonial liberalism as it was envisioned in the Imperial homeland and applied to the colonies, and the self-Orientalizing attitude that pervaded much of the Muslim world during the era of independence, nationalist struggle, and nation-building.

Here we have to remember that the scarfed woman in the late nineteenth century did not pose any threat to France or Turkey—whether to people, nation, state, government, or empire. In fact, the "scarfed woman" was the gendered other that made possible a sense of self, of "home" as different from "harem." This is not the case in the late twentieth century, albeit for very different reasons in these two places. In her account of nineteenth-century travelers between England and India, Inderpal Grewal highlights the categories of "home" and "harem" to distinguish between the characters of these concepts, as constructed by British imperialists.[15] At issue are the identities of women, both British and Indian, associated with these constructions. As with the symbol of the head scarf, the subject is complex. What is the difference between an image of oneself conferred strategically by another, as opposed to one created by and for oneself? Is it ever possible, Grewal asks indirectly, to create one's own identity at all?

With regard to these two contexts, France's attitude, may be described as an attempt to escape the geography of its own colonialism—a geography made possible through its changing borders and its attempt to incorporate its frontiers into the empire through its colonial practices. But that same geography seems now to have caught up with France's present demography, represented by the large numbers of immigrants from its former colonies as well as their second and third French-born generations. France, which cannot account for the changes to its own collective identity as a result of their presence, had to react to the scarf in a somewhat militant way that seemingly turns its back on its own liberal history.

Turkey, on the other hand, is a country which has labored for a little less than a century to distance itself from its Asian geography and Islamic heritage. Its desire, in so doing, can be described more as an attempt to escape or deny its own history. Turkey adopted a European-style democracy in form but not in content. This went hand in hand with accepting both a definition of its contemporary self, imposed from the outside, and a self-Orientalizing articulation of its own historic self occurring during its nation-building phase. Indeed, this articulation represents the dialectic tension in Turkey's identity struggle between the self-Orientalizing tendency which marked the state's definition of its Ottoman history on one hand, and its engagement in deliberate distancing in relation to its contemporary political project on the other.

Turkey, often viewed as an "in-between" place, has historically had a troubled relationship in the European imagination, as it is tied to memories of the Ottoman threat to Christendom, fears of Islamic revival, and resentment against Turkish migration. The European position, "that Turkey is not authentically of the West," has consistently resulted in the blocking of Turkish membership to the European Union.

Kevin Robins, in his consideration of Turkish identity and cultural experience, particularly through the relationship between Turkey and Europe, argues that cultural identities can best be seen in the context of cultural relationships, that only through others do we become aware of who we are and what we stand for. He believes that these interactions allow us to explore the issue of dynamism versus closure in cultural identities—what creates openness in cultural identities, and also what resists change, leading to rigidity and closure.[16]

From this point of view Robins asks what impact the changing identity of Turkey might have on its relationship with Europe today. Ataturk's policies of forced Western modernization and secularization of Turkish society beginning in the 1920s led to the suppression of difference and the erasure of Turkey's historical legacy. Recent developments have prompted the resurgence of these submerged elements in Turkish culture, as ethnic, social, and cultural differences, and Islam, in particular, have made their presence felt in Turkish life and politics. "The 'other' Turkey is making its declaration of independence," says Robins, "making its reality felt, manifesting the complexity of its social being. This has nothing to do with cultural reversion (to tradition, religion, or whatever), as many western commentators like to believe: what is at issue are precisely questions about modern identity and values in Turkey."[17] Characterizing Turkey's modernization under Ataturk as an "arid and empty affair," Robins sees the elements in this resurgence as constructing an alternative form of modernity and modern identity.

In particular, he wonders if Europeans can be open to these changes and "come to terms with the Turk." Acceptance of recent developments in Turkey by Europe could encourage the formation of a more creative and democratic culture in Turkey. At the same time, this particular historical juncture gives Europeans the chance for unprecedented change: "to meet themselves" and possibly revitalize and transform their own culture. As Robins points out, "history is created out of cultures in relation and interaction: interrupting identities."

The concept of identity and its use at the end of the twentieth century has often been seen as problematic. The term *identity* typically refers to social labels given to individuals as members of a group. This may be self-designated or assigned to individuals themselves or by others. Such a view implicitly recognizes that each person may live with a multiple sense of self and may carry disparate and contradictory identity positions. This tendency renders the "constructedness" of identity more important than its "rootedness." Kathryn Woodward has suggested there is a "crisis of identity" that has emerged from the breakdown of previously stable group membership.[18] Identity now increasingly derives from a multiplicity of sources—from nationality, ethnicity, social class, community, gender, sexuality—sources which may conflict. Much as Robins speaks of identity in terms of relationships, Woodward has insisted that identity is always about difference.

But despite the current preoccupation with globalization, the history of the world demonstrates a movement toward cultural differentiation, and not homogenization, a condition in which each individual claims allegiance to more than one culture and invokes different identities at different times and in different places. Although there may be no agreement on the nature of identity among groups that band together, groups involved in political culture behave and respond as if there are well-defined, historically established ones. Thus, as Benedict Anderson has successfully demonstrated, all national identities are constructed, and the differences between them lie mainly in the different ways in which they are imagined.[19]

Lawrence Grossberg notes that in both theoretical and political discourses, it is common to hear the assertion that the centrality of the concept of identity is a "modern" development.[20] Grossberg identifies three aspects, or logics, by which identity is constituted as modern in cultural studies: a logic of difference, a logic of individuality, and a logic of temporality. If identity is both constituted by and constitutive of modernity, then current scholarship on identity has failed to interrogate its own location within, and with the formations of modern power, he believes.[21] Challenging the direction taken by cultural studies, Grossberg posits three corresponding alternatives: a logic of otherness, a logic of productivity, and a logic of spatiality. He argues for a new sense of political identity and collective agency, based on "the concept of a belonging without identity, a notion of what might be called *singularity* as the basis for an alternative politics, a politics based on what Giorgio Agamben has called 'coming community.'"[22]

In both Middle Eastern and Western European studies, new kinds of work are being done on issues of identity and citizenship which challenge the traditional boundaries of area studies. The scholars whose works are brought together in this volume are typical of this trend. They share a view of Europe and Islam as living, historical civilizations with universal intentions. They share as well a desire to avoid reductionism, essentializing, and synecdoche. Instead, the authors tend toward a counterview which emphasizes that while Muslim scholars have historically advocated obedience even to flawed rulers, the mainstream of Islamic tradition is one of personal pietism rather than political activism. This view cautions against reifying and attributing causality to Islam, and against approaching Islam and Muslims as timeless and monolithic. In this presentation, the multivalent character of the head scarf can once again offer an instructive symbol for contemporary Islam.

We live in a world of global communication in which the parameters of tradition are changing rapidly. Local subcultures often appeal to ethnic, racial, and religious allegiances to keep from being swallowed by powerful majority cultures.[23] In this process, it is ironic that the identities of the former colonizers are undergoing major transformations in the general direction of inclusiveness, while the national identities of the formerly colonized are often becoming more exclusive and more linked to ethnic or religious association. Each individual today belongs to many cultures and has multiple identities which are in constant evolution. Stuart Hall has captured this in an apt social metaphor, comparing himself and his fellow immigrants from the Caribbean to the sugar at the bottom of the English cup of tea: although the practice of taking tea is thought of as quintessentially English, in fact both the tea and the sugar are from, respectively, South Asia and the Caribbean.[24]

## ISLAM, EUROPE, AND THE IDENTITY OF THE CHANGING NATION-STATE

In the first section of this book, we embark on discussions of identity, wherein the commonly used categories "Europe" and "Islam" are further problematized. In Middle Eastern Studies there have been two related schools of thought on Islam. Some scholars such as Bernard Lewis and Samuel Huntington have seen Islam as a totalizing force. Others have tried to interpret Islam in terms of personal pietism rather than activism.[25] In this regard, we must be cautious about reifying and attributing causality to Islam and approaching Muslims and Islam as monolithic or timeless. Similarly, the idea of a European identity is not without its problems. Indeed, one can make the argument that "Europe" is an artificial construct consisting of diverse ethnic populations and nationalities. Historically, Europe's identity emerged partially as a response to the proximity and threat of the Islamic world. And in the postcolonial era, the immigration of Muslims into Europe as guest workers, residents, and citizens has posed new challenges and possibilities of identity formation. Muslims, the citizens of Europe's various nation-states, and Europe itself now have the opportunity to rethink their identities and mold new ones.

Bassam Tibi's chapter "Muslim Migrants in Europe: Between Euro-Islam and Ghettoization," is one such attempt to rethink Muslim identity in Europe by devising a new form of Islam, one Tibi calls Euro-Islam. Tibi writes that the point of departure for understanding Islam in Europe is the recognition that Islam is not a worldwide monolithic phenomenon, but is rich in cultural diversity. Muslims in Europe have different ethnic, national, and cultural backgrounds and have adopted diverse political and social strategies for articulating their views and achieving their goals. In the past Islam has displayed a capacity to adjust to a variety of divergent cultures. There are distinct Arab, African, Indian, and South-Asian forms of Islam, which are all manifestations of the same basic religious faith. Similarly, Tibi argues, Euro-Islam is the effort to devise a liberal form of Islam acceptable both to Muslim migrants and to European societies, thus accommodating European ideas of secularism and individual citizenship. In other words, Euro-Islam is Islam that is culturally adjusted to secular European societies, much as, for instance, Islam in Africa is adjusted to local African cultures. Tibi lists major features of Euro-Islam: *laïcité*; an understanding of tolerance that goes beyond the Islamic tolerance restricted to Abrahamic believers (*ahl al-kitab*, or people of the book); and a willingness to acknowledge pluralism. In short, Euro-Islam is compatible with liberal democracy, individual human rights, and civil society.

Tibi points out that Euro-Islam is directed against both ghettoization and assimilation. According to Tibi, the German Orientalist Tilman Nagel has proposed, for example, that the German government view Muslim migrants in an arrogant way as *musta'minun*—that is, as "protected minorities" who will forever continue to be aliens. For him and other German Orientalists, tolerance lies in "keeping the aliens away from Europe in underlining the difference to them." In contrast to this xenophobic position, many multiculturalists argue from a cultural-relativist point of view, and favor Islamic ghettos in the name of communitarianism. In both cases the result is the same. Islamists among the Islamic migrants are sympathetic to multicultural positions and often willingly confuse assimilation with political integration. In contrast to both positions, Tibi advocates the democratic integration of Muslims into European society. He would like to see Muslims become members of the European body politic they live in, without, however, giving up their Islamic identity. Islamic identity and citizenship for

Muslim migrants need to become a form of European identity and citizenship. Enlightened Islamic education is a means to maintain Islamic identity, but not at the service of segregationist ends.

While Tibi articulates the principles of a Euro-Islam, Krishan Kumar, in his chapter "The Nation-State, the European Union, and Transnational Identities," argues that many non-European minorities, including Muslims, are refusing the labels imposed on them, looking beyond the nation-state to construct cosmopolitan or transnational identities. Christian Europeans have for centuries moved freely over each other's lands, contributing their distinctive patterns to the cultures of different countries. Other groups, such as Muslims, have also made major contributions but have been viewed more problematically. Old adversaries of Europe, Muslims have returned in the more modest guise of guest workers, immigrants, residents, and in many cases citizens. Kumar asks whether these are the harbingers of new identities. Is the model to be assimilation, integration, or multiculturalism? And with what implications for the future?

Kumar has no doubt that a specifically Christian European culture exists, because Europe took shape largely in response to the Muslim threat. Yet he points out that there is plenty of ammunition available to those who would deny a common European identity, arguing instead that "Europe" is nothing but an agglomeration of ethnic or national identity. And Europe's hostility toward Muslims comes partly from closeness, because Islam shares much with Christianity and Judaism. Indeed, Muslims have contributed to the formation of Europe, not just as "others," but directly, as philosophers, scientists, and scholars. The question of the impact of Muslim communities on European societies today must be seen within the context of this ambivalent history. Kumar demonstrates that European identity today is multiple—for example, one can be European, British, English, and perhaps even Cornish. For some, national identity remains preeminent, but subnational identities flourish at the same time as transnational and postnational identities. Old social models of adaptation, integration, and assimilation may be outmoded, as the present era becomes more and more characterized by hyphenization, hybridity, syncretization, creolization, and diaspora cultures.

Differences among European settings and the complex intersections of religion, race, and class make it difficult to generalize. Noting that many non-European minorities are refusing the labels imposed on them, Kumar reveals that this can lead to new dilemmas. Generally, it is difficult for non-European minorities to compete on equal terms with nationals who are adept at deploying the master symbols and cultural styles of the dominant societies. Another problem for European Muslims is that as nation-states lose control over some areas of economic and cultural life, they respond by intensifying their hold over those areas where they still remain in command, such as power to grant citizenship and nationality, visas, residence, and work permits. Kumar believes that postnational identities and transnational citizenship are undoubtedly attractive goals—and in part because not just secure and wealthy cosmopolitans can achieve them. However, he warns that a definite element of wish-fulfillment seems to have entered into the thinking of those who, in current circumstances, proclaim them to be the best or only avenues of advancement.

Next the book moves us from the subject of Muslim, European, and Euro-Muslim identities to study the broader effects of globalization on the relationship between Islam and Europe. Ashcroft et al. have defined globalization as "a process whereby individual lives and local communities are affected by economic and cultural forces that operate worldwide. In effect it is the process of the world becoming a single place."[26] The process of globalization has also promoted certain tendencies: hypercompetition, free trade, privatization, deregulated markets, unregulated cross-border financial speculation, flexible labor markets and work rules, microelectronic-based production, and subcontracting networks. Globalization has had diverse and sometimes contradictory effects. It has encouraged the formation of the EU to meet its challenges. The EU has undercut nationalism as a citizen's primary social identity, but at the same time there has been a proliferation of subnationalisms. Globalization has provided the networks and multiple identities available to Muslim communities in Europe, and for the first time it has made possible the globalization of Islam, an ideal of the *ummah* as a global community of believers. This ideal has been part of classical Islamic political theory for centuries. However, at the same time that this ideal now stands a chance of being realized, Muslim and other cultures all over the world feel their very existence threatened. While globalization was born in advanced Western economies, it has deeply affected the economies of the developing world. It also promises to bring about political and cultural change by encouraging the establishment of democratic governments and enforcing universal human rights.

In the chapter entitled "The Challenge of Islamic Networks and Citizenship Claims: Europe's Painful Adjustment to Globalization," Paul Lubeck reveals that in Europe those minding the flame of national identity now find themselves resisting globalization and challenging, not the new flows of capital or technology, but rather the attendant movement of peoples, especially Muslims, through long-standing global networks and established communities. One of the ironies facing contemporary Western Europe is that the rapid economic and cultural changes associated with regional integration and globalization have begun to undermine the once-hegemonic claims of nationalism. In an era of rising subnational identities within the EU, the nation-state no longer embodies progressive change or even determines a citizen's primary social identity. In this context, Muslim immigrant networks and multiple social identities have emerged as a vexing problem for those Europeanists wishing to pursue globalization by expanding and deepening the powers of the European Union.

Lubeck argues that to understand the meaning of Islam, identities, and citizenship conflicts in contemporary Europe, one must understand the Muslim experience of globalization. This includes the way Muslims have used the infrastructure of the new global economy, the multiple identities available to Muslims, and the structure of Muslim networks and communities within Western Europe—the new frontier of Islamdom. Despite the integrative force represented by the EU, citizenship definitions, immigration policies, and recognition of subnational communities are all defined by nation-states. Thus, definitions and policies conflict, despite the movement toward regional integration. Comparisons across European states, therefore, will illuminate understanding of citizenship, identity, and globalization among European Muslims. For Lubeck, the pivotal questions remain whether Western Europe can revitalize its demographic decline, attract skilled and entrepreneurial workers, and respond affirmatively to the diversity of the global system without reconsidering its immigration policies and its assessment of Muslims as acceptable citizens.

Writing from the perspective of Europe, Lubeck sees the rise of a unified global Islam. However, writing from Egypt, Hala Mustafa points out that national interests rather than cultural affiliation still dominate political rivalry, as can be seen in the conflicts between Iraq and Iran, or Iraq and Kuwait. Her chapter, "Islam and the West in an Era of Globalization: Clash of Civilization or Coexistence?" is a rebuttal of the work of Samuel Huntington and others, who have caused "Islam versus the West" to become a favorite theme among Western scholars. These writers have envisioned a post-Cold War era in which national and ideological differences are eclipsed or perhaps subsumed by cultural ones. In reply Mustafa argues that although possibilities of such clashes should not be underestimated, Islam and the West are not inherently inimical. In fact, such clashes and frictions should not be attributed solely to religious and cultural factors, nor should culture be reduced to religion. Mustafa argues that Islam, a major faith with millions of followers, should not be confused with the views of a small minority of militant fundamentalists who target primarily their own societies and regimes. Even militancy in its Islamic garb is but a form of social protest, more a vehicle for the expression of grievances than an underlying cause. It is certainly not the only response of Muslim societies against their regimes or against the West.

Mustafa examines these points through a number of issues. First, she discusses how the growing economic disparity between North and South has resulted in labor movement of Muslim immigrants to Europe, where they have been exploited and badly treated. Second, she points out that the Bosnian conflict, in which Europeans took no action to stop the Serbian massacres, genocide, and ethnic cleansing of European Muslims, has suggested to many that European pluralism and liberalism have no room for Islam and no tolerance for even a democratic Islamic state in Europe. Third, she argues that Western support for Israel against the Palestinians and other Arabs—especially that of the United States—feeds anti-Western sentiments in the Islamic world. Fourth, she explains that Islamic fundamentalism is closely related to the failure of political and economic modernization in the global South, which in turn is due to the absence of the social preconditions required for modernization. Finally, she writes that even during the colonial era, Muslim reformers never saw the West as a culturally hostile entity; in fact, sentiment against the West and against overly Westernized regimes is a relatively recent phenomenon.

In her conclusion, Mustafa argues that the problem with Islamic societies today is that they, unlike Europe, have not yet made the transition to secularism. This has complicated the process of democratization and the promotion of universal human rights. The argument hinges on the belief that human rights are universal and that their universality should be recognized. She believes that Islam and the West must learn how to live together, in mutual acceptance, respect, and recognition of their variant interests and needs.

## ISLAM IN EUROPE AND FARTHER AFIELD: COMPARATIVE PERSPECTIVES

In the last part of the book, contributors offer comparative and cross-cultural perspectives. Here the case studies of Muslim populations in different national contexts reveal the varied nature of Muslim experience in Europe. Government policies—whether of multiculturalism or assimilation—have uncovered the underlying assumptions about the relationship of state and religion in each national context. For example, British assumptions that religion has a role in public life and education stand in contrast to France's strident belief in secularism in these arenas. These varying contexts have informed the transformation of Islam and the Islamic practices of Muslim populations, producing new variants in Islam. On the other hand, debates around religion, secularism, and multiculturalism have also challenged and redefined the national identities of the French and British populations. Massive postcolonial migrations have led to what Rachel Bloul has described as dual ethnicization, where people are more preoccupied with collective identities as either "Maghrebi" "Muslim" or "French" "English." This ethnicization has taken place on both sides, with "the process of ethnicization" linking specific populations with distinctive cultural characteristics.[27]

Tariq Modood's chapter, "The Place of Muslims in British Secular Multiculturalism," argues that the emergence of Muslim political agency has thrown British multiculturalism into theoretical and political disarray, as religion has replaced political "blackness" as the most important source of self-identity, especially among people of South Asian origins. Britain today has a large presence

of Muslims—between one and two million—more than half of them South
Asian, of primarily Pakistani origin. This has been a result of Commonwealth
immigration from the 1950s onward, including wives and children from about
the 1970s. Modood shows that this predominantly Muslim immigration presence
has made manifest certain kinds of racism, which in turn have given rise to
antidiscrimination laws and policies since the 1960s. A main feature of early
antidiscrimination discourse, however, was that it was based not on religion, but
on race, following an American pattern. In recent years this has given way to a
multiculturalism based not just on the right to assimilate to the dominant culture,
but on the right to have one's "difference" recognized and supported in the public and private spheres. Yet, because secularism is hegemonic in British political
culture, the rainbow coalition of identity politics has become deeply unhappy
with Muslim consciousness. Modood demonstrates that the group in British society most politically opposed to politicized Muslims is not Christians, or even
right-wing nationalists, but the secular, liberal intelligentsia. In Britain, multiculturalism continues to make political headway while, paradoxically, the opposition
between its rival forms deepens.

   While Modood concentrates on the debates raised within British society
around the subject of multiculturalism, Michel Wieviorka looks at the transformation of Islam in France, arguing that "Islam is undoubtedly reproduced but it
is also produced." In "Race, Culture, and Society: The French Experience with
Muslims," Wieviorka shows that Islam in Europe is diverse—a diversity due to
the various logics explaining the migration of Muslims to Europe, and to the different influences of national contexts where migrants live and where they or their
children eventually become new citizens. In France, at least, this production has
been related to the end of industrial society and to a deep feeling of threat against
traditional French national identity. These phenomena in turn are connected
with the rise and renewal of racism. Within this French context Islam appears to
be a choice related to complex processes of subjectivization. The new identities
within Muslim communities range from the most extreme communitarian radicalism (which in a few cases leads to the embrace of terrorism), to moderation
and or total disengagement from Muslim practices. The first option often leads
actors to adopt a specific identity that makes them withdraw into community life,
possibly leading to fundamentalism or sectarianism; the second position is that of
participation in modern individualism, in which, in some cases, collective identity may be dissolved. Wieviorka argues that new forms of collective life are emerging in the invention through religion of actors who are seeking senses of themselves that may be projected into the future. In France, Islam has also become a
central element in debates about race and the growth of the National Front Party,
universalism particularism, the idea of the Republic, and the political treatment
of differences in the public sphere.

As Bassam Tibi's chapter indicated, Islam is adapting to the Western world through its attempt to formulate a Euro-Islam. In the future there may be similar attempts to describe an American-Islam. Yet, at the same time the West is changing Islam, Islam is changing the West, causing reformulations of what it means to be American, French, German, English, and increasingly, European. And in the public spheres of Europe and America, discussions on the role of Muslims and Islam are being debated not only by the political and intellectual elite from these two continents but also by Muslim intellectuals, predominately those living in the diaspora. These intellectuals have brought their own cultural and intellectual traditions into the public discourse, and in the course of these debates, Europeans and Americans have been forced to look at their own traditions in a more critical manner.

The chapter by Laurence Michalak and Agha Saeed offers a comparison of Islam in a European setting (France) with Islam in the United States. Such a comparison might at first glance seem audacious because France and the United States are so different in both scale and history. Yet this comparison does yield a number of interesting points of similarity and difference. Although there were Muslims in France and the United States before the twentieth century, the Muslim presence in both countries is mainly a phenomenon of the second half of the twentieth century, due to Muslim immigration. However, in France almost all Muslims are recent migrants or descendants of recent migrants, while in the United States a significant minority of Muslims are African American converts to Islam. Nevertheless, public understanding of Islam in both France and the United States is embedded in discourses of migration, in which people tend to use parallel arguments for and against migration. Beyond this, Muslims in France and the United States have a greater opportunity than Muslims in Islamic lands to be Muslim by conviction rather than by birth. In both France and the United States, ethnic differences that have in the past divided Muslims are giving way to interethnic Islamic solidarity, and younger generations of Muslims are less reticent in asserting Muslim identities and entering the political arena. A point of contrast is that the French tend to foreground religion in debates about the compatibility of Islam with their national culture, while Americans largely ignore religion. In such debates in France, "Muslim" is often a code word for "nonwhite," while in the United States discussions of race and discussions of religion tend to have little to do with each other. The French tend to recognize that Islam is now a permanent part of the French social landscape, whereas in the United States Islam is still seen for the most part as a foreign religion. The similarities and differences in the way that Muslims are perceived and perceive themselves in France and the United States fit into larger contexts which have to do with respective national ideologies of migration and citizenship. Here, assimilationism tends to be more dominant in France, while the United States tends more toward multiculturalism.

Of the patterns of similarities and differences identified by Michalak and Saeed within France and the United States, perhaps the most striking area of comparison is that of participation of Muslims in national politics. In both countries Muslims are increasingly engaging in electoral politics to defend and preserve their religious identities. Paradoxically but understandably, they are also increasingly open to reforming their Islamic identities. In the final analysis, for Michalak and Saeed, comparing Islam in France and the United States does not yield absolute similarities and differences so much as differences of degree arising out of different historical experience. This argument, carried a step further, suggests that the United States fits in comfortably alongside not only France, but also Britain, Germany, and other Western settings for Islam that are examined here, in a common comparative framework.

Renate Holub's chapter, "The Dialectic of Euro-Islam," is an examination of the role of intellectuals in Europe in debates around issues of Islam and Muslims. Since the fall of the Berlin Wall in 1989 these topics have gained an increasing visibility in Europe's public sphere as a result of the political mobilization of immigrant populations and the reaction of national populations to these attempts. Meanwhile, debates in the public sphere which focused around issues of migration, identity, assimilation, and accommodation are no longer the preserve of the political and intellectual elite typical of post–World War II Europe, as new agents have added their voices to these debates. Holub outlines a typology of such intellectuals' views of the future of Europe in relation to Islam: (1) European public intellectuals who address issues of migration and citizenship in general in their work, while ignoring Islam and Muslim populations; (2) right-wing intellectuals who argue that immigrants from Muslim majority countries cannot be assimilated or integrated; (3) middle-strata intellectuals, including journalists and other representatives of the media, who translate and adjust the message of intellectual leaders into a language that parallels the discourse of specific political leaders; and (4) organic intellectuals emerging from or having affinities with the migrant populations, who bring their knowledge of intellectual and cultural traditions that differ from Europe into public discourse. Holub believes that the active participation of Europe's organic intellectuals in the public sphere will not only bring a discussion of religion into the public arena, but also will force European intellectuals to rethink and critique the project of modernity. Holub concludes that rethinking "the question of Islam" will enable Europe to examine its own past, while Euro-Islam will play an important role in the self-perception of Muslims around the world.

## HYBRIDITY AND THE NEW BORDERLANDS

Of the issues addressed in this book, we may observe situations in which assumed dualities are torn open and the logic of hybridity is introduced. The process is not one which makes use of the combination or merger of incompatible elements, but instead involves the insertion of a third possibility, with the goal of connecting originally incommensurable terms and irreconcilable realities. As I have remarked in earlier work, the problem with the postmodernist celebration and endorsement of fragmentation is that it has not fully deconstructed the spatially and temporally constructed hierarchical dualities of center and margin.[28]

On the topic of multiculturalism, Homi Bhabha has claimed that a liberal-relativist perspective is inadequate in itself, advocating instead a position of liminality, according to which cultural difference is no longer accommodated within a universalist framework: "Different cultures, the difference between cultural practices, the difference in the construction of cultures within different groups, very often set up among and between themselves an *incommensurability*."[29] This example encapsulates one of Bhabha's dilemmas: while he has formulated what amounts to a universal theory of the "Third space" as a space of resistance, he has denied the credibility of understanding cultural difference within a universalist framework. To be meaningful, I believe Bhabha's formulation of Third space needs to be more grounded in common practices. European Islam and Muslim Europe may be precisely such a location.

Akhil Gupta and James Ferguson believe that, in Bhabha's account, the presumption that physical spaces are neutral grids has enabled "the power of topography to conceal successfully the topography of power."[30] According to Gupta and Ferguson, "If, however, one begins with the proposition that 'spaces have *always* been hierarchically interconnected,' a spatialized understanding of cultural differences becomes important ... [and] we can see that the identity of a place emerges by the intersection of its specific involvement in a system of hierarchically organized spaces with its cultural construction as a community or locality. Issues of collective identity today ... take on a special character, when more and more of us live in what Said has called a 'generalized condition of homelessness,' a world where 'identities are increasingly coming to be, if not wholly deterritorialized, at least differently territorialized.'"[31]

According to Kevin Robins, "The closure of European culture may be seen in terms of the loss of historical purpose: the 'End of History' fantasy. [Because] Europe no longer sees itself in terms of creation of history ... [t]here is no longer the sense of modernity as dynamic transformation. Modernity has become Europe's tradition now, to be remembered and revered, not for revision or reinvention. ... There can be no more change when the sources of change have been disavowed."[32] Robins suggests that cultural experience is always experience of the others, and that the "real others" are indispensable to transformations in historical change. "History is created out of cultures in relation and interaction: interrupting identities." Thus Robins advocates an opening up by Europe to "non-European" cultural interruption. Indeed, a future (as opposed to a continued past) is impossible without this, he believes. This rehistoricizing of European culture is the key, he says, for "redeeming the hopes of the past."[33]

Borderlands are just such a place of incommensurable contradictions: "The term does not indicate a fixed topographical site between two other fixed locales (nations, societies, cultures), but an interstitial zone of displacement and deterritorialization that shapes the identity of the hybridized subject."[34] Rather than dismissing them as insignificant, as marginal zones, thin slivers of land between stable places, we should perhaps contend with the notion that the borderland is a more adequate conceptualization of the "normal" locale in the postmodern global era. In my earlier discussion of the Third place and borderlands, I have similarly suggested that borderlands are no longer fragments anchored between two fixed and well-defined places, and that sites of the in-between, such as the Third place, no longer simply occupy the margins of the periphery.[35] I now believe that the most hybrid of places have moved firmly to the center of the core. Indeed the contributions to this book suggest that Muslim Europe may be the new but quintessential borderland, and that Euro-Islam may be that emerging Third space.

## NOTES

1. E. Cue, "For France, Girls in Head Scarves Threaten Secular Ideals," *Christian Science Monitor* (October 5, 1994), 1.
2. S. Kinzer, "Head Scarf Puts Turkish Assembly into Uproar," *New York Times*, May 3, 1999, 8.
3. For a discussion of a uniquely African Islam, see M. Watts, "Islamic Modernities? Citizenship, Civil Society and Islamism in a Nigerian City," *Public Culture* (Winter 1996).
4. C. Geertz, *Islam Observed* (New Haven, Conn.: Yale University Press, 1968).
5. A. MacLeod, "Muslim Scarf Controversy Ends," *Christian Science Monitor* (January 31, 1990), 6.
6. MacLeod, "Muslim Scarf Controversy Ends."
7. Y. M. Ibrahim, "France Bans Muslim Scarf in Its Schools," *New York Times*, September 11, 1994.
8. Cue, "Girls in Head Scarves."
9. Ibrahim, "France Bans Muslim Scarf."
10. As quoted in Cue, "Girls in Head Scarves."
11. Cue, "Girls in Head Scarves," 1.
12. As quoted in Cue, "Girls in Head Scarves."

13. No author named, "Rejecting Their Ancestors the Gauls: The Muslims in France," *The Economist* (November 16, 1996).

14. Kinzer, "Head Scarf Puts Turkish Assembly into Uproar," 8.

15. I. Grewal, *Home and Harem: Nation, Empire and the Culture of Travel* (Durham, N.C.: Duke University Press, 1996).

16. K. Robins, "Interrupting Identities," in S. Hall and P. du Gay, eds., *Questions of Cultural Identity* (London: Sage, 1996).

17. Robins, "Interrupting Identities," 72.

18. K. Woodward, "Introduction," in K. Woodward, ed., *Identity and Difference* (London: Sage, 1997).

19. B. Anderson, *Imagined Communities* (London: Verso, 1983).

20. L. Grossberg, "Identity and Cultural Studies: Is That All There Is?" in Hall and du Gay, *Questions of Cultural Identity*.

21. See M. Foucault, *Discipline and Punish: The Birth of the Prison*, 2nd ed., trans. Alan Sheridan (New York: Vintage, 1995).

22. G. Agamben, *The Coming Community* (Minneapolis: University of Minnesota Press, 1993).

23. Jurgen Habermas talks about this in the context of Euro-Islam in his *The Postnational Constellation: Political Essays* (Cambridge, U.K.: Polity Press, 2001).

24. S. Hall, "Introduction: Who Needs Identity?" in Hall and du Gay, eds., *Questions of Cultural Identity* (London: Sage, 1996), 4.

25. I refer to John Voll and John Esposito.

26. B. Ashcroft, G. Griffiths, and H. Tiffin, *Key Concepts in Post-Colonial Studies* (London: Routledge, 1998), 110.

27. R. Bloul, "Engendering Muslim Identities: Deterritorialization and the Ethnicization Process in France," in B. Metcalf, ed., *Making Muslim Space in North America and Europe* (Berkeley: University of California Press, 1996).

28. N. AlSayyad, *Hybrid Urbanism: On the Identity Discourse and the Built Environment* (Westport, Conn.: Praeger, 2001).

29. H. Bhabha, "The Third Space Interview with Homi Bhabha," in J. Rutherford, ed., *Identity, Community, Culture, Difference* (London: Lawrence and Wishart, 1990), 209.

30. A. Gupta and J. Ferguson, "Beyond 'Culture': Space, Identity, and the Politics of Difference," *Cultural Anthropology* (February 1992), 6–23.

31. Gupta and Ferguson, "Beyond 'Culture,'" 6–23.

32. K. Robins, "Interrupting Identities," 81.

33. K. Robins, "Interrupting Identities," 82.

34. Gupta and Ferguson, "Beyond 'Culture,'" 6–23.

35. AlSayyad, *Hybrid Urbanism*.

# 2

# Muslim Migrants in Europe:
# Between Euro-Islam and Ghettoization

## Bassam Tibi

Instead of rooting my discourse in the notion of an inevitable and much-publicized "clash" between Islam and Europe, I choose to underline the potential for intercivilizational dialogue. Such needed dialogue over values presupposes an awareness of difference and of its limits, that is, the limits of pluralism.[1] This, in turn, requires a willingness by those involved to open themselves to one another in pursuit of a cross-cultural consensus over values valid in the political culture. While I respect "difference," and submit that coping with it is an essential element of tolerance and pluralism, I also maintain that it is unacceptable to stop at simply acknowledging difference, as cultural relativists do, without providing prescriptions for how to deal with it.[2]

In his criticism of cultural relativism, Ernest Gellner has argued that religious fundamentalism is a variety of absolutism. Following this view, it might be expected that cultural relativists and fundamentalists would find themselves in conspicuous conflict with one another. But Gellner has noted that "in practice, this confrontation is not very much in evidence."[3] The reason for this is that cultural relativists generally apply their views only to those who espouse Western values, and they stop short of proceeding in a similar manner with non-Western cultures. Moreover, cultural relativists mostly confuse the critiques of premodern cultures with an often misconceived "cultural racism."[4]

Unfortunately, the popularity of the cultural relativist position has become so widespread that it has now been adopted even by people belonging to these non-Western cultures—for example, Islamic reformers and secularists. As a Muslim scholar who descends from a centuries-old, Muslim-Damascene notable family, but who lives today as a migrant in Europe, I maintain that the types of positions cultural relativism leads to—victimology, accusation, self-accusation, and self-denial—are inappropriate for dealing with "difference" and the issue of Islamic migration to Europe.

There is a need to overcome Western Islamophobia, but the demonization of Europe, as pursued by some, is not the proper way. If one is committed to intercultural dialogue, one should not simply replace one phobia with another.

Migration to Europe today is a new process, one that involves several actors. In common debate on the issue one often hears the demand that Europe needs to change, which is utterly correct. Indeed, Europe needs to adjust to globalization—to the very process it set in motion through the European expansion.[5] And in the present age, migration is surely one component of this globalization. However, it is not only Europe that needs to change; the migrants need to change as well. Thus, the call for a de-ethnization of European identity must apply equally to the identity of migrants. Otherwise, it would involve only "one-way change" and "one-way tolerance."

In embracing the typology of Manuel Castells concerning identity-building, I want to single out his ideal type of "project identity." By this, Castells means that social actors need to "build a new identity that redefines their position in society. . . . No identity can be an essence."[6] Thus, as much as Europeans are called upon to de-ethnicize their identity to allow the newcomers to become Europeans, it makes sense that Muslim migrants should be requested to redefine their identity in the diaspora by adding a European component. My position relies on the assumption that no prudent person would choose to be alien forever, and that the will to live in Europe is ultimately irreconcilable with a wholesale rejection of Europe, as those who demonize European civilization commonly do. In my book on Europe in the age of migration, I thus proposed that Europeans overcome their Euro-arrogance, while Muslim migrants engage themselves in the unfolding of a Euro-Islamic identity.[7] Muslims living in Europe need to find a commonality between themselves and European civilization. At the same time, the de-ethnization of Europe is a prerequisite for the feasibility of Euro-Islam.

In short, both actors are today challenged to change and redefine their identities. It is as wrong to essentialize Europe as "racist, genocidal, and so on," as it is to essentialize Islam in an Islamophobic manner. Europe and the Islamic world are separate civilizations, with centuries-old records that encompass enmity and cordiality equally.[8] In this regard, dichotomies built on this legacy—such as East versus West and First World versus Third World—are based on "artificial categories," as Nezar AlSayyad has rightly argued. AlSayyad has added that "societies are constructed in relation to one another and are . . . perceived through the ideologies and narratives of situated discourse."[9] When it comes to the construction of identities—as based on the production of meaning—academics need to free themselves from their "preoccupation with globalization" in acknowledging that "each individual belongs to many cultures, and people have multiple cultural identities. . . . Identity is always under construction and in constant evolution."[10] My vision of an Euro-Islamic identity for Muslim migrants has been developed along such lines that question constructed dichotomies—however, without overlooking real value conflicts.

## THE UNDERLYING ISSUES

The term *New Islamic Presence* has been coined to describe the increasing contemporary migration from Muslim countries to Western Europe.[11] By the end of World War II there were fewer than one million Muslim people living in Western Europe, mostly in France and the United Kingdom. This figure has now risen to about fifteen million, as Muslim migrants now live in almost all European societies, from Scandinavia to Italy.

It is, of course, wrong to relate the presence of Islam in Europe exclusively to migration. There are about eight million native European Muslims, who mainly live in southeast Europe.[12] However, since the focus of this chapter is on Western Europe, I shall set aside this native Muslim community and concentrate on Muslim migrants to Europe's west. From an American perspective, it is first important to ask why Muslims born in France, the United Kingdom, or Germany are even considered migrants at all, and not natives. The answer is that in Europe the second and even the third generation of Muslim migrants have still not been accepted as part of the polity. In many cases, being considered a migrant would actually represent an improvement in status—in particular, over the view that Muslims are merely *Gastarbeiter*, or "temporary residents." In considering their present legal and social status, I continue to address Muslims in Western Europe as migrants struggling for citizenship and acceptance.

It may be misleading to talk in general about Muslims in Europe at all. Such a broad grouping overlooks the fact the migrant community is ethnically multifaceted and strongly divided along sectarian lines. For example, Muslims living in France have been, and still are, predominantly migrants from the Maghreb.[13] Meanwhile, those living in the United Kingdom have been, and still are, mostly from South Asia (Pakistan, India, and Bangladesh). Until the early 1960s, the Muslim presence in these countries was almost exclusively related to French colonial rule in North Africa, and to British colonial rule in the Indian subcontinent. In addition, sectarian divisions in Europe are severe. Thus, for example, the Muslim Sunni community in the German state of Hessen has refused in its appeals for recognition to include Shi'is, Alevis, or Ahmadis as Muslims.

Since the 1960s the situation has been changing, as labor migration linked to the booming economies of Europe has boosted Islamic migration's statistical significance. Western European countries today need labor but lack the internal demographic growth to provide it. In this context, Western European countries other than France and the United Kingdom have started to encourage people from the Mediterranean to come there to earn money.

Until the end of the Cold War brought a loosening of Europe's internal boundaries, there was generally no talk about migration in Western Europe.[14] In Germany, for instance, the majority of workers (i.e., not simply Turks, but also

south and southeast Europeans working in German factories) were perceived
both by themselves and by Germans as guest workers—people whose presence in
the country would end when their labor was no longer needed.[15] Critically mind-
ed Germans have stated with equal prudence and repentance: "We have imported labor and have overlooked the fact that we were importing human beings."
Despite the official German slogan "We are not a country for migration," the
office of Commissioner for Issues Concerning Aliens of the former Christian
Democratic-Liberal government has introduced the very term *migration* in its doc-
umentary entitled "Foreigners Residing in Germany."[16] Among these legal aliens,
there exists a considerable Muslim community of more than three million (more
than two million being Turks and Kurds).[17] Yet, although the new Social
Democratic Green German government is more open-minded toward the
migrants, it has continued an intrinsic level of duplicity by confusing real integration with simply granting a German passport. In a country with no tradition of
citizenship, receiving a passport in line with the new German citizenship law is no
more significant than acquiring a piece of paper. A passport does not provide a
citizen identity if the cultural underpinning is lacking. Most important, it does
not convey membership in "The Club."

The majority of those who now comprise the new Muslim labor force in
Western Europe—in particular, Turks who have migrated to Germany—came, and
still come, from rural areas and have quite low levels of education and training. It
follows that such migrants not only lack in technical skills, but are also considered
by some as lacking a fundamental understanding of their own religion and culture.
Most important, because there is a lack of spokespersons among this community—
who might have been expected to come from an educated elite—such spokespersons
are now coming from outside the migrant community, without being knowledgeable
of its needs. Today such people are mostly imams who do not speak German, English,
or French, and who have no clue as to the problems and concerns of young Muslims
born in Western Europe. These imams have either been imposed on the migrants by
Islamist groups, or they have been appointed by the Muslim governments of countries such as Turkey or Morocco. In Germany, even Saudi Arabia has acquired considerable influence by using its petrodollars to fund such appointments—despite the
fact that there are no Saudi migrants there.

## HISTORY

As stated earlier, in 1945 there were less than one million Muslims living in
Western Europe. In the 1960s workers were requested to come, and those
Muslims who came were welcomed because they were needed. But by the early
1990s the situation had changed considerably, as a rapid increase in the inflow of

Muslims to Western Europe coincided with an end to the boom years for the European economies. Among other things, this meant that as unemployment rose, there was no longer as great a need for unskilled migrant labor.

The present wave of Muslim migration has had more to do with the worsening economic conditions in Muslim countries than with the need for labor in Europe. In particular, the populations of the southern and eastern Mediterranean have suffered from poverty and unemployment, and migration to Europe has been seen as a principal source of hope. In this context, the total number of Muslim migrants in Europe climbed at the end of the 1990s to an estimated fifteen million and is still increasing tremendously. At a time when most European economies have levels of unemployment that average almost 10 percent, illegal migration is thriving. In fact, illegal migration and the abuse of the right to political asylum are now the primary instruments for gaining access to Europe.[18] The common view among migrants is that it is more dignified to live on the benefits of welfare as an asylum-seeker in Western Europe than it is to live in a suburban *gececondu*, or shack, in Ankara or Istanbul, or in the slums of Casablanca or Algiers, with no income at all.

In Germany, for instance, the average monthly income of welfare benefit recipients (regardless of whether they are Germans or foreigners) is DM 1000 per adult, which does not include additional generous allowances for children, payments for free accommodation, full-scale medical insurance, and a variety of other government allowances (e.g., for clothing, furniture, fees, and even pets). According to the most recent official figures (published in August 1998), almost three million residents out of a population of eighty-two million (including legal aliens) are receiving welfare payments in Germany (7 percent more than in 1997). This amounts to a total annual expenditure of DM 52 billion. Despite the fact that only 8 percent of those eighty-two million residents are aliens (i.e., do not enjoy German citizenship), 23 percent of the recipients of welfare are aliens.[19] Furthermore, this figure includes only legal aliens who receive ordinary welfare; according to new legislation of June 1998 "tolerated illegals" are to receive special reduced payments not covered by this figure.

Such statistics, regularly published in the local press, have only furthered xenophobia in Germany, including anti-Islamic sentiments. The irony is that not only does Germany receive more unwanted migrants and asylum-seekers than almost any other European state due to extremely lax laws, but it also provides them with the most generous payments.

In regard to the above, it is important to note that a key feature of globalization is the spread of information in all directions. The most generous aspects of the German welfare system are therefore well known in the southern and eastern Mediterranean. The increasing inflow of illegal migrants and unprosecuted asylum-seekers attracted by such financial largesse has, however, exposed Muslims living legally in Germany to increased levels of xenophobia and anti-Islamism.

Thus, the existing socially and economically integrated populations of Muslims in Germany and other parts of Europe do not favor illegal migration, because it creates increasing hardships for them.

## THE INQUIRY: A CHALLENGE AND THE RESPONSES TO IT

Unlike the classical Muslim residents of France and the United Kingdom, most other Muslim workers on the continent—for example, the Turks in Germany—initially came not as migrants, but as a temporary labor force. They were looked at as staying in Europe only long enough to earn enough money to return to their countries of origin with the means to start a new existence there. The implication was that these workers would leave Europe when they were no longer needed.

In other words, apart from exceptions and some militant Muslims who relate migration to the religious obligation of *hijra*, as discussed later, most first-generation Muslims, like native Europeans, originally did not view the "presence of Muslims in Europe" as a lasting phenomenon. However, the continuing nature of their stays, and the fact that a second (and, by now, a third) generation are not only living in Europe, but have been born there, have contributed to radical changes in perception. In Germany, as in other European states, this has made migration an increasingly complicated issue for both parties. Until the legislation of the new citizenship law by the 1998 elected Social Democratic government, German law did not allow double citizenship. Even though most Turks want to acquire German citizenship, they do not want to give up their Turkish one. Therefore, they mostly do not apply for German citizenship. Adding to the problem is that Turks born in Germany are despised in Turkey as *allemanci* (something negative like "Germanized"). But neither are they considered to be Germans, even if they were born there.

Such issues concerning the interrelation of identity and migration have been dealt with extensively elsewhere. The focus here is on future strategies for addressing the risks and opportunities of Muslim migration to Western Europe. The most important issue in this regard is clearly that a large majority of the fifteen million Muslims now in Europe are there to stay and thus can no longer be considered temporary residents.[20] As indicated, this population is comprised of basically three big, comparable subgroups: Muslim Turks and Kurds (three and a half million—more than two million of them in Germany); Maghrebis (more than five million—about four million of them in France); and South Asians, basically in the United Kingdom, but also in all other European countries.

In addition to these large basic groups, there are migrants from all over the Islamic world in Europe.[21] For example, 30 percent of the residents of the city of Frankfurt are foreigners, carrying the passports of 165 different nations. Among this number are representatives of almost all the Muslim countries. The ethnic and sectarian divides among Muslim migrants in Europe are reflected in the structures of their mosques and their related religious associations.[22] These may be Sunni or Shi'i, Turkish, Bosnian, Arab, or Pakistani, again divided into Ahmadi and Sunni sects. Seldom are there comprehensive Islamic organizations. Such a fragmented structure naturally leads to concerns that the politicization of internal divides within the community of European Muslims could lead to inter-Islamic rift and violence.

Bearing these realities in mind, a central question must be whether these Muslim migrants will be able to integrate politically into Europe as citizens of Muslim faith, or whether they will continue to live in Muslim ghettos, divided along ethnic and sectarian lines.

## PROSPECTS FOR A EURO-ISLAM

The Muslim presence in Western Europe is often incorrectly viewed as monolithic, in much the same distorted manner that Western-dominated international media normally presents images of Islam outside Europe. The richness of Islam has long been related to its cultural diversity; it is a misperception to see it as an expression of a monolithic worldwide phenomenon.

Despite a unity of belief, Muslim migrants living in Europe have different ethnic, national, and cultural backgrounds. Across these lines they also subscribe to diverse political and social strategies for articulating their views and options concerning their status in society. In this regard, it is not a contradiction to speak in each case of a culturally distinct Arab, African, Indian, or South-Asian Islam. The identity of Muslims is thus the identity of culturally different people who nevertheless share the same faith. If it is therefore possible to talk about Afro-Islam for African Muslims or Indo-Islam for Indian Muslims, why should it not be possible to talk about Euro-Islam in the context of Muslims who have migrated to Western Europe?

In a project at the Institute du Monde Arabe in Paris in 1992 I outlined my concept of Euro-Islam.[23] The concept of Euro-Islam is intended to provide a liberal variety of Islam acceptable both to Muslim migrants and to European societies, one that might accommodate European ideas of secularity and individual citizenship along the lines of modern secular democracy.

In other words, Euro-Islam is the very same religion of Islam, although culturally adjusted to the civic culture of modernity.[24] In European civil societies, an "open Islam" could be as at home as, for instance, Afro-Islam, having been adjusted to domestic African cultures. As I have described them, the major features of Euro-Islam would be *laïcité*, cultural modernity, and an understanding of tolerance that goes beyond the Islamic tolerance restricted to Abrahamitic believers (*ahl al-kitab*). In addition, by acknowledging cultural and religious pluralism, Euro-

Islam would give up the claim of Islamic dominance. Thus defined, Euro-Islam would be compatible with liberal democracy, individual human rights, and the requirements of a civil society. It would also contrast sharply with the communi-tarian politics that result in ghettoization. To be sure, the politics of Euro-Islam would not allow complete assimilation of Muslims.[25] Yet it could enable the adop-tion of forms of civil society leading to an enlightened, open-minded Islamic identity compatible with European civic culture.

The presence of Islam in Western Europe has already proposed a challenge. Related realities trigger a variety of responses by the Muslim migrants and the Europeans. As a response to this situation, Euro-Islam would be directed against both ghettoization and assimilation. It is, furthermore, a democratic response directed by a commitment to individual human rights.

There have, of course, been other responses directed at the challenge. The German Orientalist Tilman Nagel has, for example, proposed that the German government view Muslim migrants arrogantly as "protected minorities." This is originally an Islamic concept describing enemy aliens who have been given tem-porary safe-conduct.[26] In other words, they are people who would continue to be aliens. For Nagel and other German Orientalists, tolerance lies in "keeping the aliens away from Europe in underlining our otherness to them."[27]

Unlike this xenophobic position, multiculturalists are usually much more benevolent, arguing from a cultural-relativist angle that presents "differences" from a favorable point of view. Nevertheless, the result is the same: Islamic ghet-tos—in this case, however, in the name of communitarian multiculturalism. Despite different positions, the outcomes are comparable.

Although by no means multiculturalists, the Islamists among the migrants to Europe are nevertheless usually more sympathetic to multicultural positions than they are to democratic integration. The reason is that they understand perfectly well how to instrumentalize multicultural views—how to make use of them for fundamentalist ends. Thus, Islamists often willingly confuse assimilation with political integration in order to rebuff the latter.

This chapter takes the view that Euro-Islamic political integration is the best response to the pending challenge. Muslims need to become members of the European body politic they live in—without, however, giving up their Islamic identity. Citizenship issues ought to be seen within this framework. And toward this end an enlightened Islamic education might serve to maintain Islamic iden-tity without promoting segregationist ends.

## SHEDDING LIGHT ON MUSLIM MIGRATION TO EUROPE: THE GLOBAL CONTEXT

Many varieties of migration have been studied by historians, and there is no doubt that migration patterns today differ from earlier patterns in many respects. The present moment has been described as a "global age."[28] And in the context of a "global village," ever-unfolding structural and institutional networks in economy, politics, transportation, and communication have brought an unprecedented degree of interaction among culturally diverse people. A novel pattern of mass migration all over the world has been one of the many by-products of this globalization.[29]

Such a level of migration implies great potential for conflict, and it necessitates the development of peaceful solutions that address identity-related issues. Generally, the emerging "global village" has been equated with the "McWorld" of consumption. But present fascination with these ideas has obscured the fact that culture refers in more basic terms to norms, values, and worldviews that result from a social production of meaning.[30] Eating hamburgers, watching videos, handling computers, wearing fashionable dress, and the like are only the outcomes of more fundamental social processes. Likewise, the development of a global culture has far more profound bases than the simple spread of an American popular culture of consumption. The rampant use of the global village notion as a sweeping critique of McWorld-culture has also led to wrong and misleading assumptions about impending cultural standardization. Despite the structural reality of the global village, there in fact exists no global culture based on outlooks shared by the entire humanity. Hedley Bull has been among the few scholars who have advanced the insight that the shrinking of the globe "does not in itself create a unity of outlook, and has not in fact done so."[31] Bull's insight has been phrased in the following manner by Zbigniew Brzezinski: "Humanity is becoming simultaneously more unified and more fragmented."[32]

On cross-regional and cross-cultural grounds, I believe it is today possible to observe both globalization and local cultural self-assertion. In my writings, I have coined the formula "the simultaneity of structural globalization and cultural fragmentation."[33] As a Muslim living in the West, I am at pains to be a mediator, seeking to establish bridges between the Islamic world and the West. In this regard, my work has addressed both entities as civilizations, and my first concern has been with their encounter, as now framed in terms of the global village. In this pursuit, I distinguish between economic interaction as bargaining; political interaction among states as negotiation; and cultural interaction on the civilizational level as cultural dialogue. In terms of the latter, it often becomes important to question the notion of "cultural racism," especially when it is implied indiscriminately. The focus of the ensuing analysis will be on the nonstate-related level of cultural interaction.

Muslim migration to Europe has revived the significance of the Euro-Mediterranean region as a classical intercivilizational basin linking the West to the core of the Islamic world. It would be dishonest to avoid the central question of whether Europe and the Mediterranean are one international society. In the understanding of Hedley Bull, an international society exists when states share "common values . . . [and] conceive of themselves to be bound by a common set of rules in their relations with one another. . . . An international society in this sense presupposes an international system, but an international system may exist that is not an international society."[34] In applying these insights to today's Mediterranean region, one may see a combination of system and society. North of the Mediterranean, the European Union forms a society of states interacting with another one. Another society, of predominantly Islamic states, exists south and east of the Mediterranean. Interaction between the two societies takes place on the grounds of an international system in which both state groupings are sub-systemic parts. However, Islamic migration to Europe has blurred the boundaries between system and society and complicated the issue.[35]

European moralists have suggested that the Mediterranean embodies the basin of a single civilization that combines a northern (European) and a southern (Islamic) component. This view was, for example, presented by several Dutch politicians at an intercultural dialogue held by the European Union at The Hague in March 1997.[36] However, an honest cultural dialogue between Islam and the West would dissociate itself from such disruptive moralistic views and meaningless mutual assurances. It would recognize instead that while both groups of states share formally in certain established international norms and values, they simultaneously belong to different civilizations, with different outlooks and worldviews.

In viewing the Mediterranean as a bridge and not a boundary (let alone a warrior frontier),[37] the need arises to determine common and shared values. My view is that such Euro-Mediterranean relations and the related migration issues are not basically interstate affairs. A prominent American student of Islam, John Kelsay, has emphasized the fact that "the rapidity of Muslim immigration . . . suggests that we may soon be forced to speak not simply of Islam *and*, but of Islam *in* the West.[38]

The outcome of this situation will ultimately be related to how Muslims and Europeans deal with cultural divergences in the course of the present civilizational interaction, of which migration is a basic part. Politicians on both sides of this issue have attempted to deny and obscure how it involves fundamental differences in worldview. Those involved must go beyond the censorship of political correctness to address impending and real issues. This must involve both an inclination to reconcile, not antagonize, divergent views, and a clear commitment to avoid concealment. Only in this manner will it be possible to realize how foolish it is to deny existing cultural differences.

Unfortunately, the debate on migration has largely been related to the concept of a "clash of civilizations" between Islam and the West. In an important

Islamic-Western dialogue undertaken in Karachi, Muslims and Westerners succeeded in going beyond the fallacy of a false sense of harmony. Instead, they assigned to themselves the task of searching for new modes of peaceful coexistence based on a proper answer to the challenge: "how to deal with differences."[39] In an interview on the occasion of that event, I argued, "The clash of civilizations was not invented, but it was used, abused for other reasons."[40] With this concern in mind, one might reconsider John Kelsay's reference to the shift in Islam's importance for the West from Islam *and* the West (an issue of neighborly relations between states) to Islam *in* the West (an issue of neighborhoods within one's own state). In this new situation there is a need to deal with persistent commonalties between both civilizations in a new manner. According to Kelsay:

> Perhaps such commonalties serve, in the main, to indicate the nature of disagreement between the West and Islam. . . . But there should be no doubt that in certain contexts, the common discourse about ethics . . . has the potential for creative and cooperative endeavor. Given the increased presence of Muslims in Europe and North America—a presence that makes for a more than intense interaction between the two traditions than ever before—it is important to see this.[41]

Among the premises of this chapter is a belief that a common discourse about ethics needs to be linked to the migration debate.[42] The outcome could be a civic culture shared by all.

## ISLAM IN THE WEST: WHAT CHOICES?

As a Muslim living in the West, I have chosen to become a European citizen—however, with a clear commitment to the French notion of *citoyen*, not to the German ethnic concept of *Staatsbürgerschaft*. I claim to maintain my Islamic cultural identity, while combining it with the political identity of *citoyennité*. In so doing, I find myself in conflict both with an inherent European racism based on exclusive ethnicity, and with an opposed trend of multicultural communitarianism that has been combined with the claims of some Islamist leaders in Europe for a separate Islamic entity within the West. In general, those Islamic migrants who want to become citizens of the West are caught between these views: between rejection, and the pressure to join a cultural ghetto. Such polarization is particularly harmful to Muslim juveniles who have been born in Europe and are seeking to unfold identities and personalities there.

Among Germans, two attitudes exist currently, which represent two extremes toward Muslim migrants: the anti-Islamic, and the philo-Islamic. German philosopher Helmuth Plessner, who found refuge in the Netherlands during the

Nazi period, has criticized the propensity of Germans to shift from one extreme to another, with no option in between. In this case, such a polarization has led on the one hand to those who demonize Islam while glorifying themselves, and on the other to those who have moved from European universalism to cultural relativism, with the result of self-denial. (In fact, the latter two views do not necessarily contradict each other, as I demonstrate below.) Siegfried Kohlhammer has depicted these attitudes as separating the "Enemies and Friends of Islam."[43] Of course, there exists a third group which combines cultural open-mindedness with a commitment to the enlightened values of European civilization. But it is unfortunate to see that the extreme views (Euro-arrogant exclusiveness, and self-denial presented as self-opening) are now being represented as dominant.[44]

Muslims like me who subscribe to the Ibn Khaldunian notion of *asabiyya*—a kind of *esprit de corps*, or civilization awareness—believe that such pseudo-opening to others in the shape of self-denial actually represents a decline in the West, concealed as open-mindedness. It is very important that Europeans grasp how a low degree of asabiyya is not the alternative to Euro-arrogance and racism. Just as philo-Semitism cannot overcome anti-Semitism, so is cultural-relativist self-denial only the other side of Eurocentric exclusivity.

Likewise, the choice that migrants make regarding the variety of "Islam in the West" will be decisive for the future of Europe. The outcome of the cooperation of the parties involved, as well as their ability to dialogue with one another, may lead to common responses to the pending challenges. In arguing that there is no such thing as an essentialist Islam, just as there is no such thing as an essentialist Europe, one must realize there exists no constant pattern of Islamic or European identity. Islam will always be an ever-changing cultural system designed by Muslims themselves. Similarly, Europe can be an open society in which there is a place for Muslims as equal citizens.

Both inclinations among Europeans—the exclusivist and the self-denying— are great obstacles to intercultural dialogue based on reason. But this dialogue is essential to determining what variety of Islam will prevail in Europe in the future. Migrants could have a multiple identity, a position I support in relation to my own multiple identity as both a Middle Eastern Sunni Muslim and a European citizen.[45]

As much as I am concerned with European exclusiveness, I am equally concerned about the maintenance of orthodox Islamic views among parts of the Muslim community in Europe, and in particular their view that migration is related to the *daiwah*, that is, the call to Islam.[46] According to this view, like missionaries, Muslims in Europe consider themselves an outpost for the spread of Islam. This belief—and, of course, the publicizing of its rhetoric—can only encourage anti-Islamic attitudes among Europeans and bolster existing prejudices. Thus, for example, among the exiled groups of Muslim extremists in London is one led by Sheikh Omar Bakri, called "Movement of the Muhajirun."[47] Bakri has clearly linked the status of migrants to the doctrine of *hijra* in the pursuit of the *daʿwah*. And like his late predecessor, the fundamentalist Kalim Siddiqi, who established the Islamic Counter-Parliament in London, Bakri has become prominent through the British media. After the terrorist attacks at U.S. embassies in Africa in 1998 and the U.S. retaliation in Sudan and Afghanistan, Bakri stated in a BBC television interview that Muslims in Europe "are all Osama bin Laden." Slogans like this have proven to be a great disservice not only to Islam, but to all Muslims living in Europe.

A dialogue is imperative to establishing the grounds for a search for commonalties. Though I oppose Euro-arrogant exclusiveness and assimilation, I do not favor cultural-relativist multiculturalism, nor that related cultural communitarianism which has clearly been abused by Islamists. My objection to multiculturalism is related to its inherent support for cultural ghettos, and to its negation of civic identity patterns and the assertion of one law for all.

I favor honest intercultural dialogue, in which both sides, with adequate standing, may seek out positive commonalties among themselves in search of foundations for a civic culture.

Honest dialogue of this sort will not overlook areas of disagreement, but address them consciously, while developing an ability to deal properly with disagreement. The goal of this combination of realism and humanism is a commitment to live together in peace, mutual respect, and self-respect, without feelings of superiority. For enlightened Muslims, it is therefore imperative to reject all kinds of Western missionarism, as well as reverse missionarism. By this statement, I address the need for Muslims to be committed to reason-based dialogue and not to confuse this with the daʿwah, as some Muslim fundamentalists in the diaspora do. The Qurʾan clearly states: "*Lakum dinakum wa liya din* [You have your religion, I have mine]." One cannot turn down Western missionarism and dialogue in favor of one's own, and at the same time be honest and committed to true dialogue and mutual tolerance.

Muslims in Europe need to decouple themselves from the Islamic tradition of associating migration with the spread of Islam, and also from the abuse of this tradition by Islamist groups. Such reason-based dialogue facilitated common understanding in a meeting among open-minded Muslims, Christians, and Jews held in Cordoba in the first week of February 1998 and again in 2000. There the *imam* of Jericho, Sheikh Rajai Abdou, said: "I am in conflict with myself. You want to dialogue and you mean by this intellectual exchange; to me *hiwar* [dialogue] is a means of *daʿwah* [call to Islam]."

## WESTERN-MUSLIM ENCOUNTERS: LESSONS FROM THE PAST

Earlier, I referred to a distinction between dialogue and negotiation. While the latter is pursued between states, dialogue is not bound to political constraints that can create gaps between rhetoric and action, word and deed. But true inter-civilizational dialogue needs to be both honest and rational—that is, reason-based. This understanding is in line with both the tradition of medieval Islamic rationalism and with the European Enlightenment. It is also in line with the current political culture of democracy and human rights.

In making the choice in favor of dialogue, it is important to learn from history. For example, Prince Hassan Ibn Talal of Jordan has stated, with crucial insight, that "Muslims and Europeans have been at their worst when they sought to dominate each other, and at their best when they looked to learn from each other."[48] Research on Muslim-Western relations supports this view. For example, in my view, the opening of the Islamic mind to Hellenism, and the ensuing Hellenization of Islam in the medieval period, were the factors that led to the height of Islamic civilization.[49] In time, European adoptions from Islamic rationalism at the eve of the Renaissance also led to beneficial new processes within European civilization. As the Berkeley scholar Leslie Lipson has written:

> Aristotle crept back into Europe by the side door. His return was due to the Arabs, who had become acquainted with Greek thinkers. . . . Both Avicenna and Averroès were influenced by him. . . . Aristotle was introduced from Cordoba. Aristotle was significant not only for what he taught but more for his method and spirit.[50]

During medieval times Muslim thinkers were able to combine Aristotle's method and spirit with their Islamic mind and identities. They thus accorded Aristotle the status of *muàlim al-awwal* (the first teacher). Such was the height of Islamic tolerance at the time that the great Islamic philosopher al-Farabi was considered second to Aristotle.[51]

As Muslims in Europe search for options, they may refer to this historical record. References to positive historical exchanges between the two civilizations continue to be both topical and relevant for the Euro-Mediterranean dialogue. Thus, just as Arab Muslims and Europeans have encountered each other positively in the past on the grounds of *aql* (reason), so might they revive such a spirit as a framework for new dialogue, instead of engaging in new varieties of *jihad* and crusade.

My friend and intellectual mentor at Harvard, the Iraqi Muslim philosopher Muhsin Mahdi, believes that al-Farabi was the greatest thinker in Islamic political philosophy. In fact, al-Farabi was by origin a Turk; but his cultural language was Arabic, and his commitment was to Islamic civilization, not to any particular ethnicity. The Farabian Islamic aql-based philosophy is a lasting indication of a Euro-Islamic encounter in its best terms, and could provide the common ground for a new Western-Muslim relationship in the age of migration.

## CULTURAL PLURALISM IS NOT MULTICULTURALISM

As a Muslim migrant to Europe, I am opposed to all varieties of monoculture, favoring instead a plurality of cultures. My commitment to civic culture is in clear opposition to that tenet of cultural relativism which denies the importance of common values. Multiculturalism is based on cultural relativism; thus, European multiculturalists look with a sense of romantic-eccentric mystification at other cultures, viewing aliens in the Eurocentric tradition as *bons sauvages*. There are multiculturalists who consider Cordoba an example for multiculturalism, when in fact they lack clear knowledge of the subject. Such mystification is extremely important in understanding the distinction between cultural pluralism and multiculturalism.

To understand the implications of the distinction, one needs to return to the question of choices. Do Muslims living in Europe want to belong to a peripheral minority, with respective minority rights? Or would they rather become members of the European polity itself, with all its respective rights and duties? I see no contradiction between being a European and a Muslim. But there are Islamist groups in Europe which have no interest in Muslim migrants serving as a bridge between civilizations. They are instead interested in using the Muslim diaspora to create political confrontation. In arguing from the point of view of an open-minded Islam, one might again refer to the words of Prince Hassan:

> Muslims respect the rule of their host states and the applicable laws. For the principles of Islam require a Muslim minority to obey a state in which it is resident, just as a Muslim state expects non-Muslims to respect and to abide by its laws. The Muslims of Europe are therefore not asking for special privileges, and do not demand what is denied to others. They are merely asking for their religion to be recognized within the European context.[52]

Muslims who are committed to this understanding of their position in Europe "view themselves as both Muslims and Europeans, seeing no essential contradiction between those identities," according to Prince Hassan. I believe it is up to Europeans whether or not such views will help Islamic migrants become Europeans. Can such an enlightened Euro-Islam become a reality at the turn of the century? Or will the opposite scenario of a ghetto Islam gain ground among migrants?

It must by now be clear that such an enlightened Muslim position does not accord with those forms of multicultural communitarianism which demand different laws and different treatment for people of different cultural communities. It should be noted that the issue is *intercultural*, not one of "multicultural discourse." The difference is determined by whether one accepts or rejects the paramount importance of a single shared civic culture. I view multiculturalism as a romantic ideology, one that is clearly distinguished from a more realistic cultural pluralism. In refuting the multicultural reference to Spain, I want to state that Islamic Spain was a society characterized by cultural pluralism; it was not a multicultural society in the cultural-relativist sense that is now spreading through Europe. In other words, Islam was the culture of Arab Spain, and Arabic was its language. No such thing as cultural relativism existed there.

## MINORITY RIGHTS AND MULTICULTURAL COMMUNITARIANISM ARE NOT AN ALTERNATIVE TO EURO-ISLAM: WHY?

In the present age of global networking, it is important to learn from the experience of others. In this regard, India, with a considerable Islamic minority, may be seen to provide a good comparative study.[53] In research completed for the project of the University of Leiden on the Islamic presence in Western Europe, I dealt with the status of Muslims in India.[54] Despite the fact that the constitution of India prescribes one secular personal law for all religious communities, the early Congress government, for reasons of political expediency and to lure Muslim votes, allowed the practice of a "Muslim Personal Law." One result has been the rise of Hindu fundamentalism, for which the elections of 1996 and again of 1998 were an alarming signal. This rise has been related to resentment toward the privileges given to minorities. While pointing at these privileges, Hindu fundamentalists have called for the desecularization of India, something that may potentially infringe even on the physical existence of Indian Muslims.

Based on my study of this case, I believe Muslim migrants to Europe should beware of minority-rights issues in light of a growing hatred toward foreigners and the danger of right-wing radicalism.[55] As in India, I fear that granting special privileges and rights to minority cultural and religious groups in Europe will be counterproductive. Such measures will not only impede the political integration of these groups, but they will encourage the growth of right-wing radicalism. Muslims could end up being treated as the new Jews of a revived European anti-Semitism.[56]

## CONCLUDING REMARKS

In this analysis, I have tried to establish a clear distinction between multiculturalism and cultural pluralism, and between political integration and assimilation. I have recommended the political integration of Muslim migrants into Europe. Granting citizenship rights and duties to migrant Muslims will have the effect both of smoothing the way for their membership in "The Club of Europe" and demanding from them loyalty to the democratic polity in which they live. In particular, the acceptance of secular European laws—and, above all, secular constitutions separating religion from politics—will require Islamic migrants to reconsider the concept of the legitimacy of the imam.[57] Cultural reforms must enable a Muslim migrant to live under the governance of a non-Muslim imam ruler. But cultural reforms are needed on the European side, as well. In particular, the process of cultural reform must make it feasible for European states to accept Muslims as citizens. Remaking the club by altering the conditions for membership is thus not only an issue that requires Europeans to change. Muslim migrants need to change, too.

Unlike political integration, however, demands that migrants be assimilated involve the effort to deny cultural identity. They thus contradict the notion of cultural pluralism. An Arab Muslim migrant may have a triple identity: religio-culturally, I am a Euro-Muslim; ethnically, I am a Damascene Arab; and politically, I am a German citizen. I believe that the combination of these identities is feasible within the framework of cultural pluralism and political integration.

The argument I have made in support of cultural pluralism clearly runs counter to those notions of multicultural communitarianism pursued equally by Muslim segregationists and European cultural relativists. My criticism of these multiculturalist views is based not only on my commitment to a shared civic culture, but on my opposition to rampant universalisms. As a Muslim with a European education, I oppose all varieties of hegemonic Western universalism, and believe that multiculturalism is just another variety of them. I share the view of David Gress, who made the following observation in his overall study of Western civilization:

> Although multiculturalism might seem to contradict universalism, the two were compatible; indeed, multiculturalism was simply universalism applied to cultural politics. . . . Universalism . . . never solved its fundamental dilemma of being both a Western idea . . . and an anti-Western idea.[58]

In my rigorous criticism of advancing cultural relativism to a rampant universalism, I also share the view of the late Ernest Gellner.

> Three principle options are available in our intellectual climate: religious fundamentalism, relativism, and Enlightenment rationalism. . . . Logically, the religious fundamentalists are of course also in conflict with the relativists.[59]

Enlightenment rationalism has already succeeded in building bridges between Islam and Europe during two previous encounters. The rationalism of Islamic philosophy was the seed of an Islamic Enlightenment that was prevented from unfolding by the Islamic *fiqh* orthodoxy.[60] It emerged out of the Hellenization of

Islam, which I have said was the first positive Euro-Islamic encounter. The second positive encounter was the impact of Islamic rationalism on the European Renaissance. In contrast, the Islamic fundamentalism of our age may succeed only in materializing the wrongful prophecy of a clash of civilizations, not in building bridges between them.[61] The spread of such an Islamism in the European diaspora will cause Muslim migrants great pains, because it will only lead to the rise of anti-Islamism and result in the isolation of Muslim migrants in dreadful ghettos.

Ethnic identities are exclusive identities. If cultivated in the diaspora, they will lead to a kind of neo-absolutism and related social conflicts. The alternative is an all-inclusive civil identity, based on cultural pluralism. Thus, while fundamentalism is a modern variety of neo-absolutism, pluralism would encourage people to represent different views while at the same time being strongly committed to shared cross-cultural rules—and, above all, mutual tolerance and respect. Tolerance can never mean that only one party has the right to maintain its views at the expense of the other. For this reason, the exclusivist bias of multicultural communitarianism stands in clear contrast to cultural pluralism and tolerance. One-way tolerance is the tolerance of the loser. Muslim migrants cannot deny others what they require for themselves.

The granting of multicultural minority privileges to Muslim migrants in Europe may prove to be a double-edged sword with far-reaching consequences. On the one hand, it may facilitate unwanted interference by mostly undemocratic Islamic-Mediterranean governments in the affairs of Muslim migrants in Europe. But its political effects could also run in the opposite direction. Thus, on the other hand, ghettoized minorities in Europe could provide the base from which exiled representatives of political Islam act to topple existing governments in the Islamic world. And these Islamists would by no means be democrats.[62]

In subscribing to the Euro-Islamic view that Muslim migrants should act as a bridge between Islam and Europe, I find myself in opposition to those who would make Europe a refuge for Islamic fundamentalists. Such fundamentalists have no interest in the integration of Muslim migrants. And in siding with the concept of civic culture for all on grounds of cultural pluralism, I also find myself in opposition to multiculturalists and their cultural relativism. I argue that the bottom line for a pluri-cultural (not a multicultural) platform is the unequivocal acceptance of secular democracy, individual human rights for men and women, secular tolerance, and civil society. In my understanding, this is exactly what is involved in Euro-Islam. It is not ghetto Islam or fundamentalist Islam. Thus it is that at the turn of the century Muslim migrants in Europe must choose the destiny they want for themselves and for their children: to continue to be alien; or to join the changed club—without, however, being forced to assimilate.

Due to the great burden of history in Europe and the view of most Europeans that their continent is not designed for migration, the study of Muslim migrants in Europe should not be confused with the same issue in the United States. In Europe these matters are more complicated, have a different scope, and need the type of sensitive insight that only people familiar with both worlds, Islam and Europe, can provide. Europe has its own strong identity, and this needs to be taken into consideration in addressing these issues.

## NOTES

1. Contributions to a debate on this topic at the Erasmus Foundation were published as *The Limits of Pluralism: Neo-Absolutisms and Relativism* (Amsterdam: Praemium Erasmianum Foundation, 1994).

2. S. Ben-Habib, ed., *Democracy and Difference* (Princeton, N.J.: Princeton University Press, 1996).

3. E. Gellner, *Postmodernism, Reason and Religion* (London: Routledge, 1992).

4. B. Tibi, *The Crisis of Modern Islam: A Preindustrial Culture in the Scientific-Technological Age* (Salt Lake City: University of Utah Press, 1988).

5. W. Reinhard, ed., *Geschichte der europäischen Expansion* (Stuttgart, Ger.: Kohlhammer, 1983–1990).

6. M. Castells, *The Power of Identity* (Oxford, U.K.: Blackwell, 1997).

7. B. Tibi, *Europa ohne Identität? Die Krise der multikulturellen Gesellscaft* (Munich: C. Bertelsmann, 1988).

8. W. M. Watt, *Muslim-Christian Encounters: Perceptions and Misperceptions* (London: Routledge, 1991); and N. Daniel, *Islam and the West: The Making of an Image,* new edition (Oxford, U.K.: Oneworld, 1993).

9. N. AlSayyad, "Culture, Identity, and Urbanism in a Changing World," in M. Cohen, ed., *Preparing for the Urban Future* (Baltimore, Md.: Johns Hopkins University Press, 1996), 109.

10. AlSayyad, "Culture, Identity, and Urbanism," 120f.

11. T. Gerholm and Y. G. Lithman, eds., *The New Islamic Presence in Western Europe* (London: Mansell, 1988; paperback, 1990).

12. W. G. Lockwood, *European Moslems* (New York: Academic, 1975); and T. Bringa, *Being Muslim the Bosnian Way* (Princeton, N.J.: Princeton University Press, 1995).

13. A. G. Hargreaves, *Immigration, "Race" and Ethnicity in Contemporary France* (London: Routledge, 1995). See also G. Kepel, *Les banlieues de l'Islam: Naissance d'une religion en France* (Paris: Edition du Seuil, 1987).

14. M. Anderson, *Frontiers: Territory and State Formation in the Modern World* (Cambridge, U.K.: Polity Press, 1996).

15. P. Martin, "Germany: Reluctant Land of Immigration," in W. A. Cornelius et al., eds., *Controlling Immigration: A Global Perspective* (Stanford, Calif.: Stanford University Press, 1994).

16. The Commissioner for Issues Concerning Aliens, *Migration und Integration in Zahlen: Ein Handbuch,* ed. C. Schmalz-Jacobsen (Bonn, Ger.: Government Publication, 1997).

17. U. Spuler-Stegemann, *Muslime in Deutschland* (Freiburg, Ger.: Herder, 1998).

18. M. S. Teitelbaum and J. Winter, *A Question of Numbers: High Migration, Low Fertility and the Politics of National Identity* (New York: Hill & Wang, 1998).

19. "Immer mehr Sozialhilfeempfänger," in *Stuttgarter Zeitung*, August 2, 1998.

20. On Muslim migrants in France and the United Kingdom, see G. Kepel, *A L'Ouest d'Allah* (Paris: Edition du Seuil, 1994). Concerning France, see also Hargreaves, *Immigration, "Race" and Ethnicity in Contemporary France*; concerning Germany, see Spuler-Stegemann, *Muslime in Deutschland*; and B. Tibi, "Les conditions d'une Euro-Islam," in R. Bistolfi and F. Zabbal, eds., *Islams d'Europe: Intégration ou insertion communautaire* (Paris: Edition de l'Aube, 1995).

21. W. A. R. Shadid and P. S. Van Koningsveld, eds., *Muslims in the Margin: Political Responses to the Presence of Islam in Western Europe* (Kampen, the Netherlands: Kok Pharos, 1996); and *Political Participation and Identities of Muslims in Non-Muslim States* (Kampen, the Netherlands: Kok Pharos, 1997).

22. Zentrum für Türkeistudien, ed., *Islamische Organisation der türkischen, marokkanischen, tunesischen und bosnischen Minderheiten in Hessen* (Essen, Ger.: Center for Turkish Studies, 1995).

23. B. Tibi, "Les conditions d'une Euro-Islam." For a case study on the Turks in Germany from the point of view of the political competition between Euro- and ghetto Islam, see also B. Tibi, *Aufbruch am Bosporus: Die Turkeizwischen Europa und dem Islamismus* (Munich: Diana Press, 1998), chapters 8 and 9; and more recently, B. Tibi, *Der Islam und Deutschland, Muslime in Duetschland* (Stuttgart, Ger.: Deutsche Verlags-Anstalt, 2000).

24. J. Habermas, *The Philosophical Discourse of Modernity* (Cambridge, Mass.: MIT Press, 1987); and *Die Einbeziehung des Anderen* (Frankfurt, Ger.: Suhrkamp, 1996).

25. P. D. Salins, *Assimilation American Style* (New York: Basic, 1997).

26. J. Schacht, *An Introduction to Islamic Law* (Oxford, U.K.: Clarendon Press, 1979).

27. The quote is taken from a lecture given by Nagel and covered by the *Frankfurter Allgemeine Zeitung* issue of June 10, 1998, N6, in the report "Das verfehlte Fremde." On Nagel, with references to his work, see my book on Turkey, *Aufbruch am Bosporus*.

28. M. Allow, *The Global Age* (Stanford, Calif.: Stanford University Press, 1997). See also B. Axford, *The Global System: Economics, Politics, Culture* (New York: St. Martin's, 1995).

29. Cornelius et al., *Controlling Immigration*. On the American debate, see N. Capaldi, ed., *Immigration: Debating the Issue* (Amherst, N.Y.: Prometheus, 1997); and Salins, *Assimilation American Style*.

30. C. Geertz, *The Interpretation of Culture* (New York: Basic, 1973). See also B. Tibi, *Islam and the Cultural Accommodation of Social Change* (Boulder, Colo.: Westview, 1990), in particular chapter 1 on the concept of culture.

31. H. Bull, *The Anarchical Society: A Study of Order in World Politics* (New York: Columbia University Press, 1977).

32. Z. Brzezinski, *Between Two Ages* (New York: Viking, 1970), 3.

33. B. Tibi, *The Challenge of Fundamentalism: Political Islam and the New World Disorder* (Berkeley: University of California Press, 1998).

34. Bull, *The Anarchical Society*.

35. Anderson, *Frontiers*.

36. B. Tibi, *Pulverfaß Nahost: Eine arabische Perspektive* (Stuttgart, Ger.: Deutsche Verlags-Anstalt, 1997).

37. F. Gabrieli, B. Lyon, et al., *Mohammed und Karl der Große: Die Geburt des Abendlandes* (Zurich, Switz.: Belser Press, 1987); and B. Tibi, *Kreuzzug und Djihad: Der Islam und die christliche Welt* (Munchen, Ger.: Bertelsmann, 1999).

38. J. Kelsay, *Islam and War: A Study in Comparative Ethics* (Louisville, Ky.: John Knox Press, 1993).

39. "Cross-Culture Talks for Peaceful Co-Existence Urged," *Dawn*, October 26, 1995; and "Ways to Avert Clash between Islam and the West Stressed," *Dawn*, October 27, 1995.

40. B. Tibi, as interviewed by T. Ahmed, "The Clash of Civilizations Was Not Invented, But It Was Used, Abused for Other Reasons," *Newsline* (Karachi), November 1995.

41. Kelsay, *Islam and War*.

42. B. Tibi, "The European Tradition of Human Rights and the Culture of Islam," in A. An-Na'im and F. Deng, eds., *Human Rights in Africa: Cross-Cultural Perspectives* (Washington, D.C.: Brookings Institution, 1990).

43. S. Kohlhammer, *Die Feinde und Freunde des Islam* (Göttingen, Ger.: Steidle, 1996); and B. Tibi, "International Morality and Cross-Cultural Bridging," in R. Herzog, *Preventing the Clash of Civilizations* (New York: St. Martin's, 1999).

44. Tibi, *Europa ohne Identität?*

45. B. Tibi, "Adventures of Multicultural Identities and the Challenge of Migration" (keynote address at the international conference Adventures of Identity: Constructing the Multi-Cultural Subject, Sidney, Australia, August 1998).

46. H. Djait, *al-Fitna* (Beirut, Lebanon: Dar al-Talia, 1992); and M. K. Masud, "The Obligation to Migrate: The Doctrine of Hijra in Islamic Law," in J. Piscatori and D. Eickelman, eds., *Muslim Travelers* (Berkeley: University of California Press, 1990).

47. "Islamists Protest in London," *al-Hayat*, August 15, 1998, 5 [Arabic].

48. Speech delivered by the then Crown Prince Hassan Ibn Talal at the European Academy of Arts and Sciences, November 1996.

49. B. Tibi, *Der wahre Imam: Der Islam von Mohammed bis zur Gegenwart* (Munich, Ger.: Piper Press, 1996).

50. L. Lipson, *The Ethical Crises of Civilization* (Newbury Park, Calif.: Sage, 1993).

51. H. A. Davidson, *Al-Farabi, Avicenna and Averroes on Intellect* (New York: Oxford University Press, 1992); Tibi, *Der wahre Imam*; and C. Butterworth, ed., *Political Aspects of Islamic Philosophy* (Cambridge, Mass.: Harvard University Press, 1992).

52. Speech delivered by the then Crown Prince Hassan Ibn Talal, November 1996.

53. M. Hasan, *Legacy of a Divided Nation: India's Muslims since Independence* (Boulder, Colo.: Westview, 1997).

54. B. Tibi, "Islam, Hinduism and Limited Secularity in India: A Model of Muslim-European Relations in the Age of Migration?" in Shadid and Van Koningsveld, *Muslims in the Margin*.

55. Tibi, "Islam, Hinduism and Limited Secularity in India."

56. B. Tibi, "Foreigners: Today's Jews?" in U. Wank, ed., *The Resurgence of Right-Wing Radicalism in Germany* (Atlantic Highlands, N.J.: Humanities, 1996).

57. Tibi, *Der wahre Imam*.

58. D. Gress, *From Plato to NATO: The Idea of the West and Its Opponents* (New York: Free Press, 1998).

59. Gellner, *Postmodernism, Reason and Religion*.

60. Davidson, *Al-Farabi, Avicenna and Averroes on Intellect*; Tibi, *Der wahre Imam*; and Butterworth, *Political Aspects of Islamic Philosophy*.

61. Tibi, *The Challenge of Fundamentalism*.

62. J. Esposito and J. Voll, *Islam and Democracy* (New York: Oxford University Press, 1996); *Journal of Religion* (1998, October issue); and A. Aiyashi, *Algerian Islamists between Rule and Bullets* (Algiers: Dar al-Hikmah, 1992) [Arabic].

# 3

# The Nation-State, the European Union, and Transnational Identities

## Krishan Kumar

[W]hat constitutes the essence of European history remains contentious and unclear. . . . Historians cannot be used to provide a simple usable pedigree for the present membership of the European Community, much less to suppose that it represents the inevitable climax of all European history.

—Keith Robbins[1]

I would defend myself, weapons in hand, if they tried to prevent our listening to Croatian sermons in church or speaking Croatian in a cafe, but I do not want my children going to a Croatian secondary school. I want them to do well, which means a job in the city, and German is the language of those they must compete with there.

—Mayor of Burgenland, a Croatian village in contemporary Austria[2]

Europeans have for many centuries moved freely over each other's lands, contributing their distinctive patterns to the cultures of different countries. The Czech and Polish cultures are unimaginable without considering the contribution of Germans; French culture is unthinkable without the contributions of Italians and Spaniards; and one cannot make sense of English culture without understanding the contributions of Huguenots, Irish, Scots, and Welsh. Even in the era of nationalism, in which states aspired to homogeneous national cultures, migrant European groups continued to settle in different European countries and affect the cultures of those countries. In France, for instance, to the earlier generations English and Germans were added; in the nineteenth century, Italians, Spaniards, and Belgians; followed in the twentieth by Portuguese, Poles, Romanians, Russians, and other

East Europeans. Each made their respective contributions to "the French melting pot"; each modified to a lesser or greater extent "French national identity."[3]

These were all, of course, Europeans, mostly of Christian belief or Christian origin. But historically, there have been other groups who have also made major contributions to the cultures of European lands even if their presence has been viewed more problematically. The Jews are one such group; Muslims are another. It would be hard to decide which of these two has had the greater impact or influence: Jews, especially in Central and Eastern Europe; or Muslims in the form of Arabs in Spain, Mongols in Russia, and Turks in the Balkans. All that can be said is that European culture would have been immeasurably different, not to say infinitely poorer, without them.

Today, the "Jewish Question" in Europe has largely been "solved," mainly by getting rid of the Jews. But Muslims present a different problem. Sent off in a series of historic encounters (from the battle of Kulikovo in 1380 to the lifting of the siege of Vienna in 1683), they have today returned in more modest guise as "guest workers," and as immigrants from the former colonies of European empires. As Turks, Tunisians, Moroccans, Algerians, Surinamese, Indonesians, Indians, and Pakistanis, they have taken up employment, residence, and in many cases citizenship among Europeans.

Muslims are not, of course, the only new workers and new citizens of Europe. There are Sikhs and Hindus in Britain, and peoples of various faiths from sub-Saharan Africa and Southeast Asia in several European countries, such as Angolans in Portugal and Vietnamese in France. But Sikhs and Hindus are largely restricted to Britain, and many of the other non-European groups are Christian. This does not necessarily lessen the problems they face in their new homes. While religion is only one dimension of ethnicity, it does serve, at least initially, to set Muslims off from all other groups. Muslims are not only the most numerous of the new immigrant populations, but culturally, they seem the most distinctive, and to many (in the host cultures, at least) they seem the most difficult to absorb. As such, they have become the new "other" of Europe, replacing the Jews of an earlier era, and the communists of more recent times.[4] The Salman Rushdie affair, expressing itself in demonstrations by outraged Muslims and resentment and bewilderment on the part of their fellow citizens, neatly encapsulated the predicament, as did, on a lesser scale, *l'affaire du foulard* (the head-scarf affair) in France.[5]

An earlier set of encounters between Muslims and Europeans permanently altered the contours of European culture and set European civilization on a new course. Can this happen again? Taking Muslims as the touchstone, will the new wave of migrants and settlers, peoples who have mostly arrived since World War II, be the harbinger of a new identity, or identities, for Europeans? Or will the migration process instead confirm the stubbornness and persistence of old identities? Is the model to be "assimilation," "integration," or "multiculturalism"? And what do these terms signify? What implications do they have for the historic role of the nation-state as the crucible of the national culture? Will the newcomers find their place within the nation-state, modifying as of old the character of the host culture without seeking to replace or undermine it? Or will they rather look beyond (or beneath) the nation-state, finding in the currents of globalization the opportunities and resources to construct cosmopolitan or "transnational" identities? Whatever the choices and constraints, one thing is clear: the adaptation of the newcomers to their European environment will have profound consequences for the longer-established inhabitants, forcing them to rethink their own identities, and perhaps invent new ones.

## EUROPEAN CULTURE AND EUROPEAN IDENTITY

Europe's new residents will undoubtedly have to adapt to Europe, even if they wish to change it in various ways. But what kind of entity is this Europe? Is it unitary, marked by a fundamental character that unites the majority of its members? Or is it plural, a thing of differences, diversity, even divisiveness? In either case, is there something that one can call a European identity, over and above common cultural characteristics? The answers to these questions will help in assessing the possible range of responses open to the new non-European groups. They will also suggest some possible responses by Europeans themselves in the face of challenges posed by the new groups.

Whether or not there is, strictly speaking, a European identity, there no doubt is something called European culture. Undoubtedly, too, the main basis of that is religion—specifically, Christianity.[6] It is, for example, this last characteristic that permits the inclusion of Russia in European civilization. Russia for many centuries guarded Europe's northern flank against invaders from the east, just as Austria guarded its southern flank. While the Habsburgs, as Holy Roman emperors, saw themselves as continuing the unifying imperial mission of Rome, Moscow claimed for itself the title "the Third Rome" following the fall of Constantinople to the Turks. It was as the champions of Christianity against the pagans that the Tsars formulated a destiny for Russia's expanding empire.

The importance of religion as a unifying factor is underlined by the consideration of how Europe was formed, what gave it its shape as a fragment of the Eurasian land mass. Europe was made by the encounter with and resistance to other religions—specifically the Muslim religion. It was largely in response to the Muslim threat—from Mongols and Tartars in the north, Arabs and Turks in the south—that Europe drew together.[7] For centuries, the only all-European enterprises were joint actions against Muslims from the Crusades of the Middle Ages to the defense of the Habsburg Empire against the Turks in the late seventeenth century.

Religion, even of the same kind, of course divides as much as it unites (contemporary Northern Ireland makes this point still, even if one does not wish to look back to the seventeenth-century wars of religion between Protestants and Catholics, or the "Great Schism" between Eastern and Western Christianity in the eleventh century). And there have been other formative European experiences that, in the unevenness of their effects, have created barriers between some Europeans, even while linking others. The Roman Empire, so crucial in the formation of European law and administration, did not include large sections of central, northern, and eastern Europe (while, in its eastern wing, it did include much of the Near and Middle East, which later fell under Muslim domination). Orthodox Europe did not, at least until quite late, share in the cultural experiences of the Renaissance, the Reformation, the Scientific Revolution, and the Enlightenment. Industrialization also divided the continent into an advanced, "developed," western half, and a backward, peasant, eastern half. Coming closer to the present time, communism and the Cold War further divided Europe into East and West, a divide fortified until recently by the role of the European Community and the European Union as an exclusively Western European club. These differences have at various times created a number of major east-west "fault lines," particularly in the elaboration of a concept of "Western civilization" from which Eastern Europe was excluded.[8]

There is clearly plenty of ammunition available to those who wish to deny that there is anything like a common European identity, who say that "Europe" is nothing but a congeries of ethnic or national identities. At best, such critics are prepared to see Europe as "a 'family of cultures' made up of a syndrome of partially shared historical traditions and cultural heritages."[9] At worst, they see the whole idea of Europe as a myth or an "ideology," perhaps a "counterrevolutionary ideology," elaborated in different ways and at different times by Western elites in the consolidation of their own power: in other words, a sham.[10]

No one would wish to deny the differences and divisions that mark European civilization; two world wars in the present century are sufficient testimony to this fact. But conflict, as is well known, tends to occur most fiercely between otherwise like-minded people: brothers, families, clans, or even nations sharing a common past. And variegated and divergent patterns might be said to be the hallmark of any culture; any culture, that is, above the most primitive. Indeed, for Francois Guizot, in his celebrated 1828 *History of Civilization in Europe*, European civilization marked itself off from all past civilizations precisely by its principle of diversity which, paradoxically, also gave it its unity.

> Modern Europe presents us with examples of all systems, of all experiments of social organization; pure or mixed monarchies, theocracies, republics, more or less aristocratic, have thus thrived simultaneously, one beside the other; and, notwithstanding their diversity, they all have a certain resemblance, a certain family likeness, which it is impossible to mistake.[11]

Conflict and diversity may therefore not be considered barriers to the idea of a common European culture. When Edmund Burke said that "no European can be a complete exile in any part of Europe," he would have been the last person to look for uniformity of character or harmony of culture.[12] There can be an idea of Europe that accepts difference, even profound divisions. What presumably holds Europe together, as an ideal or ideology at least, is some notion of a common framework of acceptance, some sense of mutual understanding and recognition based on certain historical and cultural legacies.

Such considerations of unity and diversity, distance and nearness, bring discussions inevitably back to Islam, and to religion. For it must be evident that a major reason of Europe's fear of and hostility toward Muslim peoples is the fear and anxiety that comes from closeness. Muslims have contributed to the formation of Europe, not just as Europe's "other," but directly, as philosophers, scientists, and scholars. What would the European Middle Ages have been intellectually without the works of Avicenna, Averroès, Ibn Khaldun, and the other Arab thinkers who transmitted and developed the science and culture of Greece and Rome? What is Balkan civilization but a synthesis of Slavic traditions and Ottoman culture? What, for that matter, would European cuisine be like without the oranges, lemons, spinach, asparagus, aubergines, artichokes, and pasta introduced by the Muslims in Spain?[13]

The question of the impact of Muslim communities on European societies today must be seen within the context of this ambivalent history. Hostile encounters with Muslims have to a good extent defined Europe, but Islam has also been a part, perhaps a constituent part, of European civilization. Islam is "not-Europe"; but it is also, to an extent, in Europe. The contradictions and confusions of this position affect both parties to the encounter.

## NATIONAL, SUBNATIONAL, AND TRANSNATIONAL IDENTITIES

Europeans like to be able to say such things as "I am European, but I am also British, and perhaps also English, and perhaps even Cornish." Europe-wide identities have been accompanied and, in the last two hundred years or so, often overshadowed by national identities. For some, such as Anthony Smith and Montserrat Guibernau, national identities remain preeminent, even in this era of globalization and attempts at supranational citizenship, such as with the European Union.[14] According to Smith, the arrival of non-European ethnic groups has only added to the *melange* of "distinctive *ethnies* and counter-cultures, of indigestible minorities, immigrants, aliens and social outcasts."

The sheer number of these minorities and the vitality of these divided *ethnies* and their unique cultures has meant that "Europe" itself, a geographical expression of problematical utility, has looked pale and shifting beside the entrenched cultures and heritages that make up its rich mosaic. Compared with the vibrancy and tangibility of French, Scots, Catalan, Polish, or Greek cultures and ethnic traditions, a "European identity" has seemed vacuous and nondescript, a rather lifeless summation of all the peoples and cultures on the continent, adding little to what already exists.[15]

Even those, such as Jurgen Habermas, who accept the idea of a common European civilization and urge the development of a "European constitutional patriotism" as the answer to the obsolescence of the nation-state, are inclined to stress that this is more a project for the future than something already achieved and inherited. "Our task," Habermas has written, "is less to reassure ourselves of our common origins in the European Middle Ages than to develop a new political self-confidence commensurate with the role of Europe in the world of the twenty-first century."[16] Europe, in other words, does not exist, at least as a usable identity; it has to be created. To do so, however, Europe must rid itself of a heritage of cultural exclusiveness. By a process of political dialogue among its constituent groups, it must aim at the construction of a political entity whose hallmark is citizenship, not ascriptive membership.[17]

But there is a more radical posture which has also found powerful exponents. This, too, accepts that the nation-state, as historically formed, is outmoded. But for its advocates, the future of Europe lies less in the creation of a pan-European identity than in going both beyond and beneath Europe. National identities are indeed losing their exclusiveness—if they ever really had such a character—and are now increasingly accompanied, and perhaps superseded, by other forms: subnational, regional, supranational, and "transnational." The usual position is to argue for a combination of some or all of these. Writing of Catalonia, for instance, a "nation without a state," Manuel Castells has envisaged a far-reaching pattern of interlocking and overlapping identities, based on subnational, national, and transnational institutions.

Declaring Catalunya at the same time European, Mediterranean, and Hispanic, Catalan nationalists, while rejecting separation from Spain, search for a new kind of state. It would be a state of variable geometry, bringing together respect for the historically inherited Spanish state with the growing autonomy of Catalan institutions in conducting public affairs, and the integration of both Spain and Catalunya in a broader entity, Europe, that translates not only into the European Union, but into various networks of regional and municipal governments, as well as of civic associations, that multiply horizontal relationships throughout Europe under the tenuous shell of modern nation-states.[18]

Such a conception, Castells has suggested, though historically rooted in the Catalan case, actually points the way toward a more general pattern of identity in the information age. It fits, that is, a world in which the nation-state has to find its place in a global economy and a variable and interpenetrating set of cultures. No longer can the nation-state claim a monopoly over the control of welfare and culture; nor by the same token can it demand the total and unconditional allegiance of its citizens. There are other citizenship roles to play, other arenas which provide the opportunity and resources in which to play them, and other institutions which have a legitimate claim on loyalty.

Castells does not incorporate the new non-European immigrant groups into this model, though it would not be difficult to do so. Indeed, something similar has been suggested by Yngve Lithman, in his account of how immigrant communities are reshaping the life of European cities. The model of national societies "assimilating" or "integrating" their immigrant minorities is obsolete, he has argued. The "Europeanisation of the nation state," together with the globalization of the economy and "a move from the notion of nation to more individualised . . . notions of personhood," are breaking down the ability of the nation-state to offer many of the traditional employment and welfare services which once made it necessary for immigrant groups to seek integration within that body, and which at the same time allowed the state to claim their full allegiance. "It is no longer unproblematic to see state and state policies more or less harmonize with other institutions in society to create vehicles for ambitious integration (however defined) for immigrants."[19] Especially given the difficulties that they may face in the national community, immigrant communities must see themselves as free to determine their own identities, within but also beyond the nation-state. In doing so, they may offer a new vitality and cultural richness to their host communities, by providing "a kind of self-help cultural 'smorgasbord,' where everyone is welcome to choose his or her favorite dishes, and where ethnic prejudices and stereotyping have been whittled away in the closeness of everyday interaction."[20]

An even more ambitious strategy and outcome, breaking out of the European framework altogether, is suggested by Yasemin Soysal's account of what she has described as the emergence of "postnational" and "transnational" identities among immigrant groups in Europe. She, too, regards adaptation and integration, let alone assimilation, as outmoded strategies—in any case doomed to failure. Accommodation with nation-states still remains the goal of most immigrant groups. But increasingly they are drawing the resources for group identity from the universalist discourse of human rights and their own international organizations and movements. According to Soysal, "[this represents] an underlying dialectic of the postwar global system: While nation-states and their boundaries are reified through assertions of border controls and appeals to nationhood, a new mode of membership, anchored in the universalistic rights of personhood, transgresses the national order of things."[21]

According to this logic, Turks in Germany, especially second-generation Turks, will be neither Turkish nor German. They will not model themselves on the culture either of the sending or the receiving society, but will follow a third path, build-

ing their identities out of the discrete elements of the host society, their home society, and the "postnational" possibilities made available to them in the language and
institutions of universal human rights. "Multiculturalism, the right to be different
and to foster one's own culture, is elementally asserted as the natural and inalienable right of all individuals," Soysal has written. Old particularities are now clothed
in the new human rights discourse. Thus, "Mother Tongue is Human Right"
emerged as the slogan of the Initiative of Turkish Parents and Teachers in Stuttgart,
in pressing their claims for Turkish-language instruction in German schools.[22]

The paths marked out by Castells, Lithman, and Soysal are in no way unreal or
implausible. In fact, they dovetail well with much recent thinking on migrant communities and multiculturalism. John Rex, for instance, has said that the migrant ethnic community, based on the extended family and stretched across several nations, is
today at least as important as membership in a nation. He cited as an example the
Punjabis in Britain, Canada, and the United States. The members of such a community, moreover, "belong to different social groups and different cultural systems
simultaneously and are used to the fact of multiple identities."[23] Multiculturalists,
whether or not of a "postmodern" persuasion, are also much given to talk of multiple or "nested" identities. Not just migrants, they say, but all individuals in contemporary conditions live at the intersection of several cultures, from which they are free
to select in composing their identities—and in recomposing them at a later date.
"Not only societies, but people are multicultural," Amy Gutman has declared.[24] Each
person embodies several overlapping identities, and it is bad faith to attach oneself
too exclusively to any one of them, such as national identity. In this sense, migrants
and migrant communities are the outriders of the emerging postnational society.
According to Salman Rushdie, they are no less than "a metaphor for all humanity."[25]

Part of the attraction of these positions no doubt is that they avoid the
"essentialism" of earlier writing on multiculturalism, the assumption that ethnic
cultures were primordial and fixed, and that multiculturalism consisted in a
patchwork quilt of discrete cultures, each preserving its original form and more or
less stable identity.[26] By contrast, the future appears as one of "hyphenation,"
"hybridity," "syncretization," "creolization," and the creative inventions of "diaspora cultures."[27] Immigrant communities, in an eclectic mixing of the resources at
hand, will transform not only themselves but the societies they inhabit for the
better. The goal is not "assimilation," "something immigrants or minorities must
do or have done to them," but rather "integration" as "an interactive, two-way
process [in which] both parties are an active ingredient and . . . . something new
is created." In the "plural state," as opposed to the older conception of the liberal
state, "multiculturalism means reforming national identity and citizenship."[28]

I have already mentioned how European culture is more porous and perme-
able than often thought. In fact, it is fissured through and through, and it already
has a generous leavening of non-European specifically Muslim culture as a result

of past encounters. It is not set in a rigid mold. Does this not create a space for the gradual transformation of European societies? Might not the new immigrant communities, in making and remaking themselves in their new environments, serve as a seedbed of social and cultural innovation in the wider societies they inhabit? Might they not indeed be the building blocks of a new Europe itself, undermining the nation-state "from the bottom upward," just as the European Union is attempting to do the same "from the top down"? Will the new Europe be one of "ethnic heterogeneity inserted into a multicultural suprastate"?[29]

The attractions of these and similar formulations should not draw attention from some obvious stumbling blocks. Most of these center on the persisting strength and salience of the nation-state, at least as perceived by many of their inhabitants. Soysal herself has admitted that "the nation-state is still the repository of educational, welfare, and public health functions and the regulator of social distribution."[30] It is also still the only legitimate political form recognized by the international system. This means that, in practice, many supposedly "universalistic" human rights—not just the right to vote, but the right to work, to education, to health, to housing—have to be claimed and if necessary fought for within the framework of the nation-state.[31] Most immigrant communities seem to recognize this, even if they also make use, when possible, of international agencies such as the International Court of Justice in pursuing such claims. This may partly explain why some immigrant communities, for instance those in Britain, are very ambivalent about the pull of Europe, seeing in further European integration the possible loss of hard-won gains, as much as the opportunities for new benefits.[32]

This points, in turn, to the continuing importance of citizenship. Writers in the "transnational" or "postnational" vein have argued that what matters most these days is not citizenship, but residence. Permanent residence, they say, coupled with the appeal to universal rights, have largely replaced citizenship as the basis for a claim to social rights. This suggests an ingenious reversal of T. H. Marshall's famous historical trajectory, whereby European populations moved from gaining civil and political rights to the achievement, mainly in the twentieth century, of social rights. Now, it is argued, largely through the pressure of international human rights organizations, that social and economic rights must be conferred irrespective of formal citizenship. "The transformation of 'national' rights into more universalistic entitlements that include noncitizens," according to Soysal, "undermines the categorical dichotomies patterned after the national citizenship model."[33] David Jacobson has declared that "as rights have come to be predicated on residency, not citizen status, the distinction between 'citizen' and 'alien' has eroded. . . . Citizenship . . . has been devalued in the host countries; aliens resident in the United States and in Western European countries have not felt any compelling need to naturalize even when it is possible."[34] The way forward for immigrants is not to press for political citizenship in the states in which they reside, but to urge greater recognition of their universal human rights as persons.

Of course, this could all be a dangerous illusion. In pursuing "transnational" or "universal" rather than national citizenship, immigrants may condemn themselves to passivity and to second-class citizenship within nation-states that still hold most of the levers of power and control over important aspects of their lives. As even the advocates of transnational citizenship have admitted, "the state itself is the critical mechanism in advancing human rights."[35] It is left to the state to translate into policies and bureaucratic practice the injunctions and declarations of international human rights institutions. Here is the rub. As Lydia Morris has shown, despite the efforts of the European Union, national governments in Europe have continued to act restrictively over such matters as immigration policy, the rights of migrants, citizenship of the European Union, and human rights. And several states, under the pressure of labor and other constituencies, have found ways of restricting access to welfare systems and labor markets to those who, though resident, are not citizens.[36] Noncitizens, of course, do not make up voting constituencies, and so national political parties do not therefore have to pay much attention to them. There are votes to be gained in standing against immigrants; virtually none in standing for them.

Immigrants in Europe have only to look across the water, to the United States, for a clear warning of the danger of espousing residence rather than citizenship. For a long time legal or permanent residents felt they had equal rights with citizens in the United States, and that naturalization was not only not necessary, but incurred unwanted burdens.[37] A rude awakening arrived one day in 1997, however, when by act of the U.S. Congress, legal residents found themselves deprived of most rights to Social Security benefits and subject to instant deportation if found guilty even of relatively minor criminal offenses.

Not surprisingly, many permanent residents have since been rushing to acquire citizenship (in fact, the trend started in the mid-1990s in anticipation of this and similar measures).[38] Of course, even citizenship is no guarantee these days against the infringement or deprivation of rights. But it offers at least some sort of protection if only against deportation at the arbitrary whim of immigration officials.[39] Perhaps the French are, despite the criticisms heaped upon them by the transnational theorists, right to insist upon the overriding principle of citizenship for all.[40]

If immigrant communities are compelled to face up to the realities posed by the power of the nation-state, a further difficulty for views of "postnational" or "transnational" citizenship comes from the rooted nationalism of most Europeans themselves. Although there are significant national differences here (Italians and Germans are more pro-Europe than British and French, for instance),[41] polls have repeatedly found that, despite the efforts of the European Union, despite a vast increase in social interchange and media integration, the nation-state remains the principal focus of popular identity and the main basis of legitimacy. William Wallace has summarized the evidence as follows:

A certain diffusion of loyalties, a certain expansion of horizons from the national to the European (and the global), are evident both among elites and—more faintly—among mass publics. But challenges to the legitimacy of national institutions and elites have come largely from within existing states: leading to fragmentation, not integration. Throughout Western Europe the national community remains the broadest focus for political life and group identity.[42]

Manuel Castells, too, has pointed to the fact that "since the [European] integration process has coincided with stagnation of living standards, rising unemployment, and greater social inequality in the 1990s, significant sections of the European population tend to affirm their nations against their states, seen as captives of European supranationality."[43] Political elites in the European states tend to be pro-European, their mass publics much less so, when they are not actually hostile to the European project. Some considerable time ago Johan Galtung noted the phenomenon that just as the elites of postindustrial societies were "growing out" of the nation-state, so the mass of the population was, perhaps for the first time in their history, coming to identify fully with it, and to defend it energetically against threats from both within and without.[44] A similar view has recently been expressed, rather more caustically, by Christopher Lasch.[45] The irony is that just as processes of globalization and internationalization are most profoundly affecting the lives of all groups and classes of society, some of those groups, in a defensive reaction, are feeling the need to insist more strongly than ever on their national identity. "Nationalism, not federalism, is the concomitant development of European integration."[46]

This must clearly affect the attitudes of Muslims and non-Muslim groups toward each other. Muslims, and other ethnic minorities, see native Europeans acting in the name of an often aggressively restated definition of themselves as "English," "French," "German," and so on. These definitions contain ethnic terms that generally exclude non-Europeans. Primarily they may be stated in terms of color, but they also usually include cultural elements that defy (and are meant to defy) attempts by non-Europeans to adopt or adapt to them. Thus, a former British Conservative Cabinet Minister, Norman (now Lord) Tebbit, formulated what has come to be known as the "Tebbit Test": Do "black Britons" support the "English" [sic] cricket team when it plays against India, Pakistan, or the West Indies?[47] If not, they cannot claim to be British. (The author, of course, fails to acknowledge the number of black Britons already on the English team, just as a similar test involving football in France would ignore the number of North African French on the national team). Similarly, French nationalists have denounced the wearing of scarves by Muslim schoolgirls on the grounds that this goes against French secularism—thus showing, once again, that secularism is not a neutral category, but carries a distinct cultural charge.[48]

The obvious retort to all this on the part of non-European minorities is to refuse the labels imposed on them—as incomplete or inferior British or French—and to seek identities that draw both upon past cultural origins and the new resources available to them in the international arena. That is the strategy advocated by Soysal and others. The problems in this case may be equally grave. There seems an inescapable dilemma here. One position asserts an identity that involves, for instance, retaining one's language and religion as central elements. But every person lives in a national society that defines itself predominantly in other terms, and which also controls the points of entry to the principal sources of economic opportunity and political participation. How does a person compete on equal terms with those nationals who are adept at deploying the master symbols and cultural styles of the dominant society? Following this strategy, would minorities not be condemning themselves, in practice if not principle, to second-class, if not actual ghetto, status—as members in but not of society? It is this problem, incidentally, that drives a coach-and-horses through the hallowed distinction between "civic" and "ethnic" belonging: How does one truly participate in the civic realm without possessing the requisite cultural resources to perform there successfully, and on equal terms with all citizens? What does it actually mean to press for a "French Islamic civilisation"[49]; or a "British Islam"?[50]

There is a further consideration. Many have pointed to the way in which nation-states, in losing control over large areas of economic and cultural life, have responded by intensifying their hold over those areas in which they do still remain more or less in command. These include power over the granting of citizenship and nationality, together with associated power over the issuing of passports, visas, work permits, and so forth. States now display themselves—there seems no better word for it—at borders and frontiers, controlling movement in and out, demonstrating by elaborate policing and surveillance the continued relevance of national boundaries. Older, established Europeans, at least Western Europeans, may feel that things have gotten much better for them in this respect—especially those who find themselves in the countries of the Schengen agreement. But for "new Europeans," and those still seeking citizenship, especially if they are of non-European stock, the situation is very different and can be the cause of great hardship and frustration.

This is as true of European citizenship—more precisely, European Union citizenship—as it is of national citizenship. The establishment of European citizenship was one of the most vaunted achievements of the 1992 Maastricht Treaty. At a stroke, more than 90 percent of European Union residents gained European citizenship, in addition to their national citizenship. But as Elspeth Guild has shown, of all the provisions of the treaty, those relating to nationality and citizenship are the vaguest and most open to particular interpretations (or evasions) by national governments. For instance, no right to a European, any more than to a national, passport exists: "issue and withdrawal conditions apparently remain a national prerogative."[51] European citizenship is a derivative status, dependent upon citizenship in one of the member states of the European Union. Since national governments keep control of the power to grant or withhold national citizenship, they effectively also keep control over the power to grant or withhold European citizenship, thus rendering the whole concept rather vacuous.[52]

That this can matter even to those who seem in most ways highly privileged members of European societies has been brought home with special force to one particularly keen-eyed citizen. Michael Ignatieff was, by his own account, proud to call himself a cosmopolitan in an increasingly unified and multicultural world. Anything else seemed a rejection of the Enlightenment philosophy by which he lived. But his travels in the troubled places of the earth made him realize the limits of this lofty position. Bosnia, in particular, taught him a chastening lesson in realism.

> Globalism in a post-imperial age only permits a post-nationalist consciousness for those cosmopolitans who are lucky enough to live in the wealthy West. . . . The people of Sarajevo were true cosmopolitans, fierce believers in ethnic heterogeneity. But they lacked either a reliable imperial protector or a state of their own to guarantee peace among contending ethnicities.

> What has happened in Bosnia must give pause to anyone who believes in the virtues of cosmopolitanism. It is only too apparent that cosmopolitanism is the privilege of those who can take a secure nation state for granted. Though we have passed into a post-imperial age, we are not in a post-nationalist age, and I cannot see how we will ever do so. The cosmopolitan order of the great cities—London, Los Angeles, New York, Paris—depends critically on the rule-enforcing capacities of the nation state.

> In this sense . . . cosmopolitans like myself are not beyond the nation; and a cosmopolitan, post-nationalist spirit will always depend, in the end, on the capacity of nation states to provide security and civility for their citizens.[53]

In essence, Ignatieff's discovery was that when he came to the security checkpoints and other dangerous obstacles in his travels, it was his British passport, as much as the attendant television cameras, that gave him the freedom to pass and move about the country. This is an experience shared at different levels by many who have never put themselves in such threatening situations. And it illustrates vividly the continuing power of national citizenship and the difficulties faced by those who in various ways may seek to go around or beyond the nation-state. Postnational identities and transnational citizenship are undoubtedly attractive goals. And they can be achieved in part not just by secure and wealthy cosmopolitans but, no doubt, immigrant communities seeking to protect and extend their particular identities. But a definite element of wish fulfillment seems to have entered into the thinking of those who, in current circumstances, proclaim them to be the best or only avenues of advancement.

## NOTES

1. K. Robbins, "National Identity and History: Past, Present and Future," *History* 75 (1990), 373.

2. D. Rusinow, "Ethnic Politics in the Habsburg Monarchy and Successor States," in R. L. Rudolph and D. F. Good, eds., *Nationalism and Empire: The Habsburg Monarchy and the Soviet Union* (New York: St. Martin's, 1992), 259.

3. G. Noiriel,*The French Melting Pot: Immigration, Citizenship and National Identity*, trans. G. de Laforcade (Minneapolis: University of Minnesota Press, 1996).

4. T. Bjrgo, "'The Invaders,' 'the Traitors' and 'the Resistance Movement': The Extreme Right's Conceptualisation of Opponents and Self in Scandinavia," in T. Modood and P. Werbner, eds., *The Politics of Multiculturalism in the New Europe: Racism, Identity and Community* (London: Zed Books, 1997).

5. A. Favell, "Citizenship and Immigration: Pathologies of a Progressive Philosophy," *New Community* 23, no. 2 (1997); and E. Thomas, "The New Cultural Politics of Muslim Minority Integration in France and Britain: Beyond Left and Right?" (paper presented to the Eleventh International Conference of Europeanists, Baltimore, February 26–28, 1998).

6. C. Dawson, *Understanding Europe* (New York: Image Books, 1960); and T. S. Eliot, "The Unity of European Culture," in *Notes Towards the Definition of Culture* (London: Faber and Faber, 1962).

7. M. E. Yapp, "Europe in the Turkish Mirror," *Past and Present* (1992).

8. N. Davies, *Europe: A History* (Oxford, U.K.: Oxford University Press, 1996).

9. A. D. Smith, "National Identity and the Idea of European Unity," *International Affairs* 68, no. 1 (1992), 70.

10. J. N. Pieterse, "Fictions of Europe," *Race and Class* 32, no. 3 (1991); C. Shore and A. Black, "Citizens, Europe, and the Construction of European Identity," in V. A. Goddard, J. R. Llobera, and C. Shore, eds., *The Anthropology of Europe: Identity and Boundaries in Conflict* (Oxford, U.K.: Berg, 1994); and G. Delanty, *Inventing Europe: Idea, Identity, Reality* (London: Macmillan, 1995).

11. F. Guizot, *The History of Civilization in Europe*, trans. W. Hazlitt, ed. Larry Siedentop (London: Penguin, 1997), 30.

12. Davies, *Europe*, 8.

13. Davies, *Europe*, 8.

14. A. D. Smith, *Nations and Nationalism in a Global Era* (Cambridge, U.K.: Polity Press, 1995); and M. Guibernau, Nationalisms: *The Nation-State and Nationalism in the Twentieth Century* (Cambridge, U.K.: Polity Press, 1996).

15. Smith, *Nations and Nationalism in a Global Era*, 131.

16. J. Habermas, "Citizenship and National Identity: Some Reflections on the Future of Europe," *Praxis International* 12, no. 1 (1992), 12.

17. K. Robins and A. Aksoy, "Culture and Marginality in the New Europe," in C. Hadjimichalis and D. Sadler, eds., *Europe at the Margins* (Chichester, U.K.: Wiley, 1995).

18. M. Castells, *The Power of Identity* (Oxford, U.K.: Blackwell, 1997), 50; cf. J. Keane, "Nations, Nationalism and European Citizens," in S. Periwal, ed., *Notions of Nationalism* (Budapest: Central European University Press, 1995).

19. Y. G. Lithman, "Spatial Concentration and Mobility" (paper presented to the Second International Metropolis Conference, Copenhagen, September 25–28, 1997, printed in the conference volume, *Metropolis*), 76.

20. Lithman, "Spatial Concentration and Mobility," 78; cf. L. J. D. Wacquant, "The Rise of Advanced Marginality: A Note on Its Nature and Implications," *Acta Sociologica* 39, no. 20 (1996).

21. Y. N. Soysal, *Limits of Citizenship: Migrants and Postnational Membership in Europe* (Chicago: University of Chicago Press, 1994), 159.

22. Soysal, *Limits of Citizenship*, 159.

23. J. Rex, "Ethnic Identity and the Nation State: The Political Sociology of Multi-Cultural Societies," *Social Identities* 1, no. 1 (1995), 29, 32.

24. A. Gutman, "The Challenge of Multiculturalism in Political Ethics," *Philosophy and Public Affairs* 22, no. 3 (1993), 183.

25. S. Rushdie, "In Good Faith," in *Imaginary Homelands* (London: Granta Books, 1992), 394. See also S. Hall, "The Question of Cultural Identity," in S. Hall, D. Held, and T. McGrew, eds., *Modernity and Its Future* (Cambridge, U.K.: Polity Press, 1992); and M. Wieviorka, "Is Multiculturalism the Solution?" *Ethnic and Racial Studies* 21, no. 5 (1998).

26. A. S. Caglar, "Hyphenated Identities and the Limits of Culture," in Modood and Werbner, *The Politics of Multiculturalism in the New Europe.*

27. P. Gilroy, *There Ain't No Black in the Union Jack* (London: Hutchinson, 1987); and J. N. Pieterse, "Globalisation as Hybridisation," *International Sociology* 9, no. 2 (1994).

28. T. Modood, "Introduction: The Politics of Multiculturalism in the New Europe," in Modood and Werbner, *The Politics of Multiculturalism in the New Europe*, 24.

29. Modood, "Introduction," 1; cf. P. Werbner, "Afterword: Writing Multiculturalism and Politics in the New Europe," in Modood and Werbner, *The Politics of Multiculturalism in the New Europe*; and G. Zincone, "The Powerful Consequences of Being Too Weak: The Impact of Immigration on Democratic Regimes," *Archives Europennes de Sociologie* 38, no. 1 (1997).

30. Soysal, *Limits of Citizenship*, 157.

31. L. Morris, "Globalization, Migration and the Nation-State: The Path to a Post-National Europe?" *British Journal of Sociology* 48, no. 2 (1997).

32. A. Favell, *Philosophies of Integration: Immigration and the Idea of Citizenship in France and Britain* (New York: St. Martin's, 1998).

33. Soysal, *Limits of Citizenship*, 135.

34. D. Jacobson, *Rights Across Borders: Immigration and the Decline of Citizenship* (Baltimore: Johns Hopkins University Press, 1996), 8–9. See also Favell, *Philosophies of Integration*; and R. Baubsck, "Differentiating Citizenship" (paper for the conference "Citizenship and Cosmopolitanism," University of Wisconsin, Madison, November 6–8, 1998).

35. Jacobson, *Rights Across Borders*, 11.

36. L. Morris, "Globalization, Migration and the Nation-State: The Path to a Post-

National Europe?" *British Journal of Sociology* 48, no. 2 (1997).

37. J. Goodwin-White, "Where the Maps Are Not Yet Finished: A Continuing American Journey," in D. Jacobson, ed., *The Immigration Reader: America in Multidisciplinary Perspective* (Oxford, U.K.: Blackwell, 1998).

38. Goodwin-White, "Where the Maps Are Not Yet Finished."

39. For an account of the increasing practice of this in the United States, in relation to both legal and illegal residents, see "The Immigrant Lockup," *New York Times*, December 31, 1998.

40. For the French position, see M. Silverman, *Deconstructing the Nation: Immigration, Racism and Citizenship in Modern France* (New York: Routledge, 1992); S. Hoffman, "Thoughts on the French Nation Today," *Daedalus* 122, no. 3 (1993); and Favell, *Philosophies of Integration*.

41. M. Borri, "National Identities and Attitudes Towards Europe: A Comparative Study" (paper presented to the British Council University of Silesia Conference, "Culture and Identity," Cieszyn, Poland, September 22–25, 1994).

42. W. Wallace, "Rescue or Retreat? The Nation State in Western Europe, 1945–93," *Political Studies* 42 (1994), 55–56; cf. P. Schlesinger, "Europeanness: A New Cultural Battlefield?" *Innovation* 5, no. 1 (1992); and M. Mann, "Nation-States in Europe and Other Continents: Diversifying, Developing, Not Dying," *Daedalus* 122, no. 3 (1993).

43. M. Castells, *End of Millennium* (Oxford, U.K.: Blackwell, 1998), 326.

44. J. Galtung, "On the Future of the International System," in R. Jungk and J. Galtung, eds., *Mankind 2000* (London: Allen and Unwin, 1969).

45. C. Lasch, *The Revolt of the Elites and the Betrayal of Democracy* (New York: W. W. Norton, 1995).

46. Castells, *End of Millennium*, 327.

47. J. McGuigan, *Culture and the Public Sphere* (New York: Routledge, 1996).

48. Silverman, *Deconstructing the Nation*.

49. A. M. Diop, "Negotiating Religious Difference: The Opinions and Attitudes of Islamic Association in France," Modood and Werbner, *The Politics of Multiculturalism in the New Europe*.

50. P. Lewis, *Islamic Britain: Religion, Politics and Identity among British Muslims* (London: I. B. Tauris, 1994).

51. E. Guild, "The Legal Framework of Citizenship of the European Union," in D. Cesarani and M. Fulbrook, eds., *Citizenship, Nationality and Migration in Europe* (London: Routledge, 1996), 48.

52. L. Morris, "Globalization, Migration and the Nation-State: The Path to a Post-National Europe?" *British Journal of Sociology* 48, no. 2 (1997); C. Shore and A. Black, "Citizens, Europe, and the Construction of European Identity"; and C. Brewin, "Society as a Kind of Community: Communitarian Voting with Equal Rights for Individuals in the European Union," in Modood and Werbner, *The Politics of Multiculturalism in the New Europe*.

53. M. Ignatieff, *Blood and Belonging: Journeys into the New Nationalism* (London: Vintage, 1999), 9.

# 4

# The Challenge of Islamic Networks and Citizenship Claims: Europe's Painful Adjustment to Globalization

## Paul Lubeck

It has now become readily apparent that the member states of the European Union are struggling to adjust to large-scale sources of change which are redefining the meaning of community, identity, citizenship, and nationalism within their borders. Yet while European economic and political integration is the most visible and contested of these changes, a deeper structural force at the macrolevel is globalization. As Europe adjusts to global change, the growing Muslim presence there has spawned an increasing amount of conflict. One reason is that Muslim integration into national societies is no longer a simple question of assimilation into a stable national identity.

Driven by globalization, European integration has disrupted the relationship between the nation-state and subordinate ethnonational identities. Together, the integration of Europe and the space created by the EU regional policy (i.e., a process of devolution of power) have stimulated regional autonomy movements and disrupted the accepted meanings of nationalism and citizenship across Europe. Therefore, before evaluating the significance of Muslim identities in Europe, one must review how globalization and European integration have redefined the discourse on citizenship, rights, and identities among Europeans themselves.

In different ways, European integration and the expansion of Muslim networks into Europe exemplify how globalization represents a long-term historical trend toward the integration of economies, peoples, and cultures regardless of national boundaries. Inspired first by liberal theory, globalization seeks to eliminate any institutionalized obstacle to unfettered communication, geographical mobility, and exchange. Accordingly, neoliberals favor global policies such as competitive free markets, free trade, privatization, deregulated markets, unregulated cross-border financial speculation, flexible labor markets, and subcontracting networks.[1] Yet it would be an error to assume that contemporary globalization processes are identical to neoliberalism.

What differentiates contemporary globalization processes from classical liberalism are the technological innovations generated by the microelectronic revolution. Global integration across national borders relies on the marriage of computers, satellites, and telecommunication networks. Such integration has compressed time-space relationships so that real-time interaction has become possible for a growing proportion of the world's population who are now unconstrained by distance and geographical space. The organizational heart of contemporary globalization is not the market, but rather an electronic system of computer-based information networks. These networks connect productive, financial, social, and cultural nodes of activity across national boundaries. Furthermore, these information networks have now been coordinated with transportation networks to form a global infrastructure, one that integrates a web of linked regional production centers. If mapped spatially over time, this web has expanded from a small number of regional nodes in the United States, Europe, and Japan, to an increasingly larger and more inclusive network of regional centers worldwide. Networks, therefore, are the organizational structure of contemporary globalization.

Combining transportation and electronic networks, the new global infrastructure also determines the flow of transnational immigrants today. In this chapter I argue that Muslims, to a far greater degree than many other immigrant groups, possess the institutional and cultural capital to take maximum advantage of these global networks in order to construct a web of transnational communities throughout EU countries.

## THE CRISIS OF THE EUROPEAN NATIONAL MODEL

To be sure, Europe's current adjustment problems derive in large part from the success of prior institutional arrangements. During the postwar period of social democracy, Western European states constructed a dynamic "social model" based upon a series of class compromises which, in turn, constructed a web of national regulatory institutions. Guided by Keynesian theory and Fordist coalitions, the European social model delivered rising productivity, high social investment, and generous social-welfare benefits—but only to citizens of individual nation-states. On the continent, organized market capitalism institutionalized consultation among business, labor, and government representatives, who distributed the fruits of rising productivity to capital, workers, and citizens according to agreements negotiated at the national level.

Unlike the United States, where social benefits were limited and immigration policies encouraged skilled immigrants and tolerated unskilled ones,

Western European states initially encouraged the immigration of temporary guest workers to meet the demand for unskilled labor. However, once the post-war boom ended in the 1970s, European states began to formulate increasingly restrictive immigration and citizenship policies, until the term "fortress Europe" has come to be used to describe EU immigration policy.[2] Citizenship in a nation-state has, of course, been the key to enjoying the generous benefits of the European social model, including education, social insurance, health benefits, and employment opportunities.

Regardless of success, no social model endures forever. Ever since the 1970s, the competitive economic and technical forces driving globalization have under-mined the relative autonomy of the nation-state and the class compromises that sustained the European social model. And in the last two decades, European eco-nomic growth has stagnated, especially when compared to the performance of the United States. In most EU states unemployment hovers around postwar highs, new investment and productivity gains are faint, and firms complain that inflex-ible work rules and high payroll taxes discourage domestic and foreign invest-ment. The high cost of formal-sector employment, institutionalized during moments of working-class militancy and rising productivity, is also now seen both as discouraging the employment of youths and encouraging subcontracting to the informal sector. Finally, deflationary fiscal measures, necessary to launch the Euro currency, have led to cuts in spending for social, medical, and educational needs for the most vulnerable population groups.

Demography is at the heart of the crisis of the European social model, raising questions about the continuation of Europe's restrictive immigration and citizen-ship policies. The average age of Europe's population is skyrocketing, and Europe's age structure has taken the form of an inverted pyramid, with a large number of elderly pensioners above a smaller number of younger, working-age taxpayers. There are several causal factors at work here: low immigration rates, an aging aver-age population, greater employment opportunities for women, and a rapidly declining European fertility rate. Italy provides an excellent example. Only recent-ly it was a population-exporting country, but it now has the lowest recorded num-ber of births per woman in Europe. At a little over one, this is "the lowest figure ever recorded for humans," and far below the replacement rate of two. Indeed, no European country currently fulfills the population replacement rate.[3]

Although worsened by exclusionary immigration and restrictive citizenship policies, Europe's fertility decline is a demographic time bomb that will undermine the sustainability of the social model in the longer run. Because the demand for social benefits, especially health care, disability, and pensions, rises with the average age of a population, the absolute cost of providing benefits to the aging European population is sure to rise significantly at the same time that the working popula-tion will decline as a share of the total population. Examine, for example, the ratio of pensioners to workers in Germany. McKinsey Consultants reported in 1998 that "while there were three workers for every pensioner in the 1960s, there are now two workers per pensioner, and that, by 2030, there will be only one worker for each German pensioner."[4] Some European governments have recognized the problem. For example, the Dutch Socio-Economic Council has announced, "There will be too few students to meet labour market demands by 2003," while the Dutch labor minister has favored "more people from ethnic minorities in further education."[5] European political and economic integration, by itself, will not solve Europe's demographic deficit and the crisis of the social model.

This pattern contrasts starkly with the situation in the United States, Europe's economic rival, where immigrants with higher fertility rates have replenished the productive working population base necessary for funding social programs for older-age cohorts. Indeed, in Silicon Valley, the heartland of the global information industry, high-tech firms actively recruit Asian immigrants in order to capture their professional skills and entrepreneurship.[6] Instead of being seen as a threat to the European social model, new immigration could just as easily be defined as a resource for innovative growth, one needed to fund the social-welfare system and replenish the labor force with a working-age population. The key question, given these demographic patterns, is whether European immigration and citizenship rules will adjust to take advantage of the increasingly globalized labor market through which legal and illegal immigrants continue to flow into Europe.

Global competition and the crisis of the nationally based social model combine to explain the remarkable degree of European economic and political integration, symbolized by the signing of the Maastricht Treaty (1992). But the cost to social harmony has been high. In particular, the drive for global competitiveness and fiscal austerity, so necessary to protect the value of the Euro, has generated considerable social tension. And even mediated by the new EU borders, global competition has increased economic insecurity and created new social cleavages based upon age, gender, and migrant status. The latter insecurities have sharply heightened ethnic and racial conflict between some European citizens and non-Europeans, both citizens and aliens, especially Muslims. This situation has deteriorated to a point where the extreme right's periodic violent attacks on immigrants and multicultural communities now more closely resemble North American patterns than the earlier image of social harmony, once smugly asserted by champions of the European social model. Globalization, therefore, has generated ethnic conflict, as transnational migrants have passed through social networks now interwoven within the new global transportation and communications infrastructure. And, interestingly, the tension and confusion generated by the formation of the European Union has not been limited to conflict between citizens and immigrants. European identities and the meaning of European nationalism have also been disrupted by globalization and European integration.

## IDENTITIES, RIGHTS, AND CITIZENSHIP IN THE EUROPEAN UNION

Although designed initially to bolster European competitiveness in the global economy, European integration has profoundly disrupted institutional arrangements and disturbed social identities "invented" by the centralizing states during earlier periods of national integration.[7] The nation-state and the discourse of national identity are, arguably, Europe's greatest and most far-reaching social invention, one now universalized in the international state system. But the nation-state no longer monopolizes territory, rights, and identities as it once did. Globalization processes and European integration have reduced the power of nation-states either to control activities occurring within their territories, or to define the subjective identities of residents. National identity, to be sure, remains powerful, but it is increasingly compromised by a number of competing identities and "human rights" regimes. Most of all, the structural changes associated with globalization and integration have reconfigured the meanings and practices of all that was formerly called "national"—national economies, national political institutions, and national identities. Because the rising Islamic presence in Europe has problematized issues such as identity, citizenship, and nation, it is important to review the consequences of European integration for the powers of the once-unchallenged European national state.

Let me begin with economic integration. The EU economic regulatory institutions, most notably a central bank, a common market, common tariffs, and a unified currency (the Euro), have profoundly limited nation-states from exercising sovereign powers of economic management within their territories. Deficit spending, monetary policy, currency valuations, and fiscal policy are no longer solely national prerogatives. Since Maastricht, countercyclical spending, the management of effective demand, and economic coordination in general have been severely constrained by EU economic institutions. In the political realm, EU political institutions now also parallel national institutions through European commissions, parliament, bureaucracies, and courts. And military power has increasingly been integrated into a common command structure through NATO. All of these changes have clearly circumscribed the exercise of national power over both territory and subjects to an unparalleled degree—at least since Westphalia legitimized the nation-state.

In the cultural sphere, the nation-state's power to invent cohesive community identities is now fractured by a bevy of competing identities—linguistic, regional, national, and religious. And despite the revival of an extreme, xenophobic right-wing movement, often violently targeting immigrant minorities, the formerly hegemonic discourse of nationalism remains under siege. This is especially evident on the Continent, where European integration has eliminated former border checks and other obstacles to free population flows and cross-border political associations.

## EUROPEAN IDENTITY MOVEMENTS UNDER THE EUROPEAN UNION

A number of forces now conspire to frustrate the capacity of nation-states to sustain strong national identities among their citizens. Economic and political integration within the European Union have accelerated the demand for the "devolution of powers," not only to long-recognized nationalities (Scots, Welsh, Irish, Flemish, Basques, Catalans, Sardinians), but also to other less vocal, regional identity groups sharing a common heritage, language, or complementary economic activities. In other situations, the effective abolition of national borders, together with an economic integration, have stimulated a revival of regional identities formerly divided by centralized nation-states. Throughout continental Europe the combination of open borders, a common currency, and shared linguistic and cultural traits are nurturing new regional identities.[8]

Bolstered by national policies allowing the devolution of power to regional governments, it is increasingly evident that regionally based identity groups are making very effective use of EU institutions to bypass some or all of the aspects of what were formerly defined as the prerogatives of national sovereignty. And in the future some regions will be tempted to affiliate directly with EU financial, economic, and security institutions, rather than remain under the control of existing nation-states. Indeed, many regional political parties today claim the right to opt for independence (e.g., Scotland and Catalonia). Squeezed by ethnonational regionalism from below and by EU integration from above, the discourse of national identity is giving way to a multiplicity of situational identities, and to multiple institutional mechanisms for guaranteeing the rights for European residents.

Besides opening options for regional identity groups, the European Union has disrupted national sovereignty and national identities by granting EU citizenship to citizens of member states. This means that EU citizens residing in states other than their own have the right to work without discrimination, to unify their families, to obtain schooling, to belong to trade unions, and to receive welfare benefits—at least to the level provided by their nation-state.[9] In many states, EU citizens and legal residents have the right to vote in local elections. In several states, residence rather than citizenship is beginning to determine local voting rights. In general, such benefits are especially valuable for young professionals armed with global technical and linguistic skills who, like retirees, are more mobile than established workers.

By driving European integration, globalization is indirectly eroding the grip of national identity over the residents of Europe's increasingly cosmopolitan cities. In this regard, the transnationalization of labor markets across national boundaries has been a particularly relevant and direct consequence of globalization. It has meant that non-European communities from Asia and Africa are now a permanent and institutionalized feature of the EU urban landscape—and the majority of these people are Muslims. The origins of these communities, of course, vary according to the imperial and national history of the host country—that is, through policies directed toward loyal former colonial subjects, temporary guest workers, asylum-seekers, or European integration into the global labor market. On the one hand, the permanence of multicultural communities has today added to the global sophistication of European cities by supplying a desire for cosmopolitan styles of consumption. But on the other, global immigration processes have ignited a nationalist backlash against Asian and African immigrants, including demands for restricting asylum and citizenship claims, and for the construction of an insular "fortress Europe." The cultural and religious diversity of these groups has also threatened views other than right-wing nationalism. The Islamic presence, for example, poses a serious challenge to national institutions geared to molding identities and fixing loyalties by appealing to traditional national tropes of ancestry, religion, or shared national glory (i.e., empire).

Muslims, of course, have been coded as Europe's archetypal other. They represent the largest, most diverse, and most economically marginalized immigrant group resident in the European Union. Yet European policy toward Muslims is highly contradictory. Consider the Kosovo conflict, effectively the first war waged by European states in more than fifty years. What was most ironic was that the war was waged by member states to secure the human rights of Muslims in a province in the sovereign state of Yugoslavia. Neither the "traditional" European cultural subjects, nor the direct territorial interest of EU states were at risk. Rather, the sovereign powers of a nation-state to exercise violence in its territory were compromised. Quite paradoxically, at the same time as they were waging war for the human rights of Muslims, member states in the European Union were erecting barriers to Muslim immigration based on nationalist and xenophobic declarations that Muslims are inassimilable into European culture.

## GLOBALIZATION AND NETWORKS IN ISLAMIC COMMUNITIES

Let me now shift from the fragmentation of identities within European states to assessing the effect that the Muslim presence is having on the already-fragmented European national identity. If, as argued earlier, the network represents the organizational form of globalization in the information age, then it follows that the Muslim capacity to construct and mobilize its own network of resources will become a significant factor for assessing the Islamic presence in Europe. In this regard, a number of different theoretical lines of thought may be seen to converge around the issues of global networks, the nature of "multiple situated" identities, and the rise of "human rights regimes" under globalization.

Best known as the preeminent theorist of the networked society, Manuel Castells has associated globalization processes with the increasing significance of the "space of flows" along "an interconnected node," which he has defined as a network. He has contrasted the latter with the "space of place," over which nation-states exert control and seek to define identity, citizenship, and rights of various kinds.

> Thus people do still live in places. But because functions and power in our societies are organized in the space of flows, the structural domination of its logic essentially alters the meaning and dynamic of places. . . . [A] structural schizophrenia [exists] between two spatial logics that threatens to break down communication channels in society.[10]

Assuming Castells is correct about the hegemony of the digital network over the spatial community of the nation-state, then the primacy of networks in the global age will offer significant opportunities to transnational immigrant groups who possess the requisite cultural capital and institutions. Like the Chinese, whom Castells praises for having institutionalized successful overseas networks, Muslims may also benefit from the relative decline of state sovereignty, for this trend will enable them to maximize the latent power contained in their cultural capital. Since one of the longest-standing Muslim self-definitions is membership in a global identity, it is readily apparent that Muslim cultural capital encourages the formation of networks straddling national borders and cultures.

Transnational identity theory complements Castells' conceptualization of global networks. As does Castells, this approach assumes fragmentation of once-hegemonic national identity. But it also asserts that the networks associated with globalization nurture "multiple situated subjects." Here, cosmopolitan communities may emerge from which individuals may claim multiple identities (i.e., in Castells' lexicon, membership in both the "space of place" of a nation-state, and also in a "space of flows" in a transnational community). This distinction is valuable for advancing understanding of how transnational networks shape Muslim identities, immigration patterns, and citizenship claims in Western Europe. Stuart Hall captured this situation with regard to many immigrant Muslims in the European Union when he argued that "it seems unlikely that globalization will simply destroy national identities. It is more likely to produce, simultaneously, *new* 'global' and *new* 'local' identifications."[11] Accordingly, depending on their network locations and ethnic and/or national affiliations, Muslims may occupy multiple subject positions related to context, residence, and/or their location in wider, transnational networks. Part of the reason for the vitality of global networks among Muslims thus derives from the historical legacy of Muslim transnationalism, invariably expressed as common membership in a worldwide community of believers, the *umma*.

## THE GLOBAL *UMMA* AS A TRANSNATIONAL NETWORK

Compared to other world civilizations, Islamic cultural practices, ritual obligations, and institutions encourage an unusually high degree of geographical mobility across vast distances and different political units. During the era of premodern Muslim empires, networked trading diasporas evolved, and these networks became an important institution for integrating Muslims across widely differing political units ruled by both Muslims and non-Muslims. Because networks are not fixed in the "space of place," they are notoriously difficult for states to control or tax effectively. Historically, institutionalized across Muslim and non-Muslim regions of the world, such networks continue to allow Muslims to pursue trade, scholarship, missionary activity, brotherhood ties, pilgrimage obligations, and even travel as an end in itself.

From its earliest period, Islam encouraged merchant capitalism and long-distance trade, justified as emulation of the Prophet Mohammed, a long-distance trader by occupation. Muslim long-distance trading networks extended across states ruled by Muslims, and across non-Muslim regions of Asia, Africa, and Europe. Because Islam requires every Muslim who is financially able to undertake the pilgrimage (*hajj*) to the shrines of Mecca and Medina at least once during a lifetime, the pilgrimage became the most important integrator of Muslims into transnational networks. Prior to the advent of modern transportation systems, when space was measured by a day of traveling by animal transport, the *hajj* routes institutionalized a dense network of Muslim trading diaspora and pilgrimage communities throughout Asia, Europe, and Africa. To provide for material needs across vast distances, Muslim pilgrims traded goods across the nodes in pilgrimage networks to finance the *hajj*. Hence, commerce and religion were never isolated from each other, as these networks combined commerce, brokerage, pilgrimage services, Islamic scholarship, and missionary outreach. Many of these diasporic enclaves remain today. For a comparative perspective, imagine the popular networks that would have emerged if all Christians were required to undertake a pilgrimage to Jerusalem during their lifetime.

The political and social structures of classical Muslim empires also facilitated geographical mobility. Given the absence of serfdom, and given ecological conditions favorable to seasonal migration, free peasants and nomadic pastoralist traders made up a large share of the population. According to Marshal Hodgson, population mobility and the threat of migration acted to restrain greedy tax collectors from extracting revenues from the free peasantry and merchant class.[12] Similarly, Islamic student migration to centers of Islamic learning was a common practice for male youths and adults. In contemporary West Africa, Islamic networks still play a role in redistributing dry-season rural migrants to cities, where they perform menial labor in exchange for alms.[13] The obligation of

Muslims to migrate (*hijra*) from the territory ruled by hostile or un-Islamic (tyrannical) rulers also increased the geographical mobility of popular groups. In general, Islamic religious practices interacted with long-distance trading ventures to reinforce a complex web of Islamic commercial and religious networks.[14]

Upon the foundation of these overlapping and multifunctional networks, Muslims institutionalized a "cosmopolitan" culture, where common cultural, legal, and brotherhood institutions regulated socioeconomic transactions and resolved conflicts among Muslims. Muslim cosmopolitanism assumed that trade, pilgrimage, missionary activity, and geographical mobility were normal phases of the male life cycle. Theoretically, Muslim cosmopolitanism was possible because classical Islamic political theory developed a doctrine asserting the unity of all Muslims as members of a transnational, transethnic community—the *umma*—which then, as now, recognized a universalistic Islamic law, *sharia*. Even though political rivalry and sectarian differences have blocked the unification of all Muslims, it is nevertheless true that over the long term, *sharia* has tended to undermine lineage-, ethnic-, or clan-defined inheritance patterns in favor of a more unified Muslim identity.

In the twentieth century, pan-Islamic movements sponsored by the Ottomans fell to the wayside.[15] Once Attaturk dissolved the Caliphate (1924), the symbol of a unified *umma*, most Muslim political actors focused on establishing modern, secular nation-states appropriate to Muslim societies. But transnational state organizations still do exist. For example, the Organization of the Islamic Conference (OIC), funded by the Saudis, has fifty-two member states who are committed to promoting Muslim interests, distributing aid, and promoting Muslim education. The OIC also defends Islamic minorities and mediates conflicts among Muslim states.

Despite the secular trend in the first half of the twentieth century, however, numerous Islamic theorists and political movements continued to advocate Islamic political integration through the global *umma*. Among these were Muhammed Iqbal, Maudidi, Sayyid Qutb, and the Armed Islamic Group of Algeria.[16] The influential theorist of the Muslim Brotherhood, Sayyid Qutb, known for his advocacy of militant vanguard internationalism, for example, asserted that "a Muslim's homeland is any land governed by the laws of Islam";[17] and that "our belief is that any Muslim Brothers in any country are related to us on the basis of ideology and belief. . . . When one mentions Brothers, one never asks about their nationality."[18] At the level of civil society, furthermore, a number of transnational Islamic organizations, acting independently of states, have promoted what Eickelman and Piscatori have called the "horizontal integration" of the transnational Muslim community. Among these have been the Tijaniyya, Mouridiyya, and Naqashbandiyya brotherhoods, *dawa* (call) societies, and missionary associations such as the Tablighi Jama'at.[19] All these examples illustrate the activities of Islamic networks under globalization.

Muslim cosmopolitanism, therefore, has endured as a powerful, cohesive force encouraging transnational communal integration as well as the extension of global networks for pilgrimage, trade, education, and charity. Globalization has facilitated the interweaving of transnational Islamic networks within the new global transportation and communication infrastructure. Europe, from the Muslim cosmopolitan perspective, is merely a new frontier for the extension of Islamic networks and diasporic communities. Ironically, globalization has actually increased communication and associative opportunities for the once-isolated and differentiated Muslim communities of the global *umma*. Cultural theorist Bryan Turner has made this point forcefully:

> It is the availability in modern times of effective global communications systems which makes possible for the first time a globalization of Islam. . . . While Islam had always claimed universalistic status, it was, prior to the emergence of contemporary communications systems, actually unable to impose this type of uniformity and universalism. The paradox of modern systems of communication is that it makes Islam simultaneously exposed to Western consumerism and provides the mechanism for the distribution of a global Islamic message.[20]

## PHASES OF MUSLIM IMMIGRATION: EMPIRE, GUEST WORKERS, AND ASYLUM-SEEKERS

During the twentieth century, the first Muslim communities in Europe grew out of the overlap between Islamic and global capitalist networks as well as through opportunities created by imperial institutions. At particular moments in the empires, immigrant white settlers and some of the non-European subjects qualified for citizenship and/or residence in Europe. Algeria, after all, was defined as a department of France; citizenship was once granted to the residents of four cities in Senegal; and many subjects living in the British Empire, later the Commonwealth, had British citizenship and residence rights until the 1970s, when the entry of nonwhites was restricted.[21] In general, advocates of imperial expansion tended to accept assimilation for a minority of colonial subjects who could "evolve" to accept the national culture. Additionally, Muslim members of colonial armies, typically after fighting losing wars against nationalist movements, were often repatriated to Europe. Thus, the *harkis*, a distinct identity group of Muslim Algerians who supported, and even fought for, the French against the (FLN), were settled legally in France. The Dutch did the same for Muslim colonial soldiers from Indonesia, especially the Moluccans. Once established in Europe, Muslims have unified families, established religious institutions, and maintained networks with their communities of origin.

Labor migration marked the second phase of Muslim immigration to Europe. In the immediate postwar era, Europe's high rate of economic growth exhausted the labor supply in northern European states. Muslims responded by becoming migrant workers and guest workers, often beginning in menial tasks, but soon becoming integrated into the more highly skilled and unionized sectors. In the postwar era, long-standing imperial networks, linguistic ties, and labor shortages all shaped the flow of Muslims to particular European states.

Particular patterns also emerged. Britain's ambiguous nationality laws and inconsistent citizenship policies drew Muslim immigrants from the Commonwealth, especially South Asia.[22] Today most Muslims in Britain are citizens.[23] France recruited Muslim workers from Southern Europe and from North and West Africa, especially Algeria. Its immigration controls were lax, and eventually illegal immigration became so widespread that "by the end of the 1960s, 70 to 80 percent of all immigrants entered France 'spontaneously'" (i.e., on tourist visas that were made permanent upon employment).[24] Likewise, the Netherlands recruited from Surinam and Indonesia, and later from Morocco. Finally, drawing on long-term informal imperial ties, Germany recruited Muslims from Turkey and the Balkans.

Since Britain was already composed of diverse nationalities, Muslims were defined first as a racial minority, and later as a new community within a multicultural polity. In contrast, France's secular, evolutionary tradition recognized no communal group mediating between the individual and the state, requiring instead that all new citizens be assimilated into French culture. Initially, the incorporation of Muslims and other noncitizens into the French industrial labor force was not accepted by European trade unions. In 1970, there were 600,000 Algerians, 140,000 Moroccans, and 90,000 Tunisians without citizenship in France.[25] But after immigrant workers launched wildcat strikes for "recognition" (1971), French trade unions and left political parties reached out and incorporated the millions of immigrants employed in the manufacturing and organized industrial sectors. Progressive elements of the French church also affirmed immigrant rights by forming solidarity groups, not unlike the German Greens. Finally, competition among Communist, Socialist, and Catholic organizations and the rise of experienced immigrants to trade union offices gradually led to the incorporation of established immigrant workers into French society and political processes.[26] With the victory of Mitterrand's Socialist government (1981–1991), French policy then moved toward securing family unification for immigrant workers and naturalizing immigrants after five years of residence, while blocking new immigrants by stricter enforcement of new immigration laws.

Unlike France, where assimilation, birth, and residence enable immigrants to become naturalized citizens in a contractual relationship between states and individual citizens, eligibility for German citizenship requires membership in the German *Volk*, which usually requires descent from German blood relatives. For this reason, guest workers were never assumed to have a claim to permanent residency. However, the views of German trade unions and solidarity groups followed a trajectory similar to that of the French: union resistance to incorporation of immigrants at first, followed by strikes for "recognition" by immigrants, and finally incorporation of immigrants into unions and the Social Democratic Party. In both the German and French cases, industrial actions served as the first step toward recognized political participation. Currently, Germany's national trade union federation (DGB) "has taken an increasingly inclusive position that has propelled it toward an alliance with churches and welfare organizations."[27] Meanwhile, the Greens have spearheaded a campaign for the recognition of rights for immigrants. Today, Turks represent the largest Muslim group in Germany, numbering almost two million out of a total foreign population of six and a half million.[28]

By the middle of the 1970s, the crisis of the European social model and economic stagnation had halted the active recruitment of guest workers. In response to these economic changes, states tightened citizenship requirements, restricted immigration, and even financed the repatriation of guest workers. Yet, the global pressures driving transnational migration did not cease. Rather, migration has sought out new routes, including family unification, asylum-seeking, and clandestine entry. Observe these facts: the number of legally resident aliens in the twelve EU states rose from seven and a half million in 1985 to eleven and a half million in 1993 (an increase of 66 percent), while illegal aliens were estimated at more than a million and a half in 1992.[29] Applications for political asylum in Western European countries increased from 65,400 in 1983 to 544,400 in 1991.[30] In the member states of the European Union, asylum applications rose 420 percent between 1987 and 1992. Sorensen has concluded that "asylum seeking then proves to be a very good way of circumventing normal immigration procedures. . . . [A]sylum has become a parallel immigration route."[31] Rogers estimated that 30 percent of applicants are granted asylum in Europe, but more importantly, "75 to 80 percent of those rejected stay in the country of asylum, nonetheless."[32]

These facts are forcing reconsideration of the relationship between citizenship and rights. After observing that millions of permanent residents of Europe are not citizens, and that identity has increasingly been decoupled from the national state, Soysal argued that the world is entering a "postnational" era. In the postnational model, the boundaries of membership are fluid and networked rather than territorially fixed in citizenship. The process of global integration and the signing of human rights accords by states "means that national citizenship is no longer the main determinant of individual rights and privileges."[33] Instead, "International conventions and charters ascribe universal rights to persons regardless of their membership status in a nation-state."[34] Thus, nation-states have signed into international law a number of codes and laws affirming a global human rights discourse that confers rights based on universal "personhood," not "citizenship." This argument is discussed further in the conclusion.

## GLOBAL SOURCES OF MUSLIM MIGRATION AFTER MAASTRICHT

To be sure, during the 1980s xenophobic and anti-immigrant political movements shifted state policies against asylum-seekers and non-EU immigration in
general. For example, Britain and other EU states implemented the following
controls: stricter documentation for entry visas, greater discretionary power for
immigration officials at entry, commercial carrier responsibility and fines for
transporting illegal aliens, denationalization of airport space to block application
for asylum, limitation of appeal procedures, and stricter detention and deportation procedures.[35] A number of formal and informal immigration agreements
(TREVI, Schengen and Dublin) designed to harmonize policies among EU
states having open borders after 1993 will further restrict entry of political
refugees, largely because traditionally liberal countries can now justify such
restrictions due to the harmonization requirements of EU agreements.
Henceforth, asylum-seekers will be limited to one application to any EU state,
and a computer database at Strasbourg will make accessible a list of previously
rejected applicants. This means that unelected officials will have enhanced discretionary powers to "amend the regulations on a day-to-day basis."[36]

   While these restrictions may constrain the flow of immigrants and refugees
temporarily, they will ultimately be insufficient in light of global and structural
pressures channeling immigrants to Europe. The reasons are demographic, political, and economic. Within Europe, demographic decline and age structure will
continue to create a demand for new immigrants to provide labor and sustain
social services. Of course, Western European states may choose to recruit from
Eastern Europe or other culturally similar populations rather than from the
Muslim world. But this assumes that immigrants from these places will be willing
to take the low-wage, low-status jobs (i.e., in agriculture, services, and the informal economy) that are now typically occupied by Muslims.

   Realistically, it is also clear that political instability will continue to drive
political refugees to EU states. Many areas with close ties to the European Union
are currently embroiled in insurrection and civil war: Algeria, eastern Turkey,
Yugoslavia (Bosnia, Macedonia, and Kosovo), and, more distantly, Iraq, Sudan,
Somalia, and the Central Asian hinterland. Most of the remaining states bordering the European Union to the south and southeast are ruled by authoritarian,
patrimonial regimes, often led by geriatric leaders without legitimate successors.
Such states are further increasingly challenged by a new generation of Islamist
political movements. Indeed, NATO's air war against Yugoslavia alone has propelled hundreds of thousands of Muslim refugees across EU borders. Political
forces in the region, therefore, guarantee that a steady stream of Muslim political
refugees and illegal immigrants will seek entry into the European Union by legal
and clandestine routes.

Nor is there any evidence that rates of economic growth or institutional reform in these foreign states will suffice to absorb new, youthful entrants to the labor force, who will likely choose instead to swell the ranks of economic immigrants illegally seeking work in Europe. Richards and Waterbury have painted a particularly grim picture of the Middle East and North Africa (MENA) region. Among their findings was that MENA is second only to Africa in rates of population growth; that the region's population is expected to double in twenty-seven years; and that Islam and fertility are positively correlated universally.[37] The age pyramid in the region is also the opposite of Europe's: "Most Middle Easterners are less than twenty years old."[38] "Everywhere in the region the labor force is growing faster than the demand for labor," and in most cases exceeds 3 percent a year.[39] State educational budgets are also biased toward tertiary and secondary education, geared to the state employment of males.

In Egypt, for example, Richards and Waterbury found that increases in secondary-school enrollments average 14 percent annually; tertiary enrollments roughly doubled between 1971–1984; and universities consumed 38 percent of the education budget in 1984–1985, while nearly a quarter of the girls were not enrolled in primary school.[40] In Algiers, a survey found that 75 percent of youth aged sixteen to twenty-nine were seeking work while, at the same time, "the educational system produced 270,000 unemployed diploma holders. Some 80 percent of this age group continued to live with their families, often eight persons to a room."[41] Finally, in an era governed by global competition and neoliberal structural adjustment programs, neither international investment nor internal economic reform is on the horizon. "As MENA countries procrastinate on reform, the stresses of lagging incomes, slow job creation, and tenuous food security mount," Richards and Waterbury concluded.[42] Such a view would indicate that the demographic, economic, and social forces in the region virtually guarantee more, not less, clandestine economic migration to Europe in order to escape the misery of a stagnating regional economy ruled by authoritarian elites.

## INCORPORATION AND IDENTITY AMONG EUROPEAN MUSLIMS

Generalizations are difficult to make about the identities of European Muslims, mostly because of the geographical variety of their origins. Few sources even agree on the actual numbers of Muslims living in Europe and the European Union, and rising illegal immigration further renders accurate estimates difficult. Vertovec's national estimates, presented in Table 1, are conservative: nearly twenty-four million Muslims in Europe and nearly seven million in the EC (European Union). Shadid and van Koningsveld's estimates are slightly higher for some states.[43] Tibi's (1998) estimates are significantly higher: fifteen million Muslims in

Western Europe and eight million in southeast Europe. Nor can Muslims be described as an integrated community in any sociological sense. Differences arise from ethnonational origin, language, sectarian beliefs, legal status, social class, and generational cohort. A major distinction lies between legal residents, including citizens, who have been incorporated into the European polity, and the growing number of illegal and temporary immigrants who are more deeply integrated into transnational networks of the Islamic community.

Muslim identities correlate with migrant status and national modes of incorporation into European societies. Generally speaking, there are several major groups of European Muslims, however. A first group consists of those Muslims who have been incorporated as naturalized citizens in a European state. As rec-

Table 4.1. Estimated Muslim Population by EC State.

| COUNTRY | YEAR | POPULATION (x one thousand) |
|---|---|---|
| Belgium | 1990 | 244 |
| Denmark | 1990 | 60 |
| France | 1990 | 2,619 |
| Germany | 1990 | 2,012 |
| Greece | 1981 | 140 |
| Italy | 1991 | 250 |
| Netherlands | 1990 | 442 |
| Portugal | 1975 | 30 |
| Spain | 1990 | 40 |
| U.K. | 1991 | 1,000 |
| EC | | 6,837 |
| Europe | | 23,589 |

Source: S. Vertovec and C. Peach, eds., *Islam in Europe: The Politics of Religion and Community* (Basingstoke: Macmillan, 1997).

ognized minorities, their identity and degree of political participation depends in large part on those national institutions that regulate their incorporation and political representation. Typically, these people are immigrants or converts, but their children represent a distinct generation, often identifying as "Euro-versions" (e.g., British Muslims, Beurs, Euro-Muslims) of their parents' generation. A second major group of European Muslims is composed of immigrants possessing temporary or permanent residence rights—that is, holders of work permits, contract workers, spouses, students, and asylum-seekers awaiting decisions. Because the average length of immigrant residence exceeds fifteen years, and because naturalization rates are very low (e.g., only 6 percent of Germany's foreign population naturalized between 1975–1984), millions of Muslims in this second group are legal residents but lack citizenship rights.[44] A third group consists of those immigrants who entered by clandestine means and who live and work outside the regulation of formal European institutions. Generally unskilled, they are largely employed in agriculture and the informal sector. Because the supply of such migrants is so high in the wider Mediterranean region, a key question for the future is whether this group will ultimately encourage the continued expansion of the informal underground economy in places such as Italy where regulation is weak or absent, especially the sectors of agriculture, restaurants, construction, domestic services, and sweatshops.[45] A fourth group of Muslim migrants are the cosmopolitans: highly skilled, professional, artistic-intellectual, media, and entrepreneurial workers recruited by subsidiaries of transnational corporations or professional networks for work or formal training. Labeled as "denizens," their geographical mobility makes them indifferent toward citizenship because they possess the talent or capital to perform in the globalized marketplace.

While such migrant statuses reflect differences among Muslims residing in Europe, each nation-state has also institutionalized different immigration and naturalization policies, as well as different institutions to incorporate migrants into the state. As the following review of national incorporation strategies in Britain, France, the Netherlands, and Germany indicates, variation in terms of mechanisms of Muslim incorporation into European states is extreme, posing a great problem for the future harmonization of immigration and citizenship policy within the European Union.

Most Muslims in Britain are citizens of South Asian origin. Despite Britain's liberal tradition, all revisions of nationality and citizenship acts since 1948 have made it more difficult for nonwhites to become citizens. Today, therefore, incorporation of Muslims is only achieved through interest-group lobbying, alliances with other racial minorities, and by demanding equal rights as individuals to secure employment, education, and religious institutional resources. The Muslim strategy is often oriented toward local governmental units, and toward securing individual rights in ways other than through the formal institutions of the national government.[46]

France, too, allocates citizenship on the basis of birth and residence, but it demands that individuals achieve a high degree of cultural assimilation. Unlike Britain, which recognizes nationalities and an official Church of England, the French political tradition rejects all intermediary corporate groups which are based upon religion or ethnicity. The result has been that, until recently, Muslim immigrants tended to be incorporated through national-level trade unions, political organizations, and antiracial movements. Kepel, however, has chronicled a shift toward communal-identity politics, as Muslim youths have become marginalized economically and global Islamic networks have exerted their influence.

After describing the linkage of domestic Muslim movements to international Islamist networks, Kepel also documented how the French state has tried to undermine what it defines as "communalist" political groups. Nonetheless, he has also acknowledged that this trend "has considerable potential," because schools and labor unions are failing to integrate Muslims. "The demand for communalist identity gathers force with the spread of systematic social exclusion in postindustrial [i.e., global] society," he has concluded.[47]

Different still is the case of the Dutch, who have institutionalized a state-centered, corporatist model of incorporation that grants official recognition to religious organizations. In effect, organs of the Dutch state organize, consult with, and even fund Muslim organizations. Comparatively, Dutch citizenship is relatively easy to obtain, and dual citizenship is allowed. Official state policy is called "pillarisation," whereby state ministries recognize and fund religiously/spiritually defined corporate groups, and then allocate state revenues for education, clergy salaries, and media. Once recognized by the state as a corporate religious group, equivalent to Christian sects or Jews, Muslims have been eligible to receive subsidies for Islamic activities, including a Muslim broadcasting station.[48] In the Dutch case, the social democratic corporatist tradition, together with a series of historical compromises among confessional groups, has combined to incorporate Muslims, so that Muslim identities are institutionalized in state policy.

In contrast to this policy is the case of Germany, where naturalization rates are low because, until recently, German national identity, and thus citizenship, was defined strictly according to descent from blood relatives, that is, the German *Volk*. At the same time, unlike France, and until recently Britain, Germany is a federation of states whose center does not recognize immigrant groups; rather, it relies on nationally linked institutions such as trade unions and educational and training institutions to incorporate immigrants. Not surprisingly, the globally linked and more cosmopolitan German states—Berlin, Hamburg, Hessen, and Bremen—recognize and promote immigrant organizations and rights.[49] Given the racial basis of German national identity, one of the great paradoxes of this situation is that Germany has absorbed the largest number of asylum-seekers, and incorporated immigrants to a far greater degree than states with more liberal citizenship regimes. The German Green Party, for example, has made immigrant rights a foundation of its platform. Jacobson's explanation for this condition is insightful:

> Paradoxically, the ethnonationalistic basis of German nationhood and citizenship led the Germans to turn more readily to international human rights codes to account for the foreign elements in their midst; for the Germans, unlike the Americans or the French, concepts of nationhood left little room for "internally" accounting for the migrants.[50]

Whatever the rhetoric of EU harmonization of member states' immigration policies implies for Muslims, what this brief overview indicates is that the European Union contains highly variable and contradictory policies across nation-states. And since nationality and citizenship are determined at the national rather than EU level, it is unclear whether multicultural policies based on human rights regimes will become policy, or whether "fortress Europe" will prevail. But harmonization of EU policies toward Muslims will certainly be contradicted by the residual effect of those ways in which European nation-states have so far dealt with internal ethnonational, regional, and religious minorities at critical historical moments. What was necessary for a centralizing nation-state, however, is highly unlikely to be enlightened policy for a multinational confederation trying to position itself within the new global economy.

## EUROPEAN MUSLIM IDENTITIES UNDER GLOBALIZATION: SOME CONCLUSIONS

Earlier in this chapter, the European national state is described as being squeezed by ethnonational regionalism from below and by EU integration from above. The EU resident is subject, therefore, to overlapping and competing authorities, each claiming loyalty and conferring rights. What is unclear is how the fracturing of nation-state identities will influence the acceptance and incorporation of Muslims in the European Union. For example, does the acceptance of Scottish and Welsh nationalism create greater acceptance of multicultural society? Is Spanish acceptance of considerable regional autonomy for Catalans likely to increase tolerance toward Muslim migrants, the historical antagonist of the Spanish nationalist narrative? What of Muslim migrants in bureaucratically challenged Italy, with its strong regional identities? Will Italians continue to tolerate Muslim participation in the black economy, as they have to date? While it is clear that EU residents are experiencing a fragmentation of authority, one could also argue that the fracturing of national identity has created the possibility for alliances among the multicultural groups, perhaps led by the postnational Greens who favor extending human rights regimes. Alternatively, the squeezing of the state from above and below may harden the border between EU citizens and Europe's marginalized Muslim neighbors.

Although it is impossible to answer these questions with certainty, several trends are readily apparent. Driven by demographic, political, and economic forces, the Muslim presence will continue to increase in Europe at a time when both the Islamic revival and the global infrastructure are extending the reach and cohesion of Muslim networks. By expanding the boundaries of the European Union and eliminating internal immigration controls, moreover, the control of illegal immigrants will become more difficult, becoming, in essence, a matter for the local police after entry. What this means for a high-income country such as Germany is that immigration control will shift from the Rhine to such locations as the Spanish border, maritime Italy, or the Turkish frontier. Given variations in organizational discipline and bureaucratic commitment to managing influx controls, it is difficult to see how this shift will not lead to further increases in the number of Muslims living in Germany, where a large Muslim community already exists and into which new aliens can be absorbed. All of these trends can only lead to a larger population of Muslim immigrants without either citizenship or the right to legal residence.

The other trend of importance is the cumulative accumulation of judicial and regulatory powers by EU institutions. Many skeptics believe that economic integration will require greater political integration. The existing fragmentation of national polities and contradictory immigration policies will make it difficult for any single regulatory policy to be effective. In the past, nation-states regulated immigration by developing a diverse array of incorporation institutions that more or less regulated immigration. Therefore, as the political and economic integration deepens, it is likely that EU-wide regulatory institutions will need to be developed to monitor, recognize, and incorporate Muslims and other immigrants. In turn, just as Muslim organizations have emerged at the national level to pursue Muslim interests, one may expect that economic and political integration will stimulate EU-wide Muslim organization, probably led by second- and third-generation Euro-Muslims.

One must recall both Sorensen's conclusion that "asylum-seeking has become a parallel immigration route," and Soysal's argument that the rise of "postnational" rights regimes may explain why very few asylum-seekers are actually expelled. As has been mentioned, postnational rights are universal human rights conferred on individuals on the basis of universal personhood and not on the basis of citizenship in a nation-state. In the European Union, the enabling legislation is the European Convention on Human Rights (ECHR), which thirty-five states had ratified by 1995, including all member states of the European Union. Moreover, as Jacobson has pointed out, "the European Union's Court of Justice has determined that the convention forms part of Community Law. Hence the convention is the nucleus of a European constitution and a European Bill of Rights."[51] Located at Strasbourg, the ECHR's institutions are the Commission of Human Rights and the Court of Human Rights. But the ECHR is not an EU institution, for its commissioners are appointed by the Council of Europe. Just as Soysal's theory of postnational rights would predict, a series of rulings by ECHR institutions have recognized the human rights of aliens over those of states. Not surprisingly, according to Jacobson, "From 1976–1983, about a quarter, on average, of the applications registered by the Commission on Human Rights were lodged by aliens."[52] The combination of global immigration pressure, the activism of advocacy groups, and judicial review by ECHR institutions, therefore, has forced EU states to be "accountable to international rules and institutions for the treatment of people in its jurisdiction." Given these precedents, nothing will prevent EU institutions in the future from proposing laws and incorporating institutions that override the immigration policies of member states toward Muslims in the wider Mediterranean region.

## NOTES

1. K. Ohmae, *The Borderless World* (New York: Harpers, 1990).

2. R. Cohen, *Frontiers of Identity* (London: Longman, 1994); and J. Sorensen, *The Exclusive European Citizenship* (Aldershot, U.K.: Avebury-Ashgate, 1996).

3. M. Specter, "Population Implosion Worries a Graying Europe," *New York Times*, July 10, 1998, 43.

4. Quoted in R. Blackburn, "The New Collectivism," *New Left Review*, no. 233 (January–February 1999), 13.

5. *Times Higher Education Supplement*, April 16, 1999, 9.

6. A. Saxenian, *Regional Advantage: Culture and Competition in Silicon Valley and Route 128* (Cambridge, Mass.: Harvard University Press, 1996).

7. E. Hobsbawm and T. Ranger, eds., *The Invention of Tradition* (Cambridge, U.K.: Cambridge University Press, 1983).

8. J. Newhouse, *Europe Adrift* (New York: Pantheon, 1997).

9. E. Meehan, *Citizenship and the European Community* (London: Sage, 1993); and E. Guild, "The Legal Framework of Citizenship of the European Union," in D. Cesarani and M. Fulbrook, eds., *Citizenship, Nationality and Migration in Europe* (London: Routledge, 1996).

10. M. Castells, *The Rise of the Network Society* (Oxford, U.K.: Blackwell, 1996), 376ff.

11. S. Hall and P. du Guy, eds., *Questions of Cultural Identity* (London: Sage, 1996), 624.

12. M. Hodgson, *The Venture of Islam* (Chicago: University of Chicago Press, 1974), vol. 2.

13. P. Lubeck, "Islamic Protest Under Semi-Industrial Capitalism: Yan Tatsine Explained," *Africa: Journal of the International African Institute* 55, no. 4 (1985).

14. D. Eickelman and J. Piscatori, eds., *Muslim Travelers: Pilgrimage, Migration and the Religious Imagination* (Berkeley: University of California Press, 1990).

15. J. Landau, *The Politics of Pan-Islam: Ideology and Organization* (New York: Oxford University Press, 1990).

16. D. Eickelman and J. Piscatori, *Muslim Politics* (Princeton, N.J.: Princeton University Press, 1996).

17. E. Sivan, *Radical Islam, Medieval Theology and Modern Politics* (New Haven, Conn.: Yale University Press, 1985), 45.

18. F. Ajami, "In the Pharaoh's Shadow: Religion and Authority in Egypt," in J. Piscatori, ed., *Islam in the Political Process* (Cambridge: Cambridge University Press, 1983), 95.

19. Eickelman and Piscatori, *Muslim Politics*.

20. B. Turner, *Orientalism, Postmodernism and Globalism* (London: Routledge, 1994), 86.

21. Cohen, *Frontiers of Identity*.

22. Cohen, *Frontiers of Identity*.

23. J. Nielsen, *Muslims in Western Europe* (Edinburgh: Edinburgh University Press, 1992).

24. P. Ireland, *The Policy Challenge of Ethnic Diversity: Immigrant Politics in France and Switzerland* (Cambridge, Mass.: Harvard University Press, 1994), 40.

25. D. Jacobson, *Rights Across Borders* (Baltimore, Md.: Johns Hopkins University Press, 1996).

26. Ireland, *The Policy Challenge of Ethnic Diversity*.

27. W. Barbieri, *Ethics of Citizenship* (Durham, N.C.: Duke University Press, 1998), 43.

28. S. Vertovec, "Berlin Multikulti: Germany, 'Foreigners' and 'World Openness,'" *New Community* 22, no. 3 (1996).

29. Sorensen, *The Exclusive European Citizenship*.

30. Y. Soysal, *The Limits of Citizenship: Migrants and Postnational Membership in Europe* (Chicago: University of Chicago Press, 1994).

31. Sorensen, *The Exclusive European Citizenship*, 93.

32. R. Rogers, 1991, cited in Soysal, *The Limits of Citizenship*, 24.

33. Soysal, *The Limits of Citizenship*, 12.

34. Soysal, *The Limits of Citizenship*, 145.

35. Sorensen, *The Exclusive European Citizenship*; and Cohen, *Frontiers of Identity*.

36. Cohen, *Frontiers of Identity*, 184.

37. A. Richards and J. Waterbury, *A Political Economy of the Middle East*, 2nd ed. (Boulder, Colo.: Westview, 1996).

38. Richards and Waterbury, *A Political Economy of the Middle East*, 89.

39. Richards and Waterbury, *A Political Economy of the Middle East*, 91.

40. Richards and Waterbury, *A Political Economy of the Middle East*, 91.

41. Eickelman and Piscatori, *Muslim Politics*, 116.

42. Richards and Waterbury, *A Political Economy of the Middle East*, 250.

43. W. A. R. Shadid and S. van Koningsveld, *Religious Freedom and the Position of Islam in Western Europe* (Kampen, the Netherlands: Kok Pharos, 1995).

44. Soysal, *The Limits of Citizenship*.

45. E. Pugliese, "Italy between Emmigration and Immigration and the Problems of Citizenship," in D. Cesarani and M. Fulbrook, eds., *Citizenship, Nationality and Migration in Europe* (London: Routledge, 1996).

46. P. Lewis, *Islam in Britain: Religion, Politics and Identity among British Muslims* (London: Routledge, 1994).

47. G. Kepel, *Allah in the West* (Stanford, Calif.: Stanford University Press, 1997), 232–33.

48. Shadid and van Koningsveld, *Position of Islam in Western Europe*.

49. Soysal, *The Limits of Citizenship*.

50. Jacobson, *Rights Across Borders*, 10–11.

51. Jacobson, *Rights Across Borders*, 80–81.

52. Jacobson, *Rights Across Borders*, 88.

# 5

# Islam and the West in an Era of Globalization: Clash of Civilizations or Coexistence?

## Hala Mustafa

While the concept of globalization began in the cradle of advanced Western economies, it affects ways of governance in the developing world as the latter is drawn, willy-nilly, into its vortex. If things turn out well, globalization may bolster the burgeoning democracies of the Third World and redress social grievances worldwide. Indeed, the growing appeal of human rights is nothing if not proof of the potency of human rights advocacy on a universal scale.

Western democracy was only born several centuries ago, after the conflict between the state and the church was resolved in a manner that rebutted the claims of the clergy to Divine Rights. This turning point for Western democracy continues to inspire social scientists to this day. During the modernization trend of the 1950s in the West, political theorists went so far as to assume a correlation between democracy and modernity, and they made the relation between religion and the state a central point of their analysis. Development at the time was seen as a panacea for a variety of social ills, and liberal democracy was deemed a safe-guard against social injustice. Theorists of that era drew heavily on the ideas of Max Weber, which contrasted traditional societies with the modern state.

Economic change in developing societies has always been relatively easier than social and political change. The latter eventually always encounters resistance when it locks horns with entrenched sets of values and traditions. As globalization—which has so far translated into the inexorable advance of capitalist values—gathers pace, countries in the Third World will continue to face unfamiliar challenges, not the least of which will be the issue of human rights.

Since Samuel Huntington presented his theory of the "Clash of Civilizations," Islam versus the West has become a favorite theme for many Western writers.[1] Huntington envisioned the post-Cold War era as a time when national and ideological differences would be eclipsed by cultural ones. But is this truly inevitable? Are Islam and the West inherently inimical? This chapter attempts to refute those beliefs.

Although the possibility of a clash between Islam and the West must not be underestimated, the roots of such friction should not be attributed solely to religious or cultural factors, as Huntington suggested. There are a host of political and economic grievances inherent in relations between the North and the South, the rich and the poor. Religion may actually be more of a vehicle for expressing these grievances than one of their underlying causes.

The allure of Huntington's hypothesis must not allow a number of essential facts about the Muslim world to be forgotten. Key among these are the following seven points:

Islam, a major faith with millions of moderate followers, should not be confused with the views of militant Muslim fundamentalists, who primarily target the very Muslim societies and regimes in which they live. Algeria, Tunisia, and Egypt are clear examples of countries where such militant views are today directed at local regimes. Militancy, in its Islamic garb, is but a form of social protest against the absence of genuine political participation—a sorry but dominant phenomenon in developing countries, including Muslim ones. It is a symptom of a social crisis that has less to do with religion, per se, than with the failure of development models to produce social equity. Many adherents of Islamic militancy are college graduates who hail from rural areas and have turned to militancy in protest against their lack of social mobility. The West is often viewed with suspicion in developing countries. Not only is the West associated with colonialism, but with exploitation and apathy in the postcolonial era. It should not, however, be forgotten that political Islam has not been the only response of Muslim societies to the perceived Western threat, that pan-Arabism filled the same need for the generations of the 1950s and 1960s.

The gap between developed and developing countries is rather the result of disparities in growth of development levels between the two sides. Many developing countries find themselves contrasted with other countries—sometimes geographically near—that have taken major strides in terms of historical, political, economic, and cultural experience. Those places supposed to be integrated into the global capitalist system through interaction and mutual dependence measure themselves as far from the Western, modernist model (and its implicit characteristics of economic freedom, democracy, and individualism). Developing countries, by definition, are undergoing that transition, still living in agricultural, pastoral, or preindustrial societal patterns. On the opposite side are developed countries that live in the postindustrial era; places that have experienced "complete modernity" relative to those just entering its throes. This gap cannot be easily overcome even with the astounding advancement in the field of communications and media, or the mere integration into the global free market. Bridging the gap will involve a long-term, multidimensional process.

In pre-Renaissance Europe, the march toward democracy and human rights was slow and tedious. The Muslim world, however, has seen an entire phase of this process foreshortened through the accelerated copying of Western values. Secularism in Europe preceded democracy. The Muslim world is now striving for democracy without benefit of a similar process. In Algeria, for example, democracy has been stunted as it has been faced with a conflict between religion and the state, and the normal sequence of a historical process has been reversed, with unpleasant consequences.

Culture is a broader concept than religion. Just as today's Western culture cannot be reduced to Christianity, one should not attempt to do the same with Islamic culture. History abounds with examples of coexistence between the two cultures. Both, for example, interacted comfortably with Greek culture, and the twelfth-century Arab thinker Averroès (Ibn Rushd) was an avid advocate of Greek philosophy. Cultural interaction is not only possible, it has been ongoing and pervasive.

National interests, rather than cultural affiliation, still dominate the scene of political rivalry. Globalization may have given more leverage to multinational businesses and nongovernmental organizations (NGOs), but the national state still has the last word in matters of political conflict, and has so far made no marked distinction between Western and Islamic rivals. Take, for instance, Turkey and Syria, the Taliban and Iran, Iraq and Iran, Iraq and Kuwait. National interests, not creed, are still the ultimate decider of political rivalries.

The Middle East has long been a melting pot of cultures, a convergence point of major religions. But now it is also a political powder keg, with religion providing a smoke screen for a more general malaise. The stalemate in the Israeli-Palestinian peace process has provided fertile soil for fanaticism, and has fed extremists across the political divide (Hamas and Jihad are only a humble match for Jewish extremists who adamantly oppose Israel's return to its 1967 borders). The continuation of the stalemate threatens to turn the region into a site of confrontation not only between Arabs and Israelis, but between Arabs and Israel's unquestioning supporter, the United States. Washington's position on Israel's nonaccession to the Nuclear Nonproliferation Treaty is only one example of the partiality of its Middle East policies.

Ethnic and national strife following the end of the Cold War has transcended the scope of the West-versus-Islam formula. As oppressed minorities have tried to break away from the political straitjacket of the Cold War and redress long-standing grievances, clashes have ensued in many places. Some have had an outward religious appearance (Bosnia, Kosovo), but even then strife may owe more to economic and political factors than to religious ones.

Among the endless possibilities of Islam-West relations, I focus on five issues: the North-South divide, ethnic rivalries, the Middle East conflict, modernization, and Islam's political discourse.

## NORTH-SOUTH RELATIONS

National and cultural variables do indeed influence the course of international relations, but in relations between countries of the North and the South, economic factors often take the lead. The disparity between the advanced economies of the North and the fledgling economies of the South—including Muslim countries—is a major determinant of international politics. Tension between South and North occasionally takes on a religious character, but its underlying roots are economic.

Disparity, however, is not only in evidence across the North-South divide. There are disparities among countries of the South as well. Within the latter, the gap in income between countries with emerging economies and those with lesser developed economies may be particularly substantial. Unfortunately, Muslim countries are rather heavily represented at the lower end of the economic scale.

For the purposes of this analysis, it is useful to differentiate between the following categories of Southern countries:

1.   Emerging countries such as South Korea, Singapore, Mexico, and Argentina, which have achieved high, although sometimes unsteady, growth over the past two decades. These economies have faced some difficulties in negotiating their terms of trade with the North (e.g., import barriers), but they do not lack a certain leverage on the international scene.
2.   Oil-rich countries, including the Gulf states and some Latin American countries, which—despite their current economic doldrums—have had a smooth ride for most of the last two decades.
3.   Countries with developing economies, such as Egypt, Syria, Morocco, Tunisia, Turkey, and (formerly oil-rich) Iraq and Iran. A promising diversification is taking place in the economies of these countries, but most have yet to resolve their debt problems.
4.   The poorest, raw-material-exporting nations, such as Sudan, Yemen, Somalia, Mozambique, and Mali.

Each of the above four groups is differently affected by globalization, and each has its own set of grievances toward the North. It used to be that the Non-aligned Movement (NAM) acted as the rallying point for many of these countries. But since the decline of NAM, Islam has emerged as an ideological meeting point for Muslim nations, a banner under which to fight "Western domination" in the post-Cold War era.

One field in which this battle is being fought is the labor market. As wave after wave of impoverished workers have sought better lives in the relatively affluent West, Islam has appeared in Europe in the person of the immigrant. The trend has been impressive: the number of Muslim immigrants in Europe has risen from just less than six million to approximately fifteen million in less than two decades. Such northbound movement continues to this day, fueled by overpopulation and lack of political freedom in countries of the South.

The tide of immigrant labor has given rise to political resentment in host countries. Resentment now greets Muslim as well as non-Muslim immigrants everywhere, but it is more acute in Europe, where unemployment is higher, than it is in the United States.[2] As Moroccans have headed to France and southern Europe, Turks to Germany and the Scandinavian countries, and Indians to the United Kingdom and North America, large Muslim communities have formed on Western soil. The backlash in countries such as France and Germany has led to the rise of right-wing politics, and to increased pressure on governments to reverse the tide of immigration.[3] Of course, it has not helped that a large proportion of these Muslim immigrants hail from rural areas, such as southeast Turkey, and have found it particularly hard to blend into Western societies. Not infrequently, the ethnic divide has also acquired racial overtones.[4]

Nor has the process of assimilation been made easier by the fact that many of the immigrants have brought the political fervor of their often-volatile regions with them, threatening to turn their host countries into proxy battlefields. The World Trade Center bombing, the assassination of Rabbi Kahane, attacks on Israeli targets, and the liquidation of Iranian and Kurdish dissidents have all fueled fears that Muslim immigrants are bringing Middle Eastern turmoil to Western countries.[5] Thus, as the growth of Muslim communities continues in Western countries, so do Western fears of its social and political implications. The obvious reluctance of the European Union to admit Turkey to its fold is only one reminder of such persistent tensions between Muslims and the West.[6]

One way to address this problem is for the European Union to take a more active role in promoting development and investment on the southern shores of the Mediterranean, and thus alleviate the motive for southerners to move northward. Meanwhile, the way Europe treats its Muslim residents will inevitably shape the future relations between Islam and the West. Anti-Muslim violence and fanaticism in France, Germany, and Italy could have serious long-term consequences.

## ETHNIC CONFLICT: THE BOSNIAN CASE

The collapse of the Soviet Union in many cases facilitated the emergence of new republics, some Muslim, in a peaceful manner. But peaceful political evolution to a post-Soviet world has not always been the case. In Chechniya, Bosnia, and Kosovo, bloody confrontations have deepened the mistrust between Islam and the West.

In particular, the Bosnian conflict has communicated to Muslims that Europe—a presumed oasis of liberalism, democracy, and human rights—is adamantly opposed to any collective, political Muslim presence taking shape on its soil, and that it is ready to go to any lengths in order to stymie this possibility. Is Europe still fighting its old battles against Islam? Is this a contemporary version of the Crusades, Andalusia, and the Balkan Wars? Such suspicions have been justifiable. Europe, indeed the Christian West, will never be able to shrug off the responsibility for what happened to Muslims in Bosnia.[7] And many Muslims still believe that Western, Christian countries were actually satisfied with the Serbian onslaught against this population, the better to rid a Greater Europe of the future with a Muslim presence in its middle. Indeed, the recent tragedy of Bosnia was not unique even in this century: Bosnian Muslims also came under attack in 1912 and 1945.

It would be useful here to refer to the manner in which the majority of Muslims perceive Western policy on Muslim minorities and the broader ideological ramifications of that policy. When former Yugoslavia disintegrated in late 1991, Europe and the United Nations Security Council intervened swiftly to stop Serbia's offensives against Croatia and Slovenia, and succeeded in doing so. Serbian-Croatian differences at the time were at least as serious as Serbian-Bosnian differences, which only came to a head later. Nevertheless, Slovenia won its independence without a fight, and the United Nations never imposed an arms embargo on Croatia.

Serbia dealt with the independence of these two prosperous republics largely by accepting the red lines drawn on the map of former Yugoslavia by other Western nations. This is why the conflict remained limited and short-lived. The Croats had behind them the support of Germany (unified and with more leverage than ever), Hungary, Austria, Italy, and the Vatican. Slovenia also could count on France, Italy, and the Vatican. But once Bosnia declared itself independent, it was a new ball game.[8]

For the first months of the conflict involving Bosnia, Europe kept its distance. The United Nations, for its part, imposed a full embargo that, practically speaking, only affected the Muslims, since Serbia already had immense military power and could count on the backing of neighboring Balkan states. Was it evenhanded for the United Nations to try to stop all weapons arriving to the warring sides? The Serbs were in a position to manufacture all types of weapons, including planes, tanks, and missiles, whereas the Muslims had nothing but modest defense capabilities.

From the beginning of the war in Bosnia, international organizations and UN observers knew of Serb atrocities against Muslims: detention camps, ethnic cleansing, killing of prisoners, murder of women and children, rape, and pillage. But this information was not released to the public for months—not until the media finally began to present the story. Even then, European countries and the United States failed to take timely action to stop the massacres.

The UN Security Council also refrained from making any serious commitment to protect the Muslims, apart from ordering the Serbs to cease from using their air force in the fighting. And even that measure was not enforced, when the UN Security Council failed to agree on action that might force the Serbs to stop using air power in Bosnia. The only practical measure taken by the United Nations was to instruct Britain's Lord David Owen and America's Cyrus Vance to call on both sides to reach a negotiated solution—a solution that, in all probability, would have been more inspired by balance-of-power considerations than by the dictates of international law. In the end, no action was taken to stop the massacres or end a war that was revealed as an act of genocide and ethnic cleansing.

One Muslim writer defined the elements of the Western position in the year-long Bosnian strife as follows: besieging the Bosnian Muslims, and blocking any assistance to them with the exception of UN-provided humanitarian aid; giving the Serbs a free hand to annihilate the Muslims; obstructing any international action—through the United Nations or the Islamic world—to rein in the Serbs; imparting legitimacy on Serbian actions—including violations of international law and human rights—through political conferences and the "mediation" conducted by the U.S. and U.K. envoys. Serbian acts were thus portrayed as measures taken in the normal course of a crisis, and the best reaction to them was seen as political mediation rather than forceful retribution, distancing the United Nations from the crisis while turning it into a tool of pressure on the victim rather than the aggressor. This was accomplished first through the arms embargo, and then through lopsided mediation that treated the Muslims as if they were rebels acting against international law.[9]

To many Muslims, this Western position only confirmed the suspicion that Christian Europe has never accepted an Islamic political entity in its midst in the past, and would not do so any time soon. Further, the Bosnian case can hardly be assessed in isolation from other trends in Europe, such as a growing negative attitude toward Muslim immigrants, a low level of tolerance for Muslim traditions, and a tendency to equate Islam with violence and terror.

To many Muslims, European pluralism and liberal democracy have no room for Islam. Human rights, although mostly respected in European countries, are seen as the privilege of membership in an exclusive club, to which Muslims are denied access. Moreover, the Western policy on Bosnia, according to many Muslims, was little more than the expression of a growing tide of racism against Muslim and Arab minorities in Europe.

A great number of Muslims suspect that Europe—a continent which fails on a daily basis to treat its small Muslim communities with grace, let alone acceptance—will never tolerate the presence of a Muslim state nearby. It would not matter if this state were democratic, or if it professed and promised to act as a cultural bridge between Europe and the Muslim world.

Unified Europe, according to many Muslims, is where the three major Christian churches and possibly Judaism may feel at home; but not Islam. Europe's position toward Islam, many Muslims contend, is a foregone conclusion. It has not changed since the Crusades, since Andalusia, and since the Ottoman wars. This is why Turkey remains an outsider to the European Union despite seven decades of secularism, and despite its fervent efforts to forge closer economic and political links with the West.

## THE ARAB-ISRAELI CONFLICT AND ANTI-WESTERN SENTIMENTS

The conflict between Arabs and Jews over Palestine, which erupted at the beginning of this century, and which acquired international dimensions following the establishment of Israel in 1948, has never failed to fuel Islamic-Western mistrust. Muslims in general, and Arabs in particular, have attributed Western support for Israel to a Jewish-Christian conspiracy against the Muslim world. It is a common impression among Arabs and Muslims that Jews Israelis exercise disproportionate influence over Western decision making and are overrepresented in Western research centers and academic departments specializing in Arab and Islamic affairs.

Arab and Muslim analysts frequently point an accusing finger at the perceived "alliance of Christian and Jewish fundamentalism against Islam," and they blame this alliance for the Jewish success in establishing a homeland in Palestine. A central tenet of this position is that Protestant clerics since the nineteenth century have pressed U.S. presidents to resettle Jews in Palestine on grounds that "the Jews are a people without land, and Palestine is a land without a people."

As early as the 1880s, the United States approached the Ottoman Empire with the view of creating a Jewish national home in Palestine. Pressure to carry through with this plan culminated immediately following World War I, during the presidency of Woodrow Wilson. Meanwhile, fundamentalist Christianity in Europe succeeded in obtaining the famous Balfour Declaration, recognizing Jewish national aspirations over Palestine. The declaration was approved in 1920 by the San Remo conference and in 1922 by the League of Nations, and British authorities took steps to implement it during their mandate in Palestine. The declaration's wording was most probably inspired by a strain of Christian fundamentalism with roots extending back to the Reformation. Specifically, it ignored the existence of Arabs in Palestine, referring only to "non-Jewish communities currently living in Palestine." Christian fundamentalists have maintained since the Reformation that Palestine is not a Muslim, but a Jewish country.[10]

According to one Muslim writer:

The Zionist entity in Palestine is not just a realization of a presumed celestial promise, but a consequence of the interplay of colonial interests in the region, an outcome of a guilt complex that developed in the West.... The Zionist entity is a knife which the West has stuck in the heart of the Middle East, with the full support of the United States. It is no secret that political Zionism uses the Bible as an ideological means to an end.... Will the West ever comprehend the magnitude of the wrong it had done the Muslims? ... A Christian cleric once admitted that the establishment of the so-called Israel of the Old Testament is at odds with the New Testament. For, with the death of Christ, the Holy Land became a property of all people.[11]

Israel has managed to normalize its relations with such Muslim countries as Malaysia, Indonesia, and the Islamic republics of the former Soviet Union. Its relations with India are improving; it has a strong presence in Africa; it participates in all the economic forums in the Middle East and North Africa. Yet, the Judeo-Christian, or Western-Israeli alliance is a source of continued consternation in the Muslim world.

Israel, an integral part of the international capitalist system, is still seen as a threat to the Arab and Islamic world in that it has in the past waged war and used its military power to achieve strategic ends. Many Arabs and Muslims now fear it desires to promote these same objectives of domination and supremacy through the policies of normalization.[12] So far, Israel has not reversed its policy of gobbling up Palestinian land; it insists that Jerusalem is its undivided and eternal capital; and it is dragging its feet in the peace process. Arabs and Muslims, not unjustifiably, suspect that Israel is using the Jewish lobby in the United States to distort the views of U.S. policymakers regarding Arabs and Muslims.

U.S. officials have publicly admitted that the reason the United States opposes the acquisition of nonconventional weapons by Arab and Muslim countries is the fear that these weapons may be used to threaten Israel. Despite these views, U.S. officials have rarely been known to challenge Israel's own version of its security needs.

Although U.S. officials routinely deny that Israel affects U.S. policy in the Middle East, according to analyst William Quandt, U.S. decision makers rarely cross the line Israel draws for U.S. policy in the region. A great deal of political analysis concerning the Arab-Israeli conflict has been written by pro-Israeli experts. Their views, directly and indirectly, affect U.S. decision makers. Thus, when a decision is about to be made concerning the Middle East, Quandt has argued, only one side of the story is normally heard. This imbalanced representation gives Israel a commanding hold over U.S. policy.[13]

## THE FAILURE OF MODERNIZATION AND THE RISE OF POLITICAL ISLAM

It is hard for scholars discussing Islam in the second half of the twentieth century to separate the phenomenon of Islamic revival and the resurgence of fundamentalism from the failure of modernization in most Islamic societies. For my purposes here I define the modernization process as that set of social, economic, and political changes which took place in Western Europe and North America between the seventeenth and nineteenth centuries, and which spread to Latin America, Asia, and Africa during the nineteenth and twentieth centuries.[14] Modernization involves the existence of a high degree of differentiation in the activities of individuals and institutions. This specialization means that individuals and institutions may perform their activities in a manner free from the rigid control of clan, sect, or class. Under modern administrations, institutions such as the market, public elections, and political parties take their prominent place in society and regulate the performance of its main activities. As a result, political, social, and economic changes occur in an organized and relatively smooth manner.

Traditional systems of government, however, tend to resist radical changes. This is particularly true with regard to political participation, social justice, and equality. For modernization to take root, societies must be able to digest continued change with regard to such social and political issues.[15]

Muslim societies have undergone a number of major modernization attempts, not the least of which began with the French campaign in Egypt in the early nineteenth century. However, looking back at developments in Asia, Africa, and Latin America, both in Muslim and non-Muslim countries, one is forced to admit that the modernization process has often failed to achieve its objectives. Many political systems, while poorly copying the Western ways, have failed to provide efficient or fair governance. Samuel Huntington was one of those who detected this phenomenon and, therefore, moved his focus from democracy to public order.[16]

According to Huntington, there are three major elements to political modernization. One is the rationalization of authority, which means that the multiple traditional authorities (clergy, clan, and tribe) should be replaced with a unified secular and national political authority. The second is the development of new political functions and the creation of specialized institutions for the performance of these functions. The third is increased political participation by various social groups.[17] Huntington also stressed the importance of public order and political stability. He pointed out that the most crucial political factor in differentiating between various countries is not the form of government, but the degree of government intervention. The difference between democracy and dictatorship is less important than that between countries that form their policies in a collective, lawful, organized, and stable fashion, and those that do not.

As for the concept of free and fair elections, Huntington has argued that this formula is not entirely indispensable in a society aspiring to modernization. For elections to be effective, he argues, a certain level of political organization should be in place. The problem is not in having elections, but in having these organizations. Some or many developing countries use elections to strengthen the hand of reactionary forces, he pointed out. What matters is not liberty, but the creation of legitimate public order. It is possible to have public order without liberty, but it is impossible to have liberty without public order. Therefore, it is important to create and establish authority, and then impose controls on this authority.

Huntington's ideas reflect the general frustration felt by scholars who have focused on political modernization in the 1950s, a time when political pluralism and democracy failed to take root in many newly independent countries, and when military, one-party systems proliferated instead. That trend eventually spawned ethnic and civil conflicts and multiple rebellions and coups, during which the administrative structures inherited from colonialism gradually deteriorated and the political organizations that had fought for independence were often weakened and torn apart.[18]

The Islamic world provided many good examples of such processes. Those Western-style institutions which have appeared there have mostly remained ineffective. One-party systems came to control all state bodies, stifling opposition and extinguishing hopes of pluralism. And parliaments were created to pass custom-made laws protecting the ruling elite.

Such was the sad course of events in many newly independent states, where the traditional social fabric and economy were dismantled, while modern economic and political institutions failed to materialize. Extended-family systems that provided security against unemployment and marginalization disappeared, without a modern social security system to replace them. Most modern institutions in the Islamic world never gained appropriate public approval, and have therefore remained fragile. For example, there are more members of Sufi societies in many Islamic states than there are members of political parties. And a greater number of people participate in religious festivals than in elections. As democracy has remained a mirage and legal and human rights abuses have abounded, ordinary citizens have shunned the state's modern institutions.[19] As has already been mentioned, one should not therefore look at the Islamic revival and the rise of fundamentalism as an isolated cultural phenomenon. In large part, the failure of political and economic modernization has been responsible for providing the right soil for this phenomenon.

In particular, although the Islamic revival may derive its cultural inspiration from anti-Western fundamentalist beliefs, it also owes much to the failure of nationalist movements in the Arab world. One might note how the rise of Islamic movements gathered pace after the defeat of Arab armies in the 1967 war, a defeat which threw into question the legitimacy of nationalist regimes. Since then, political forces associated with social and doctrinal modernization have been in retreat, leaving room for the advance of conservative political trends.[20]

But nationalist and leftist forces have also refused to admit their shortcomings, often blaming their difficulties on external, or even governmental, conspiracies, and denouncing the surge of Islamic groups as counterrevolutionary. Thus, nationalists and leftists have accused governments of siding with the Islamic groups, and they have even linked the growth of Islamic trends to Western designs and oil money. The Islamic revolution in Iran forced a change in this thinking, of course, as the *mullahs* backed anti-Western Islamic groups and were less than friendly to the oil-rich states of the Arabian peninsula.

Iran's involvement in political and doctrinal maneuvers in the Arab and Islamic worlds, however, have not fully deterred leftist and nationalist conspiracy theorists from attempting to explain away the Islamic trend. Some initially accused the United States of staging the Iranian revolution. Others claimed that Israel was secretly backing religious movements in order to revive sectarianism and tear apart Muslim societies. Such views, however, assume complete political ineptitude on the part of the general Muslim public, which is envisioned as unquestioningly following the political elite, politically unable to differentiate between empty slogans and proper vision. A certain measure of self-criticism has only recently begun to appear in leftist and Arab organizations, which now may admit their failure to find an effective strategy to lure and mobilize the masses.[21]

The rise of political Islam and fundamentalist trends has also coincided with deteriorating economic conditions and rising social inequality in Arab states—a state of affairs variously blamed on the failure of socialist-style development programs, the collapse of raw material prices, state mismanagement, and rampant corruption. At heart, political Islam is mainly a reaction to a state of social disorder, an expression of protest against dominant but incapable regimes.

The triggering crisis for political Islam was ultimately the economic suffering linked to the failure of raw material prices and industrialization plans to correspond. Eventually, this may mean the present religious revival with its social and political doctrines based on Islam will be seen as nothing but a puritan and unrealistic response to a material problem. Political Islam may not be able to formulate a practical economic and political program that will turn it into an effective historical trend.

Hasan Hanafi, an Egyptian expert in political Islam, has identified seven objectives for Arab modernization efforts common among reformist, liberal, and secular writers:

* To liberate the land from occupation and defend it against invasion and colonialism.
* To defend the citizen against oppression and injustice.

* To unite the nation against fragmentation and establish Arab or Islamic unity.
* To establish an independent identity vis-à-vis the West.
* To achieve independent development and self-reliance.
* To mobilize the masses and end their social and political apathy.[22]

Realizing these objectives, some of which date back almost two centuries, has clearly failed to happen. As for the first objective (liberating the land), Israel has occupied all of Palestine plus parts of Syria and Lebanon, and has waged attacks on faraway targets, hitting a nuclear reactor in Iraq and Palestinian officials in Tunisia. The second objective (defending the citizen) has fared no better: oppression abounds and prisons are full of political dissidents, while human rights are hardly respected, pluralism is denied, and freedom-busting emergency laws are common. The same dismal state of affairs applies to the remaining objectives. Sectarian and civil wars are common, dependence on the West is evident, and political apathy is the norm.

By contrast, Islamic groups have succeeded in mobilizing the masses and in connecting with ordinary citizens. They have been as active in universities as in mosques, and they have combined political ambition with a ruthless willingness to achieve their objectives through violence.

Politics has often played a central role in Islam. The concept of Islam as a religion and a state is not new. As far back as the ninth century, the Khawarij represented the first Islamic dissident movement based on political demands, and in the last two centuries the Wahabi (Hejaz), Sinnusi (Libya), and Mahdi (Sudan) movements all made a practice of resisting imperialist occupiers. Such movements have always been a part of the Arab political fabric, but the recent failure of leftist and nationalist movements, in addition to the weakness of the liberal streams, has only strengthened their political power. And although some of their policies actually benefit the West, there is always an element of unpredictability in their methods that has worried Western decision makers.

Historically, the revolutionary aspect of Islamic movements was more linked to political and social factors rather than purely religious ones. In historic times it was mainly directed against political leaders. What is new is that violence is no longer reserved for the political elite. Ordinary citizens—local and foreign, Muslim and non-Muslim—are often now the victims. But it is necessary to recall that this violence is a reaction to the deteriorating economic conditions and the lack of democracy in most contemporary Muslim societies.[23]

## POLITICAL ISLAM AND THE WEST

In his analysis of the functions of religion in social life, Brian Turner has challenged the conventional view that religion is a tool of control serving to maintain the status quo.[24] He said that the historic and sociological appeal of religion may best be understood by examining the relation between religion on the one hand, and social classes, family, and property systems and the legitimacy of the state on the other. The function of religion depends on the type of society and social class at hand. In traditional societies, religion is used to maintain the economic and political unity of the ruling classes. But in modern industrial societies, where the role of the family in societal control is minimal and government and business agencies are in control, religion has lost some of its social appeal. In other words, in modern society religion no longer plays a significant role in maintaining the cohesion of the ruling classes, and its message is more individual and personalized. It is possible, therefore, to argue that fundamentalist movements are trying to defend certain religious concepts in the face of the changes brought about by "modernization." These movements have associated modernization with the West, and have perceived the latter as a threat.

This view of contemporary fundamentalist movements contrasts sharply with the Islamic reform trends of the late nineteenth and early twentieth centuries. At that time, scholars such as Sheikh Hussein al-Attar, Rifa'ah al-Tahtawi, Muhammad Abdu, and Sheikh Ali Abd al-Razeq lamented the stagnation and backwardness of the Islamic and Arab world under Ottoman rule and took their progressive cues from Europe. For them, the West sent a complex message. It was a symbol of colonialism, but it was also a beacon of culture and science.

Islamic reformers a century ago blamed Mamluk and Ottoman rule for the ills of their nations and questioned the right of the Ottomans to govern the Muslim world. In his work "Islam and the Principles of Government," Sheikh Ali Abd al-Razeq contested the role of religious authorities in government. He called for creative interaction with modern science and for coexistence with the West.

It is hard to claim that the Islamic reformers of the early twentieth century produced a theoretical basis for contemporary reform. What they did, however, was endorse openness to modern culture. Furthermore, they never saw the West as culturally hostile, and therefore they never advised the formation of an Islamic counterculture to resist it.

But in clear contrast to such reformers there has also been a militant strain to Islamic thinking about the West since the beginning of the twentieth century. The Muslim Brotherhood of Egypt was among the first fundamentalist groups to turn Islam into an anti-Western ideology. Its scholars saw the West as a threat, particularly after the Caliphate system was abolished in 1924, and they denounced Western culture as secular, material, and imperialist. Still, the Brotherhood accepted the technological achievements of the West. In other words, its approach toward the West was a pragmatic and selective one. Hasan al-Banna, the founder of the Brotherhood, built his political message on general concepts, never bothering to formulate a rigorous and systematic doctrine for the group. The group has advocated Islam as a universal doctrine, but its attitude toward the West has never been entirely close-minded.

According to Hasan al-Banna, it is the duty of Muslims to revive the glory of Islam, adopt its laws, and spread its message. He saw the West as a possible threat to Islam's universal message, and he was quick to denounce it as a "materialistic civilization," devoid of spirituality and therefore inherently inadequate.[25]

The Brotherhood's thinking has undergone no major change since then. Mohammad Hamid Abu al-Nasr, another former leader, once stated that "the West is cursed by immorality and materialism." The Brotherhood's current leader, Mustafa Mashur, has agreed:

> The West has created and backed the ruling regimes in most Muslim countries and made those places dependent on it. The Islamic nation is weak because of European invasion and because Western enemies have designs upon this nation and want to drag it away from true Islam . . . they want us to remain dependent on them for food and weapons and want our rulers to obey their orders.[26]

This same trend of thought is still dominant among the Brotherhood followers. In its platform, the Brotherhood-dissident Wasat (Center) Party in Egypt—not yet approved by the government—says that the world order is "a state of universal search for a new framework of international relations that would allow the United States to create a unipolar system which it can dominate." Wasat also rejects Israel's integration in Middle East cooperation forums and calls for a continued boycott of Israel and the liberation of Palestine.

Other militant Islamic groups are even more hostile toward the West. Inspired by the writings of Ibn Taymia, a thirteenth-century scholar whose hard-line ideas were fashioned in response to the Mogul invasion and destruction of Muslim lands, they have denounced the West as responsible for the "secularization" of Muslim societies and the retreat of Muslim values. They have also seen the West as an obstacle to the spread of Islam's "legitimate" universal leadership. Following are the core beliefs of these groups:

* The world's two superpowers (before the collapse of the Soviet Union) are atheist entities that seek to exploit other nations.
* The United Nations is a product of modern-day atheism and only serves the interests of atheist forces.
* Modern slogans, such as human rights, world peace, liberty, fraternity, and equality, are empty words aimed to deceive the gullible.
* All nations are repressed, and their only deliverance is through Islam.

* The Jews have international designs which they implement through their effect on decision-making centers around the globe.
* International capitalism is a new form of veiled occupation, aimed at depriving nations of their beliefs and exploiting their resources.[27]

Since they believe that conventional history has been corrupted by secular methodology, theorists of armed Islamist groups have called for an alternative history of the Islamic world. Only such a revised history, they claim, will enable Muslims to see the truth about themselves and the world.

In this context, Al-Jihad group has denounced the U.S. military presence in the Gulf as a symptom of the "evil Western onslaught" against the Islamic nation. The group urges the Muslim public to differentiate between the allies of the United States and those who would establish an Islamic state, presenting itself as the "model of salvation" in the region.[28]

*Jihad* (holy war) against the West and modern-day atheism (a.k.a. the new international order) take center stage in the thinking of such radical Islamic groups. During the 1970s and 1980s, however, militant groups adopted a multiphased strategy to achieve their goals. The foremost and immediate task was defined as establishing Islamic governments in Arab and Muslim countries and supporting the Palestinian resistance against Israeli occupation.[29] After that, the struggle against the "distant enemy," or the West, would begin.

A reversal of these priorities took place in the 1990s, when militant groups decided that their primary battle was against a "foreign invasion" of the Islamic world, and that a corollary battle was to liberate Muslim nations from their secular rulers. Some think that the final battle would be to liberate Islamic holy places in Palestine, a task which could not conceivably be achieved by secular governments.[30] Remarkably, the 1990s brought no marked change in the doctrine of militant groups concerning the West.

## PROSPECTS FOR COEXISTENCE

Having reviewed the undercurrents of friction and potential enmity between Islam and the West, I would like to conclude by considering several examples of what can be done to promote the prospects of coexistence between the two.

Rather than focusing on religious or cultural conflict, it is more constructive to think of an ongoing clash of interests that is not irreconcilable. The non-Western world should be permitted, and indeed encouraged, to play a larger role in shaping the post-Cold War era.

Fundamentalism is at least in part a reaction to the failure of the modernization process in most developing countries. This failure is suffered on the economic, social, political, and cultural levels. Only the elite benefit from moderniza-tion, which to underprivileged classes means the West, and contributes to the for-mation of anti-Western sentiments. Measures should be taken to accelerate and broaden the scope of the modernization process in a step to provide more justice, thus reducing the gap between the Islamic world and the West.

Anti-Western discourse expresses the view of some Islamic political trends, not the Islamic world in general. The West need not overestimate these views, mistaking them for the standpoint of the Islamic world as a whole.

Crucial to the coexistence between the Islamic world and the West in the era of globalization is the attainment of a common ground with relation to the form and content of political and economic systems worldwide. This requires modern-ization, industrialization, education, and a scientific technological base, in addition to improved means of transmitting culture and knowledge. Also required is the development of traditional cultures to achieve a modern civil culture.

The values of democracy and human rights should be persistently promoted worldwide. That a common denominator of these values may be accepted by the broad spectrum of Muslims should not be ruled out.

Double standards must not be accepted as a routine way of conducting inter-national affairs. U.S. policies favoring Israel and seeking to find fault with Islamic states constitute an obvious provocation to Muslim sentiments.

To sum up, democracy is a crucial element in global, multicultural coexis-tence. Likewise, human rights is an integral part of a "universal ethics" that should be accepted by all civilizations, regardless of their ideological leanings.

The issue here is that most Islamic societies, unlike Europe, have not yet undergone a transition to secularism. This, in turn, complicates the process of democratization and hinders the promotion of human rights.

The promotion of democracy and human rights is not the sole responsibili-ty of the West. Political and cultural elites in Islamic countries should actively advocate the values of reason, tolerance, and freedom. This task is not easy in view of the present fundamentalist backlash against intellectuals (writers and artists have been threatened and killed in Egypt, Algeria, and Turkey), but every effort should be exerted so that this important work is not left undone.

The claim that human rights is a Western concept and that alternative, non-Western codes of human rights must be developed is spurious. Human rights should be universal, unified, and common to all humanity.[31]

Islam and the West must learn how to live together, in mutual acceptance, respect, and recognition of their variant interests and needs. Steps must be taken on both sides to narrow their differences. The Muslim world should endeavor to reverse the trend to politicize religion. And the West should respond by revising its policies toward the Muslim world, particularly those involving elements of domination and double-dealing.

## NOTES

* FOR THE ARABIC SOURCES WHICH FOLLOW, THE TITLES OF ALL BOOKS AND ARTICLES ARE GIVEN IN ENGLISH.

1. S. P. Huntington, "The Clash of Civilization," *Foreign Affairs*, no. 3 (Summer 1993); and "The West Unique, But Not Universal," *Foreign Affairs*, no. 6 (November–December 1996).

2. J. S. Passel and M. Fix, "Myths About Immigrants," *Foreign Policy*, no. 95 (Summer 1994).

3. R. Escalier, "les Chiffres de L'immigration Maghrebine en France," in *l'Etat du Maghreb, sous la direction de Camille et Yves la Coste* (Paris: La Decouverte, 1993).

4. G. Gornel, "Migrations Toward Western Europe: Trends, Outlook, Policies," *International Spectator*, Rome (April–June 1992).

5. O. Loescher, "Refugee Movement and International Security," *Adelphi Paper*: no. 268 (London: IISS, Summer 1992).

6. M. C. Dunn, "Islamic Activists in the West: A New Issue Produces Backlash," *Middle East Policy*, no. 1 (1994).

7. M. Khalifa, "The Yugoslav Crisis and the Bosnia Disaster in the New World Order," *El Mustaqbal El Arabi*, 3, no. 10–11 (Spring–Summer 1993) [Arabic].

8. Khalifa, "The Yugoslav Crisis and the Bosnia Disaster."

9. Khalifa, "The Yugoslav Crisis and the Bosnia Disaster."

10. R. El-Gamaal, "Islam and the West: Between the Civil Gap and the Fundamentalist Confrontation," *Mustaqbal El-Alaam El Islami*, no. 9 (Winter 1993) [Arabic].

11. Z. Abdel-Aziz, "The Western Stance vis-à-vis Islam and the Clash of Civilization," *El-Mustaqbal El-Arabi*, no. 9 (Winter 1993), 92 [Arabic].

12. N. El Guassour, "The Islamic Summit in Tehran: The Common Islamic Work and the Future Perspective," *El Mustaqbal El-Arabi*, no. 225 (November 1997) [Arabic].

13. G. Fawaz," The American and the Political Islam," *El-Mustaqbal El-Arabi*, no. 217 (March 1997) [Arabic].

14. S. N. Eisenstadt, *Modernization: Protest and Change* (Englewood Cliffs, N.J.: Prentice-Hall, 1966).

15. J. A. Bill and C. Leiden, *Politics in the Middle East* (Boston: Little Brown and Company, 1979).

16. S. P. Huntington, *Political Order in Changing Societies* (New Haven, Conn.: Yale University Press, 1968).

17. Huntington, *Political Order in Changing Societies*.

18. Huntington, *Political Order in Changing Societies*.

19. M. Abdel-Hafez, "The Islamic Fundamentalism: Is It an Aspect of the Echo of Modernization?" *Quadaya Figria*, no. 13–14 (October 1993) [Arabic].

20. B. Gualioun, "The Political Sociology and the Islamic Movement: An Interpretation," *Quadaya Figria*, no. 13–14 (October 1993) [Arabic].

21. H. Hanafi, *The Tradition and the Renovation* (Cairo: al-Markaz al-'Arabi lil-Bahth wa-al-Nashr, 1980) [Arabic], and *The Contemporary Islamic Movements in the Arab World* (Beirut: Center for Arab Studies, 1987) [Arabic].

22. H. Hanafi, "Al-Hakyimiia in Defiance, Cairo," *Quadaya Figria*, No.13–14 (October 1993) [Arabic].

23. Hanafi, "Al-Hakyimiia in Defiance"; and Abdel-Hafez, "The Islamic Fundamentalism." Also see M. Abed-El Guabri, *Tradition and Modernity* (Beirut: Center for Arab Studies, 1991) [Arabic].

24. B. Turner, *Religion and Social Theory*, 2nd ed. (London: Sage, 1991).

25. H. Mustafa, *Political Islam in Egypt from Reformist Movement to Militant Groups* (Cairo: Center for Political and Strategic Studies, 1992) [Arabic]; "The State and the Islamic Opposition," *El Mahroussa* (1995) [Arabic]; and "The Islamist Movements under Mubarak," in L. Guazzone, ed., *The Political Role of Islamist Movements in the Contemporary Arab World* (Berkshire, U.K.: Ithaca Press, 1995).

26. An interview with M. Mashur. Cairo, 1996.

27. "Al-Jihad and the Features of Revolutionary Work," unpublished document, Al-Jihad Group, 1991.

28. S. Sariyah, "A Message of Advocacy," unpublished document, Al-Jihad Group, 1991.

29. A. Al-Zumur, "The Battle of Islam and Secularism in Egypt," unpublished document, Al-Jihad Group, n.d.

30. A. Al-Zumur "The Basis of Tomorrow's Battle," unpublished document, Al-Jihad Group, n.d.

31. B. Tibi, *The Challenge of Fundamentalism: Political Islam and the New World Disorder* (Berkeley: University of California Press, 1998).

# PART II

## ISLAM IN EUROPE AND FARTHER AFIELD: COMPARATIVE PERSPECTIVES

# 6

# The Place of Muslims in British Secular Multiculturalism

## Tariq Modood

The large presence of Muslims in Britain today—between one and two million people, of whom more than half are of South Asian, primarily Pakistani, origin—is a result of Commonwealth immigration from the 1950s onward. These immigrants were initially male laborers from small farm-owning and artisan backgrounds who met the demand for unskilled and semiskilled industrial workers in the British economy, and whose wives and children began arriving in the 1970s. By contrast, the proportion of urban professionals among South Asian Muslims has historically been small, though it did increase with the arrival of political refugees from East Africa in the late 1960s and 1970s. The majority of this group, however, were Hindus and Sikhs. Britain, and especially London, as a cosmopolitan center, has also been an attractive destination for some members of the rich and professional classes of the Middle East, especially from the 1970s onward, and many of them now have large investments in property in the city. Waves of political refugees have also come to Britain since the 1970s from other parts of the Muslim world—Somalia and Bosnia being two notable recent cases.

The presence of such new population groups has made manifest certain kinds of racisms in Britain, and, in response, antidiscrimination laws and policies have been put into place since the 1960s. These laws and policies, however, have been influenced by contemporary thinking and practice in relation to antiblack racism in the United States, which has largely assumed that the grounds of discrimination are "color" and ethnicity. Thus, prior to the last decade or so, when Muslim assertiveness became a feature of majority-minority relations, racial-equality discourse and politics were dominated by the idea that the dominant postimmigration issue was "color-racism."[1] This perspective was epigramatically expressed by the writer Salman Rushdie. "Britain is now two entirely different worlds and the one you inherit is determined by the colour of your skin," he wrote in 1982.[2] Together with most antiracists, Rushdie has now come to adopt a more pluralistic perspective, and one in which the Muslim presence is seen as a fact to be ignored at one's peril. Nevertheless, in pure or mixed form, the U.S.-derived racial dualism continues to be an influential force in British social science and radical politics.[3] One consequence of this has been that legal and policy frameworks still reflect the conceptualization and priorities of racial dualism.

## RACE AND EQUALITY

To date, therefore, it is still lawful to discriminate against Muslims as Muslims, because the courts do not accept that Muslims are an ethnic group (even though, oddly, Jews and Sikhs are recognized as such). While initially unremarked upon, such an exclusive focus on race and ethnicity as a basis for antidiscrimination policy—and the exclusion of Muslims, but not Jews and Sikhs, from the definition of ethnic identity—has today come to be a source of resentment among Muslims. Muslims do enjoy some limited indirect legal protection as members of ethnic groups—such as Pakistanis, Arabs, and so on. And over time, groups like Pakistanis have become an active constituency within British "race relations." (By contrast, Middle Easterners tend to classify themselves as "white"—as in the 1991 census—and are not at all prominent in political activism of this sort, or in domestic politics generally.) One of the effects of this politics has been to highlight the issue of race.

    In Britain a key measure and indicator of racial discrimination and inequality has been numerical underrepresentation in prestigious jobs, public office, and so on. To verify the existence of such discrimination, people have had to be (self)classified and counted. This practice has inevitably led to arguments about which group labels are authentic, and these arguments have now become a common feature of certain political discourses. Yet by these inequality measures it has also become apparent over the years that it is Asian Muslims—not Afro-Caribbeans, as policymakers had originally expected—who are the most disadvantaged and poorest groups in the country.[4] To many Muslim activists, the misplacing of Muslims into "race" categories and the belatedness of the recognition by policymakers of the severe disadvantages that Pakistanis and Bangladeshis face mean, at best, that race relations are an inappropriate policy niche for Muslims.[5] At worst, it has been interpreted to reveal the existence of a conspiracy in Britain to prevent the emergence of a specifically Muslim sociopolitical formation.[6] To see how such thinking has emerged, one must consider the career of the concept of racial equality.

    The initial development of antiracism in Britain followed the American pattern, and indeed was directly influenced by American personalities and events. Just as in the United States the color-blind humanism of Martin Luther King, Jr., came to be mixed with an emphasis on black pride, black autonomy, and black nationalism as typified by Malcolm X, so did these concepts mix in the United Kingdom. Indeed, it is best to see this development of racial explicitness and positive blackness as part of a wider sociopolitical climate which was at the time not confined to race and culture or nonwhite minorities. Feminism, gay pride, Quebecois nationalism, and the revival of Scottishness were some prominent examples of new identity movements which also emerged at the time, especially in those countries where they could fill the gap left by the decline in class politics.

In fact, it would be fair to say that what is often claimed today in the name of racial equality, especially in the English-speaking world, is more than would have been recognized as such in the 1960s. Iris Young expressed this new political climate well when she described how an ideal of equality has now emerged based not just on allowing excluded groups to assimilate and live by the norms of dominant groups, but based on the view that "a positive self-definition of group difference is in fact more liberatory."[7]

The shift here is from an understanding of equality in terms of individualism and cultural assimilation to a politics of recognition: to equality as encompassing public ethnicity. Equality thus defined means not having to hide or apologize for one's origins, family, or community; rather, it requires that others show respect for these aspects of identity and adapt public attitudes and arrangements so that the heritage they represent may be encouraged rather than contemptuously expected to wither away. Two distinct conceptions of equal citizenship would seem to underlie these positions, each based on a different view of what is "public" and "private." These two conceptions of equality may be stated as follows: (1) the right to assimilate to the majority/dominant culture in the public sphere, and toleration of "difference" in the private sphere; (2) the right to have one's "difference" (minority ethnicity, and so on.) recognized and supported in the public and the private spheres.

It should be noted that these are not alternative conceptions in the sense that to hold one, the other has to be rejected. Multiculturalism (as recent antiracism has come to be known), however, requires support for both. The assumption behind the first conception is that participation in the public or national culture is necessary for the effective exercise of citizenship—the only obstacles to which are exclusionary processes preventing gradual assimilation. The second conception also assumes that groups excluded from the national culture have their citizenship diminished as a result. It, too, offers to remedy this by accepting the right to assimilate, but it adds the right to widen and adapt the national culture and the public and media symbols of national membership to include the relevant minority ethnicities.

It may be thought, therefore, that the second conception of equality involves something of a contradiction: at the same time that it accepts that participation in the national or shared culture(s) is necessary for effective equality, it encourages individuals to cultivate minority identities and practices. There is indeed a genuine tension here, one that may perhaps only be resolved in practice through finding and cultivating points of common ground between dominant and subordinate cultures, as well as developing new syntheses and hybridities. The important emphasis in the second conception, however, is that the burden of change (or the costs of not changing) should not be assigned exclusively to one party.

## BEYOND A LIBERAL POLITICS

This new, emergent notion of equality has created some dissonance with preexisting political concepts. It does not fit in easily, for example, with a Tory British nationalism. But more to the point, it is at odds with some of the center-left ideas that underpinned earlier notions of racial equality.[8] The politicization of "racial" and ethnic groups (as well as women and homosexuals) has thus been interpreted as introducing "particularism" into "universalistic" conceptions of justice, as, for example, defined by meritocratic individualism, liberal citizenship, or socialist equality. (Why class solidarity or national citizenship would be considered "universalistic," while identification with the female half of the species or black internationalism would be "particularistic," I fail to understand.) But, overall, the success of the new concept of multicultural equality, at least on the left, has been made possible because it is not anomalous, but has fit in well with wider challenges to liberal individualism. For example, it has coalesced with feminist arguments that ostensible gender-neutral conceptions of the political, of citizenship, and of the domain of law and legal norms—as well as a host of substantive laws and policies—represent covert but systematic expressions of male perspectives that have ignored the needs and capacities of women.[9] According to this view, the abstract, rational individual of liberal politics and jurisprudence has, in fact, been a man (as evidenced by the fact that this individual doesn't seem to have any domestic or child-rearing obligations). The very definition of the political (i.e., the activities appropriate for public discourse, political campaigns, and legal control) has thus favored male interests, leaving male power in domestic and sexual relations unchallenged. Hence, an alternative politics has been born out of the slogan "the personal is the political."

The politics that I have just described is both a theoretical, discursive politics as well as one of institutional reform, competition for office, and social policy. But my concern here—as a way of approaching the political-normative climate of opinion in which British Muslims can and are mounting a case for Muslim rights—is particularly with the theoretical dimension of the politics of "difference" as a critique of the 1960s notions of liberal equality. It is therefore worth mentioning some other theoretical sources in order to emphasize how important this politics has become among center-left egalitarians, especially in book-writing and book-reading circles in Britain and elsewhere. This is above all a movement that has received considerable underpinning from the rise of philosophical antiessentialism in the social sciences.[10] Such antiessentialism originated in the (very different) work of thinkers such as Nietzsche, Heidegger, and Wittgenstein, but it was given a certain indeterminate radicalism in the hands of such more recent theorists as Foucault and Derrida.

Antiessentialism in one form or another has been used to critique such hegemonic ideas as nation-state, community, and class—and even such counterhegemonic notions as woman, black, and so on.[11] These views have been promoted to such an extent that an appreciation of perspectivism—of the essentially contested nature of concepts, of fluidity and multiplicity of meanings, of cultural pluralism, and perhaps even aporia—has quickly established itself as a new form of orthodoxy in social theory.

Of relevance here is how this antiessentialism, when married to a theory of political equality as participation in a discursive public space, can define inclusion into a political community.[12] It is now argued such inclusion may take place not only in terms of accepting the rules of an existing polity and its hallowed public-private boundary lines—an attitude many European politicians have adopted with regard to Muslims—but through an opposite course. Public space is thus defined as essentially contested. Indeed, it may be created through ongoing discursive contestation and political struggle, where the rules of appropriate concern and the terms of political debate, far from being fixed in advance, themselves become the object of political discourse.[13]

Typically, in such an approach, the public-private distinction is seen to work as a "gag-rule" to exclude matters of concern to marginalized and subordinated groups. The political integration of these minorities on terms of equality therefore inevitably involves a challenge to existing boundaries of "publicity." Real political integration is thus seen to flow from a process of discursive engagement, as marginal groups begin to confidently assert themselves in the public space, and others begin to argue with them and forge new agreements, as new laws, policies, and so on, are eventually enacted.

Indeed, laws and policies may be of lesser importance in the long run to such a view than the very process of dialogue, since these theories explicitly repudiate the classical liberal identification of the political with the realms of law and the state. Rather, a more expansive understanding of the political is seen to be more compatible with the idea of shifting boundaries and politics as debate. It also allows for the changing of certain attitudes, stereotypes, stigmatizations, media images, and national symbols to become primary political goals. Hence, it becomes clear that there is today a new concept of equality, one in which the issues of "representation" have not just had to do with the numbers of various categories of people in certain jobs or positions of power, but with "representation" as the public imagining of groups as groups.[14]

## RACIALIZATION AND IDENTITY

Apart from the rather abstract concepts which contribute to the story of the emergent politics of Muslim identity in Britain, it is important to briefly mention some of the events that have been taking place "on the ground." The "minorities" politics, the cutting-edge antiracism that developed in Britain in the 1970s and early 1980s (first in radical activism and ultraleft corpuscles, then, following the Brixton riots of 1981, in some local governments, trade unions, radical public-sector professional associations, and the Labour Party), was based on a concept of political blackness. It viewed the British population as divided into two groups—black and white—in which the former consisted of all people who were potential victims of color-racism (though in both theory and practice such people were disproportionately assumed to have the characteristics of the Afro-Caribbean population).[15]

This political movement played an important part in opening up the question of "race" in Britain, and eventually came to define the identity of many people (less so now than at its height in the mid- to late 1980s). Whether at any point this political identity was embraced by the majority of South Asians or Muslims is an open question. Two things, however, are clear. First, this identity was embraced by Asian political activists in the 1980s, especially those whose activism concerned mainstream British society rather than the organization of their own communities. Second, from the late 1980s onward, if not earlier, most Asians emphasized a more particular ethnic or religious identity than this all-inclusive nonwhiteness.

Several factors were at play here: time, numbers, and confidence. As the Asian communities became more settled and thought of themselves less as sojourners, as they put down familial and community roots, and as some Asian groups, especially African Asians, began to acquire a prosperity and respectability that all Asians sought, they began to express their "own" identities rather than the borrowed identity of blackness, with its inescapable Afro-Caribbean resonances. Movements outside the United Kingdom also became relevant (for example, the Sikh battle for Khalistan, the growth of Hindu cultural nationalism, and the rise of Islamism in various parts of the world). Additionally, the multicultural climate described earlier began to encourage people to define and publicly project themselves in terms of authenticity, "difference," and victimhood, and gave them the confidence to reject opposing arguments (such as advocating that newly settled groups be seen and not heard, or "when in Rome do as the Romans do"). This was probably especially the case with middle-class professionals who had some choice in whether to emphasize "integration" or "difference" in their public discourse and political personas.[16]

Political blackness, therefore, began unraveling at a grassroots level at the very time it was becoming hegemonic as a minority discourse in British public life (the 1980s). The single event that illustrated this most dramatically was the battle over

*The Satanic Verses* that broke out in 1988–1989. This was seen by all concerned as a battle pitting Muslims versus the West. On the Muslim side, it mobilized an impassioned activism that no previous campaign against racism had been remotely able to stir.[17] Thus, many "lapsed" or "passive" Muslims (especially the nonreligious, whose Muslim background had hitherto not been particularly important) (re)discovered a new community solidarity. Yet what was even more striking was that when the public rage against Muslims was at its most intense, Muslims neither sought nor were offered any special solidarity by any nonwhite minority. It was, in fact, a group of white liberal Anglicans who tried to moderate hostility against angry Muslims, and it was in interfaith fora rather than in political-black organizations that space was created for Muslims to state their case without being vilified. Political blackness, seen until then as the key formation in the politics of postimmigration ethnicity, thus emerged as irrelevant to an issue which many Muslims insisted was fundamental to defining the kind of "respect" or "civility" appropriate to a peaceful multicultural society—that is to say, to the political constitution of "difference" in Britain.[18]

The fundamental problem for political blackness came from the internal ambivalence I mention earlier—namely, whether blackness as a political identity was sufficiently distinct from and could mobilize without blackness as an ethnic-pride movement. This black identity movement, in a growing climate of opinion favorable to identity politics of various kinds, was successful in shifting the terms of the debate from color-blind individualistic assimilation to questions about how white British society had to change to accommodate new groups. But, unlike black America or South Africa, its success in imposing or making a singular identity upon or out of a diverse ethnic minority population was temporary. In particular, probably at no time did a majority of Asians think of themselves as part of a positive black identity. What it did was pave the way to a plural ethnic assertiveness, as Asian groups, including Muslims, borrowed the logic of ethnic pride and tried to catch up with the success of a newly legitimized black public identity.

Historically, an oppositional identity depends upon emotionally welding together a disparate population; to do so, one must draw upon the traditions and beliefs of the oppressed, especially in a way that is readily communicable to the ordinary mass of people. Where the relevant population embodies one or more major historical cleavage, the task is difficult. For example, in British India the mobilization of the Indian masses required an appeal to past Hindu glories, to Hindu symbols and customs—in short, to a form of Hindu nationalism. But the beating of that drum led through group competition, and "me-too-ism," to a rival oppositional identity. This Muslim nationalism eventually led to the creation of Pakistan. And the more populist it had to be—that is to say, the more it had to mobilize mass action—the more religious it also became in rhetoric, imagery, and so on. If the matter could have been left to an Anglicized Indian elite, communal passions would not have been aroused. But the politics of anti-imperialism required the mobilization of the masses, and the political struggle had to be couched in terms that made sense to the masses and could elicit their support and sacrifices.

I hope the significance of this historical point is clear: just as the development of an Indian oppositional identity was confused with Hindu nationalism, so, too, was the development of a contemporary British "black" (i.e., nonwhite) opposi-tional identity confused with the development of a black ethnic-pride (African roots) movement. This, in turn, triggered other ethnic assertions, such as "Asian," "Muslim," and so on, and reduced a political "black" to an ethnic blackness.

Not only have British ethnic minorities failed to unite under a single identity capable of mobilizing them all, but the number of identities which generate inten-sity of commitment and community mobilization has continued to grow. Of course, much of this has had to do with context, and in particular what people feel they need to react against. Thus, Pakistanis were "black" when it meant a job in a racial-equal-ity bureaucracy; "Asian" when a community center was in the offing; "Muslim" when the Prophet was being ridiculed; and "Kashmiri" when a nationalist movement back home was resulting in bloodshed. These identities may be read both as pragmatic moves as well as definers of the field in which moves could be made. And yet all this leaves one question unanswered. Why is it ethnic?

At a time when social theory and research is dominated by constructivism and anti-essentialism of various sorts, it is with some trepidation that I raise the question about whether, among alternative identities, certain ethnicities or col-lectivities may be more "real" than others, and thus have a greater durability or ability to resurface—in short, whether they may not have some characteristics that cannot be accounted for by radical constructivism. When I try to explain to myself why, say, Pakistanis mobilize around the term "Muslim" with a conviction, intensity, and solidarity that they do not around "black," I use the distinction between a group's mode of oppression and mode of being. Thus, even if it were the case that white British society saw and treated Muslims as a "colored Other," it doesn't follow that Muslims accept that description of themselves. Excluded groups seek respect for themselves as they are or aspire to be, not simply a soli-darity on the basis of a recognition of themselves as victims. In other words, they resist being defined by their mode of oppression and seek space and dignity for their mode of being.[19] All the identities that are being discussed here are in some sense reactive and are shaped by a situation that the minorities do not control (though I am impressed by the degree to which the minorities are active in these identity formations). I am not contrasting situationally or politically construct-ed identities with something primordial. My point is that a minority will respond to some forms of exclusion or inferiorization and not to others. The ones it will respond to are those which relate in some way to its own sense of being. Again, this sense of being is not atemporal, and can change; but it does mean that neither the oppressor nor the oppressed are totally free to set the terms of a reactive identity. Specifically, the oppression must "speak" to the oppressed; it must reach their sense of being.

Thus, part of the answer as to which identity will emerge as important to a group at a particular time lies in the nature of the minority group in question. That Caribbeans have mobilized around a color identity and South Asians around religious and related identities is not chance nor just a "construction," but has been based on something deeper about these groups. That Muslims in their anger against *The Satanic Verses* found a depth of indignation, a "voice" of their own—in a way that most had not found in relation to events and in mobilization in the previous decades—cannot be explained just in terms of issues to do with political leaderships, rivalries, tactics, and so on. Certainly, some individuals and organizations exploited the situation, but they could not have done so if there had not been a "situation" to exploit.

## MUSLIM IDENTITY POLITICS

Since the cork was pulled from this bottle, it has not been possible to get the genie back inside. In a very short space of time "Muslim" has become a key political minority identity, acknowledged by right-wing and left-wing bigots and the open-minded media and government. It has become integral to local community politics, and it has continued to thrive through romantic, global solidarities, as wars and massacres in Palestine, Bosnia, the Gulf, Chechniya, Kashmir, and India have filled newspapers and television screens, and led some young British-born Muslims to reinvent the concept of the *umma* to give a global identity to the victims. This politics has meant not just a recognition of a new religious diversity in Britain, but it has brought new or renewed importance to religion in public policy. In Britain, recent empirical evidence shows overwhelmingly that the religion of one's family is the most important source of self-identity among people of South Asian origin, especially Muslims. The large, nationally representative Fourth Survey of Ethnic Minorities (of which I was the principal researcher) found that, although skin color remained prominent in the self-descriptions of Caribbeans, religion was most prominent in the self-descriptions of South Asians.[20]

Granted, this distinction may owe as much to a sense of community as to personal faith, but the identification and prioritization of religion is far from nominal. For example, the Fourth Survey also found that very few Asians marry across religious and caste boundaries, and that most expect that their children will be inducted into their own religions. At a time when a third of Britons say they do not have a religion, the survey also found that nearly all South Asians said they have one, and 90 percent said that religion was of personal importance to them (compared to 13 percent of whites). And while about one-quarter of whites said they attend a place of worship once a month or more, the survey found that more than half of Hindus and seven out of ten Sikhs attend once a month or more, and that nearly two-thirds of Muslims attend at least once a week. Even among the young, expressions of commitment were found to be exceptionally high. The survey found that more than a third of Indians and African Asians, and two-thirds of Pakistanis and Bangladeshis between sixteen and thirty-four years of age, said that religion was very important to how they led their lives, compared to 5 percent of whites (though nearly a fifth of Caribbeans took this view).

There are two important points to make here about these identities, especially Muslim ones. First, they cannot be characterized as belonging to private life, and therefore as being irrelevant to public policies and resources. For example, half of all Muslims interviewed said that there should be state funding for Muslim schools. Second, religious and ethnic identities are not simply an expression of behavior or participation in distinctive cultural practices. Across the generations and in relation to time spent in Britain, there has in fact been a noticeable decline in participation in the cultural practices (language, dress, attendance at place of worship, and so on) that go with particular identities. Yet the decrease in self-identification with a group label (black, Muslim, etc.) has been relatively small. In other words, there are many people in Britain who say of themselves that they are Muslim, but who may not be at all religious.

In one sense, there is nothing new or peculiar about the above distinction. In another, however, it marks the arrival of a new conception of ethnoreligious identity, for these are not passive or fading identities. Such a conclusion would overlook the pride with which these identities may be asserted, the intensity with which they may be debated, and their capacity to generate community activism and political action. People may still feel passionate about the public recognition and resourcing of aspects of their community identity, even though as individuals they may not wish that resource for themselves. So, for example, the demand for public funding of Muslim schools has been a source of Muslim grievance—with some secular, as well as religious, Muslims highlighting the injustice of a system that funds Christian and Jewish, but not Muslim, schools. Nevertheless, the Fourth Survey found that, given the choice, only half of Muslims who support funding of Muslim schools would prefer to send their own children there. And, once again, the young were not much less likely to want such funding, even if they were much less likely to indicate they would choose this option for their own (future) children. Muslim purists might disparage these ambivalences, but in fact the success of the Muslim campaign partly depends on the political support of non-fully-religious Muslims, on the extensive mobilization of the Muslim community. Hence, it would be wrong to think of non-fully-religious Muslims as only token or "symbolic" Muslims.[21]

I have given some account of what terms such as "equality," "inclusion," and "recognition" mean in contemporary discourses, but what do they mean in practical terms? What kinds of specific policy demands are being made by or on behalf of religious groups when these kinds of terms are being deployed? I would here suggest that these demands have three dimensions, which get progressively "thicker" and are progressively less acceptable to radical secularists.

## NO RELIGIOUS DISCRIMINATION

The very basic demand is that religious people, no less than people defined by "race" or gender, should not suffer discrimination in job and other opportunities. So, for example, a person who is trying to dress in accordance with his or her religion or who projects a religious identity, such as a Muslim woman wearing a head scarf (*hijab*), should not be discriminated against in employment. At the moment in Britain there is no legal ban on such discrimination, and the government has said that a case for it is not proven. The legal system leaves Muslims particularly vulnerable, because while discrimination against yarmulke-wearing Jews and turban-wearing Sikhs is deemed to be unlawful as racial discrimination, Muslims, unlike these other faith communities, are not deemed to be a racial or ethnic group. Nor are Muslims protected by the legislation against religious discrimination that does exist in the United Kingdom, for that, being explicitly designed to protect Catholics, only covers Northern Ireland.

The best that Muslims are able to achieve is to prove that the discrimination against them was indirectly against their ethnic characteristics—that they suffered an indirect discrimination by virtue of being, say, a Pakistani or an Iraqi. While it is indeed the case that the discrimination against Muslims is mixed up with forms of color racism and cultural racism, the charge of indirect discrimination is a much weaker offense in law, carrying with it no compensatory requirements for the victim.[22] Moreover, some Muslims are white, and so do not enjoy this second-class protection, and many Muslim activists argue that religious freedom, being a fundamental right, should not be legally and politically dependent on dubious concepts of race and ethnicity.[23] Campaigning for religious discrimination legislation in Britain thus has an importance for Muslims greater than for other minority faiths. The same applies to the demand for a law in Britain (again, it already exists in Northern Ireland) to curb and punish incitement against religious hatred, to parallel the law against incitement to racial hatred (which extends to certain forms of anti-Jewish literature).[24]

## PARITY WITH NATIVE RELIGIONS

Many minority faith advocates interpret equality to mean that minority religions should get at least some of the support from the state that older, established religions do. Muslims have led the way on this argument too, and have made two particular issues politically contentious—namely, state funding of schools and the law of blasphemy. They have so far failed to get the courts to interpret blasphemy to cover offenses beyond what Christians hold sacred. And after some political battle, the government did recently agree to fund a few Muslim schools on the same basis enjoyed by hundreds of Anglican and Catholic, and some Methodist and Jewish schools.

Some secularists have been unhappy about this. They have said they accept the argument for parity, but that they believe this should be achieved by withdrawing state funding from all religious schools.[25] Most Muslims reject this form of equality, in which the privileged lose something but the underprivileged gain nothing (except perhaps the resentment of the newly dispossessed). More specifically, the issue between "equalizing upwards" and "equalizing downwards" here is about the legitimacy of religion as a public institutional presence. This leads to the third dimension.

## POSITIVE INCLUSION OF RELIGIOUS GROUPS

The demand here has been that religion in general, or at least the category of "Muslim" in particular, should be a category by which the inclusiveness of social institutions should be judged—in the same way, for example, that antiracists use "black" and feminists use "female." Thus, employers should have to demonstrate that they don't discriminate against Muslims by explicit monitoring backed up by appropriate policies, targets, managerial responsibilities, work environments, staff training, advertisements, outreach, and so on. Similarly, local authorities should provide appropriately sensitive policies and staff, especially in relation to (non-Muslim) schools and social and health services. They might, for example, fund Muslim community centers or Muslim youth workers in addition to the existing Asian and Caribbean community centers and existing Asian and black youth workers.[26]

One could see this same issue in another way. An organization such as the BBC currently believes it is of political importance to review and improve its personnel practices and its output of programs—including its on-screen "representation" of the British population—by reference to making provision for and winning the confidence of, say, women, ethnic groups, and young people. Why should it not also use religious groups as a criterion of inclusivity, and have to demonstrate that it is doing the same for viewers and staff defined by religious community membership? In short, such a standard would demand that Muslims be treated as a legitimate group in their own right (not because they are, say, Asians), whose presence in British society has to be explicitly reflected in all walks of life and in all institutions. Thus, whether they are so included would become one of the criteria for judging whether Britain is an egalitarian, inclusive, multicultural society.

## A RETREAT TO A LIBERAL PUBLIC-PRIVATE DISTINCTION

If the emergence of a politics of difference out of and alongside a liberal politics of assimilationist equality has created a dissonance, as indeed it has, the emergence of a British Muslim identity out of and alongside ethnoracial identities has created an even greater dissonance. Philosophically speaking, one might expect the opposite, for a move from the idea of equality as sameness to equality as difference would seem to involve a more profound conceptual shift than the simple creation of a new minority identity in a field already crowded with such identities. But this would be to naively ignore the hegemonic power of secularism in British political culture, especially on the center-left. While black and related ethnoracial identities were welcomed by (and indeed were intrinsic to) the rainbow coalition of identity politics of the 1980s, this coalition has been deeply unhappy with Muslim consciousness in the 1990s.

While for some this objection has been specific to Islam, the ostensible reason why others have disagreed with it has involved the assertion of an outwardly religious identity. If taken at face value, what is most interesting in this latter objection is that it implies that difference theorists, activists, and paid professionals have reverted to a public-private distinction they spent two or three decades demolishing. In this regard, the unacceptability, the bad odor, of Muslim identity no doubt has partly had much to do with the conservative views on gender and sexuality professed by Muslim spokespersons—not to mention the issues of freedom of expression that arose during the Rushdie affair.[27] But these are objections to specific views, and as such, it would seem they could be argued with on a point-by-point basis.[28] In other words, they aren't objections to an identity. The primary stated objection to Muslim identity is rather that it is a politicized religious identity.

The fundamental assertion here is that religion belongs to the private sphere, and does not therefore provide a legitimate basis for a political identity. This is a classical liberal distinction, though it has never been followed in a pure form—except, in different ways perhaps, in France and the United States. It is, of course, incompatible with the politics-of-difference perspective on the essentially contested nature of the public-private distinction I have described. It is also a distinction that does not fit with contemporary British society, in which there is an "established" church, the Supreme Governor of which occupies that post by virtue of being the monarch and head of state. Hence, in the last few years many liberal and radical multiculturalists have declared that they think it is time to "disestablish" the Church of England.[29] Most extraordinarily, it is said that the inclusion of religious minorities, like Muslims, into the British polity requires not just the abolition of the Church of England's constitutional privileges, but the severance of any relationship between state, local, or central government, and religion. One explicit implication of such a policy would be the phasing out of state funding for denominational schools, of which there are thousands (four Muslim schools having joined these ranks since 1997).

Initially, few members of religious minorities joined this discussion, and so the secular multiculturalists were taken to be speaking for these religious minorities. However, more recently, spokespersons for a number of non-Christian religious minorities have begun to argue for the importance of maintaining a symbolic and substantive link between religion and the state.[30] In fact, somewhat surprisingly, besides arguing for various benefits for minority religions (and for the importance of religious-discrimination legislation to complement legislation on racial discrimination), these spokespersons have neither challenged Anglican privileges, nor even the conception that Britain is ought to be a Christian country.[31]

It is once more worth emphasizing that the panic that the rise of Muslim assertiveness has caused among secular multiculturalists has resulted in knee-jerk reactions and inconsistencies.[32] By forcing the debate about religion and politics into the polar options of establishment-disestablishment, multiculturalists have obscured other options, such as replacing the Anglican Christian link with the state with a pluralized religions-state link, or developing other forms of institutionalization which would give political and administrative expression to a multifaith society. Nor have they suggested any lay or secular forms of representation for Muslims and related groups. In fact, the latter would be just as or more consistent with the ethos of Sunni Islam. Most mosques in Britain are run by local lay committees, with the *mullah* or *imam* usually being a minor functionary. At the national level, too, very few of those who aspire to be Muslim spokespersons and representatives have religious authority, and they are not expected to have it by fellow Muslims. Thus, the argument ought to be more about the recognition and support of communities, rather than necessarily about ecclesiastical or spiritual representation in political institutions.

These debates would indeed be more consistent with the notions of group "recognition" and publicity that inform much multiculturalist thinking. Instead, multiculturalist disestablishmentarians have suggested that if a religious denomination is not "established," it is effectively a matter of private religious observance and conscience, and therefore has no place among public, political identities. But in so doing, they have applied a different standard of publicity to religion than to ethnic and other forms of identity. The result is a mixed-up situation. On the one hand, secular multiculturalists may argue that the sex lives of individuals—traditionally a core area of liberal privacy—are a legitimate feature of political identity and public discourse (and they seem to generally welcome the sexualization of culture, if not the prurient interest in the sexual activity of public characters). Yet on the other hand, they maintain that religion—a key source of communal identity in traditional, nonliberal societies—must be regarded as a private matter, perhaps as a uniquely private matter. And most specifically, Muslim identity is seen as the illegitimate child of British multiculturalism.

Indeed, the Rushdie affair has made evident that in British society the group most politically opposed to (politicized) Muslims is not Christians, or even right-wing nationalists, but the secular, liberal intelligentsia.[33] While hostile press reporting and inflammatory headlines about black people are more characteristic of the tabloids than the broadsheets (with the latter usually castigating such journalism), Muslims are frequently criticized in the op ed pages of the broadsheets in a way that few, if any, other minority groups are. Muslims often remark that if in such articles either the words "Jews" or "blacks" were substituted for the word "Muslims," the newspapers in question would be attacked as racist, and indeed risk legal proceedings.[34] The Fourth Survey also found that nominal Christians and those without a religion were more likely to say they were prejudiced against Muslims than those Christians who said their religion was of importance to them.[35]

Yet, just as the hostility against Jews, in various times and places, has taken on a varying blend of anti-Judaism (hostility to a religion) and anti-Semitism (hostility to a racialized group), so, too, is it difficult to gauge the extent to which contemporary British Islamophobia is "religious," and the extent to which it is "racial." Nevertheless, it is generally acknowledged that of all groups today, Asians face the greatest hostility, and that Asians themselves feel this is related to a more targeted hostility toward Muslims.[36] But these matters are not at all easy to disentangle, and have hardly been researched. Furthermore, anti-Muslim racism is only just beginning to be acknowledged by antiracists. One has also to acknowledge that there must be analytical space for forthright criticism of aspects of Muslim doctrines, ideologies, and practice without it being dismissed as Islamophobia—this being exactly the parallel problem of distinguishing anti-Zionism from anti-Semitism.

## CONCLUDING NOTE

The emergence of Muslim political agency has clearly thrown British multiculturalism into theoretical and practical disarray. This is worrying, because based on any objective reading, there cannot be what one might call a race-relations settlement in Britain that does not include Muslims, since nearly half of all nonwhites in Britain are Muslims. On the other hand, Muslims cannot prosper without political allies and without the goodwill of the educated classes, both of which are denied to them at the moment.

What may be of international and comparative interest here is that, as far as I know, in no other country at the moment is this debate taking place in quite this way. In particular, Britain can be contrasted to France, where the Muslim presence has stimulated a neorepublican anti-multiculturalist consensus.[37] In Britain, multiculturalism continues to make political headway while, paradoxically, the opposition between rival versions of multiculturalism deepens.[38]

## NOTES

SOME OF THE WORK ON WHICH THIS CHAPTER IS BASED WAS MADE POSSIBLE BY ESRC AWARD R000222124, FOR WHICH I AM GRATEFUL. FURTHER DETAILS OF THIS ESRC PROJECT, ENTITLED "ETHNIC DIVERSITY AND PUBLIC POLICY," ARE AVAILABLE IN *SOCIAL COMPASS*, VOL. 47, NO. 1 (MARCH 2000).

1. J. Rex and R. Moore, *Race, Community, and Conflict* (Oxford, U.K.: Oxford University Press, 1967); CCCS (Centre for Contemporary Cultural Studies), *The Empire Strikes Back* (London: Hutchinson, 1982); A. Sivanandan, "RAT and the Degradation of the Black Struggle," *Race and Class*, 26 no. 4 (1985); and P. Gilroy, *There Ain't No Black in the Union Jack* (London: Routledge, 1987).

2. S. Rushdie, "The New Empire Within Britain," *New Society* 9 (December 1982).

3. M. Luthra, *Britain's Black Population: Social Change, Public Policy and Agenda* (Aldershot, U.K.: Ashgate, 1997).

4. T. Modood et al., *Britain's Ethnic Minorities: Diversity and Disadvantage* (London: Policy Studies Institute, 1997).

5. UKACIA, *Muslims and the Law in Multi-faith Britain: Need for Reform* (London: U.K. Action Committee on Islamic Affairs, 1993).

6. Muslim Parliament of Great Britain, "Race Relations and Muslims in Great Britain: A Discussion Paper" (London: The Muslim Parliament, 1992).

7. I. Young, *Justice and the Politics of Difference* (Princeton, N.J.: Princeton University Press, 1990), 157.

8. H. Goulbourne, "Varieties of Pluralism: The Notion of a Pluralist, Post-Imperial Britain," *New Community* 17, no. 2 (January 1991); and *Ethnicity and Nationalism in Post-Imperial Britain* (Cambridge, U.K.: Cambridge University Press, 1991).

9. C. Pateman, *The Sexual Contract* (Stanford, Calif.: Stanford University Press, 1988); and Young, *Justice and the Politics of Difference*.

10. T. Modood, "Anti-Essentialism, Multiculturalism, and the 'Recognition' of Religious Minorities," *Journal of Political Philosophy* 6, no. 4 (December 1998), 378–99; reproduced in W. Kymlicka and W. Norman, eds., *Citizenship in Diverse Societies* (Oxford: Oxford University Press, 2000).

11. D. Fuss, *Essentially Speaking* (New York: Routledge, 1989).

12. As articulated, for example, by Hannah Arendt and Jurgen Habermas. See H. Arendt, *On Revolution* (New York: Viking, 1963); *Human Condition* (London: University of Chicago, 1968); J. Habermas, *The Theory of Communicative Competence, Vol. 1: Reason and the Rationalisation of Society* (Boston: Beacon, 1983); and *The Theory of Communicative Competence, Vol. 2: Lifeworld and System* (Boston: Beacon, 1987).

13. S. Benhabib, *Situating the Self* (New York: Routledge, 1992); and N. Fraser, "Rethinking the Public Sphere," in G. Calhoun, ed., *Habermas and the Public Sphere* (Cambridge, Mass.: MIT Press, 1992).

14. S. Hall, "New Ethnicities," in J. Donald and A. Rattansi, eds., *"Race," Culture and Difference* (London: Sage, 1992).

15. T. Modood, "Political Blackness and British Asians," *Sociology* 28, no. 3 (1994).

16. This was even truer of the Caribbeans than the South Asians. However, at least superficially, they were able to (and did) combine an ethnic assertiveness ("black" as pride in African roots) with a wider political solidarity ("black" as inclusive of all nonwhites) without a new identity vocabulary.

17. T. Modood, "British Asian Muslims and the RushdieAffair," *Political Quarterly* 61, no. 2 (1990), reproduced in Donald and Rattansi, *"Race," Culture and Difference*.

18. Modood, "Political Blackness and British Asians."

19. T. Modood, "Catching up with Jesse Jackson: Being Oppressed and Being Somebody," *New Community* 17, no. 1 (October 1990); reproduced in T. Modood, *Not Easy Being British: Colour, Culture, and Citizenship* (Stoke-on-Trent, U.K.: Runnymede Trust, 1992).

20. Modood et al., *Britain's Ethnic Minorities*.

21. J. Rex, "National Identity in the Democratic Multi-Cultural State," *Sociological Research Online* 1, no. 2 (1996), http: www.socresonline.org.uk socresonline 1 2 1.html.

22. T. Modood, "Difference, Cultural Racism and Anti-Racism," in P. Werbner and T. Modood, eds., *Debating Cultural Identity* (London: Zed Books, 1997).

23. UKACIA, *Muslims and the Law*.

24. CRE (Commission for Racial Equality), "Free Speech: Report of a Seminar" (London, 1990); and T. Modood, "Muslims, Incitement to Hatred and the Law," in J. Horton, ed., *Liberalism, Multiculturalism and Toleration* (London: Macmillan, 1993); reproduced in UKACIA, *Muslims and the Law*.

25. It has even been argued—though in the name of integration rather than multiculturalism—that this should be done expressly to prevent state-funded Muslim schools.

26. Muslim Parliament of Great Britain, "Race Relations and Muslims."

27. Modood, "Muslims, Incitement to Hatred and the Law."

28. It is noticeable that Muslim homophobia gets far more condemnation than, say, black homophobia. Likewise, Muslim sensitivities against offensive literature get far less sympathetic treatment than that of radical feminists against pornography, or Jews against holocaust revisionism—not to mention legal restraints against incitements to racial hatred. See Modood, "Muslims, Incitement to Hatred and the Law."

29. G. Saghal and N. Yuval-Davis, *Refusing Holy Orders: Women and Fundamentalism in Britain* (London: Virago Press, 1992).

30. T. Modood, ed., *Church, State, and Religious Minorities* (London: Policy Studies Institute, 1997).

31. Modood, *Church, State, and Religious Minorities*.

32. Women Against Fundamentalism, "Founding Statement," *Women Against Fundamentalism Journal* (1992); and Saghal and Yuval-Davis, *Refusing Holy Orders*.

33. The feeling is mutual: it is not Christian hegemony but radical secularism and sexual liberalism that Muslims, in private and public, fulminate against.

34. Cf. Runnymede Trust Commission on British Muslims and Islamophobia, *Islamophobia: A Challenge To Us All* (London: The Runnymede Trust, 1997).

35. Modood et al., *Britain's Ethnic Minorities*, 134.

36. Modood et al., *Britain's Ethnic Minorities*, 134.

37. T. Modood and P. Werbner, eds., *The Politics of Multiculturalism in the New Europe: Racism, Identity and Community* (London: Zed Books, 1997); and A. Favell, *Philosophies of Integration: Immigration and the Idea of Citizenship in France and Britain* (London: Macmillan, 1998).

38. Modood, "Anti-Essentialism and Religious Minorities;" and "British Multiculturalism: Some Rival Positions and Thoughts on the Way Forward," seminar paper to the Commission on the Future of Multi-ethnic Britain (London, July 1998).

# 7

# Race, Culture, and Society: The French Experience with Muslims

## Michel Wieviorka

Islam in Europe presents a changing and relatively heterogeneous picture. This diversity has resulted primarily from two sets of factors: Muslims have come to Europe for a variety of reasons; and these reasons have mobilized populations whose practice of Islam was already diversified. In addition, the national and even the local contexts into which Muslims arrive, or where people have discovered or rediscovered Islam, have exerted influence on an already-varied religion.[1] But immigration by Muslims to Europe cannot be fully explained by religious factors alone. Rather, Islam has merely been the chosen religion of certain groups of immigrants who have come to Europe since the 1950s, and who in some cases were coming to Europe before then.

Some of these immigrants have arrived as a direct result of decolonization, which created conditions in their homelands that encouraged them to choose residence in the former mother country over the former colony. In France, one such group was the so-called *harkis*, backup troops in the French army during the Algerian war. There was clearly no place in an independent Algeria for these mainly Muslim former soldiers and their families who were accused of having chosen the enemy camp.

Other arrivals throughout the 1950s, 1960s, and early 1970s, however, came in response to a demand for labor. This demand originated both in the private sector (big firms, employers' organizations, etc.) and, as a last resort, in the public sector. Migration to satisfy this demand for labor sometimes involved close cooperation between local European organizations and their counterparts in the original countries. In the cases of France, Germany, and Belgium, in particular, a majority of such workers from Islamic countries also intended, at least at the outset, to return. They were largely single men who often lived in hostels or in furnished rooms, where the landlords exploited them.

Although such workers were socially integrated in terms of labor relationships, they were politically and culturally excluded. Such incongruity between economic and social integration and political and national exclusion has been particularly evident in Germany, where it has been based on *ius sanguinis*—a principle which is supposed to disappear under the government of Gerhard Schroeder. But in France during the 1960s, 1970s, and early 1980s, the Islamic beliefs of immigrants were also sometimes used by employers to divide workers and weaken trade unions. Above all, the Islam of these migrant workers was never significantly different from that of their home countries, and it was not considerably shaped or transformed by the host societies.

More recently, a new trend has emerged among those who emigrate for work. Whereas the arrival of foreign workers was once organized, legal, and desired by the authorities in both the receiving and original countries, this is often no longer the case. And one result of the rise of new illegal or clandestine labor networks has been the dreadful dramas which recall the experience of the "boat people" of Asia. This has particularly been the case with Moroccans, who may leave their country in small, woefully inadequate boats. This immigration, which remains fundamentally one of labor, but which is not legally organized, is now further suspected of involving motives other than work. The main suspicion has been that such immigrants desire to take unfair advantage of the fruits of modernity—in particular, to live off the largesse of welfare payments in European societies. Racist and xenophobic discourse constantly reiterates this type of accusation.

Finally, political reasons may also play a role in the immigration of many Muslims to Europe. Thus, for example, many recent immigrants to France from Algeria may simply be seeking to escape that country's vicious circle of terrorism and counterterrorism.

From one country in Europe to another, these various reasons have had different weights at different points in time. But the main reality is that there is a wide range of reasons for the arrival of Muslim migrants in Europe, and they involve individuals and groups whose backgrounds in Islam are already diverse. Such diversity is one of the main reasons why national and local authorities in France, for example, have encountered such difficulties in their efforts to institutionalize Islam. French Muslims today adhere to many separate Muslim doctrines, and it is very difficult to get them to agree when it comes to either opening or operating a place of worship. This disparity of views made it difficult for the government of France to set up an arrangement for Islam comparable to that which has existed since the time of Napoleon for Jews—an arrangement which some have claimed is itself in crisis.

## FROM NATIVE ISLAM TO AN ISLAM OF SETTLEMENT

For the reasons outlined above, Islam should be understood as a religion which comes with Muslim migrants, who then ensure its reproduction. This in no way means, however, that the phenomenon of Islam has been stabilized for centuries. In reality, the Islam migrants bring is only that which represents the most recent state of the religion in their home countries—an Islam which may have undergone considerable local transformation. This observation is particularly true with regard to those originating countries which have experienced a steady rise in radical Islam in the context of large-scale economic and political change.

Above all, the Islam practiced by the immigrants is not a phenomenon which is by definition stable and likely to be reproduced identically in the receiving countries. On the contrary, Islam in Europe is fluid, and its career has been fraught with many changes attributable to its functioning within European host countries. Thus, it is possible to say that Islam has undoubtedly been reproduced in Europe, and it has also been produced.

What this reality means for young people in France, in particular, is that their form of Islam may not be the same as that of their parents, or of preceding generations—that it may convey other meanings and take different turns. More specifically, following from the work of Farhad Khosrokhavar, in France it is today possible to differentiate between a number of major forms of Islam. Among these one might note the traditional Islam of older people, which is highly ritualized, apolitical, and sometimes (in the case of immigrants of rural origin) amalgamated with forms of sorcery (maraboutisme). A second form is the institutionalized Islam represented by the Paris Mosque, which is apolitical, but republican in spirit. There is also the Islam of the peripheral suburbs, which is primarily the outcome of a lack of social integration among young people of immigrant origin, and of which there are various versions. Finally, there is a political form of Islamism, which advocates a sociopolitical conception of the religion based on anti-Westernism. This last form is very rigid in its practices, encouraging a refusal of democracy and a radicalism that sometimes leads to violence.

If one thing is clear from such an emerging typology (of which this is a mere sketch) it is that the various forms of Islam in France have more to do with issues in French society than with issues from the originating societies. In other words, it suggests that a proper analysis of Islam in Europe should take the host society and the way it deals with Islamic populations into account. It also suggests that such an analysis should take into account the nature of the individuals who have chosen Islam, and the meaning such a choice conveys.

## AN IN-DEPTH TRANSFORMATION: DESTRUCTURING

I begin my analysis of these issues by examining the host countries— and, more specifically, the example of France (it is not very difficult, if not to generalize these remarks, then at least to transpose them with some adjustment to the other countries of Western Europe).[2] The society of France, in its own way, and those of the other countries of Western Europe in theirs, have all undergone in-depth transformations over the past thirty years, which can be described as having two main elements. On the one hand, these societies have experienced, and are still living through, a process of destructuring of the forms of community life and protest. Among other things, this has led to a weakening of the various models for national integration, which once ensured close correspondence between society *stricto sensu*, political and institutional systems, and the nation. On the other hand, new forms of community life and protest have been emerging—themes which I consider in the next section.

The most spectacular aspects of these changes have involved the destructuring of traditional social life. Among the key changes destructuring has brought has been the end of industrial society and the conflict inherent in it between a working-class movement and employers. Destructuring has also generated a crisis over those institutions which formerly ensured solidarity and equality, to the extent that since the 1980s the issues of socialization, public order, and public service have become important subjects of discussion. A third manifestation of destructuring has been a decline in the open idea of the nation. This first became perceptible in the 1980s, when the Front National, until then a minority extreme-right group, began to promote a closed, racist, and xenophobic conception of the nation. These views have now gradually crowded out more open and democratic approaches and their parallel faith in the future.

Amid these broad social changes, Islam appeared as an extraordinary phenomenon—which the French only discovered, dumbfounded, in the mid-1980s with the publication of Gilles Kepel's important book *Les banlieues de l'islam*.[3] Until then, Muslims had been single, male workers who lived apart, foreigners who were preparing to go home sooner or later. But from then on, French society could no longer ignore how the process of family reunification, inaugurated in the mid-1970s, now meant that Muslims were young boys and girls, unemployed and "having a hard time," living in the so-called *banlieues* (peripheral estates) and deprived inner city areas. Such people usually were themselves French, or likely to become so; and if they were not French, their children would certainly be. Islam thus became the second religion of France, and a source of great anxiety.

In hindsight, one can see several reasons why Islam raised such troubling concerns. Among these were the success of the Iranian Revolution, the rise in numerous countries of radical Islamism, and the increase in international terrorist groups which claimed to adhere to Islam. The past also gave form to the imaginative world of the French: both the recent past, involving the difficulties associated with decolonization; and the distant past, with the historical recollections of Charles Martel and the Crusades. At the same time, one of the effects of the destructuring process, which was translated into acute feelings of social and cultural threat, was a fear that Muslim immigrants would take advantage of the social crisis to undermine national identity. In France, the effects of globalization were detected very late. And when they were, they were described as being a threat from the outside world to the economic capacity of the country, and to its cultural being and national identity. Ultimately, these forces were attributed to international cultural industries under North American hegemony. But the very threat brought a classical search for a scapegoat. In this regard, the immigrant (to a greater extent, albeit, than simply the Muslim) served as a ready-made target.

The problem of Islam thus appears today as merely one among many by-products of the destructuring of French national society. One might have thought that a new population of immigrant origin would have been expected—like other immigrant groups before them—to give up their original cultural characteristics and sooner or later be integrated into France. But the anxieties of the period, a rise in unemployment and social exclusion, and a hardening of nationalism affected this population differently. In response to both racial and social discrimination, some members of this group began to seek new forms of meaning, opting for increased religiosity as a deliberate expression of their subjectivity. But the fact that they chose Islam, and not a communitarian solution (thereby merely reproducing tradition), paradoxically meant they were also opting for modernity. The key distinction in this case was that religion was an invention which took place in modernity, and it did not represent something left over from the past which would be resistant to modernity. The actors thus became the subjects, not the objects, of their existence. Their goal was to produce identity in a modern context, even if this meant borrowing material from tradition—and, as it happened, from a religion, Islam.

## AN IN-DEPTH TRANSFORMATION: BEYOND THE CRISIS

The above remarks show how the present changes cannot be reduced to notions of decadence. This is why I consider the notion of transformation so appropriate. At the same time that traditional forms of social life have been disintegrating (with unemployment and insecurity taking hold in the wake of a decline in the production relations of classical industry), and at the same time that a crisis has emerged in those institutions which previously defined society, new forms of protest have emerged, with new actors coming to the fore who have defined themselves primarily in cultural terms.

When political action began to reappear in France in the 1960s, it was initially weakly determined in social terms. Some observers even considered it to be uniquely the expression of the middle classes, who were politically and culturally active, but not socially defined. Among the movements, the Jews of France visibly occupied the public arena. The movements of women and homosexuals posed the question of gender and of the tension between equality and difference. Regionalist movements expressed an "ethnical revival," in the words of Anthony Smith.[4] And ecologists began to express doubts and criticisms about industrial society, which announced entry into what Ulrich Beck was later to refer to, in Germany, as the risk society.[5] From the early 1980s, however, the actions of these groups (in which Alain Touraine has sought the characteristics of new social movements specific to a postindustrial society)[6] became imbued much more distinctly with social preoccupations. Their proponents thus became heavily involved in denouncing inequalities, sometimes putting aside any ethnic, or more generally, any cultural definition of the actor. Such was the case in the main with the involvement of the *"Beurs"* in the marches for equality, and against racism, in 1983 and 1984.

At the same time, however, the new actors who emerged stressed their cultural specificity. This eventually took place to such an extent that they kindled fears among all those who saw their assertions as a challenge to universal values of reason and human rights.

It is in this new context, in which all sorts of actors have been shaped, or re-shaped, that Islam has played an important role. Here Islam may not be considered only the by-product or consequence of the destructuring of traditional forms of social life. It has also provided new forms of identity, ones which have demanded recognition. As such, it has presented a whole set of orientations, ranging from the most extreme communitarian radicalism (in the last resort, extending into terrorism), to a moderation bordering on alienation. From this point of view, the tensions internal to Islam are inevitable, and may be seen to convey choices and endeavors which are organized from diametrically opposed positions. One of these positions is that of having a specific identity, which can lead a person to withdraw from society and opt for a form of communitarianism, which is likely to lead to fundamentalism or sectarianism. The other position is that of participation in modern individualism, in which, in the last resort, collective identity may well be dissolved.

Such realities are far from Islam as a tradition or its reproduction, or even from Islam as the by-product of the destructuring of a declining industrial society. They indicate the emergence of new forms of collective life, involving the invention through religion of an actor who is seeking to project himself or herself into the future.

This invention is incomprehensible if one does not consider the three factors around which action is organized. The first two have already been described, and correspond to the contrasting orientations above. Thus, in some cases, the cultural characteristics associated with the new forces of identity formation may lead to withdrawal into communitarianism; while in others, they may lead to the dissolution of identity. But the most frequent situation is one in which people move within a triangular space, endeavoring at the same time to belong to a religious collective identity (the first pole) and to participate in daily life as citizens, consumers, and workers (the second pole). This in turn implies, as Alain Touraine has demonstrated, a capacity to make choices, to construct oneself—in short, to be a subject (the third pole).[7]

## THE PROCESS OF BECOMING A SUBJECT

From the above discussion, and considering how France is not the only country with such experiences, it is easy to see how the idea of Islam in Europe, while obviously having its fundamental source in the processes of reproduction associated with the arrival of immigrants, must be considered an invention, in which the theme of the subject has played a role.

This role may be the outcome of a considerable personal and collective effort. It is, moreover, a form of work on the self which begins with a situation in which the individual is excluded and despised. Thus, the youth who is refused entry to a club because he is a little too dark, who is the victim of discrimination in employment, or who is systematically stopped by the police to check his identity, may be attracted by a religion that offers him resources defined in terms tending to the communitarian. Islam in this instance offers him a space, which may be practical and materialized around a place of worship, but which protects him from what in other respects is a hostile outside world. The choice of Islam may also provide him with the personal strength to confront this society, and endeavor to find a place therein. Islam then becomes inseparable from a discovered and asserted subjectivity which enables the individual to go much further than merely reverse the stigmata of racism and discrimination. Here, the individual does not simply create an insuperable difference, an alterity which in fact prohibits any communication, but asserts himself or herself while simultaneously demonstrating a desire and capacity to participate in social, political, and general cultural life.

This observation is true for both sexes. It is also valid for young people, as illustrated in a recent book incorporating data collected during research carried out on the RATP's *Grands Freres* program (a "big brother" scheme operated by the Paris public transport).[8] As part of this program, young people from difficult parts of the city and of immigrant origin were paid by the Paris region public transport system to travel in groups of three on local buses to ward off incidents of conflict and reduce feelings of insecurity. Most of these youths were Muslims, and they explained during the course of the study that their choice of Islam gave them the strength to do a job which was trying and sometimes dangerous. They also said their one dream was to be socially integrated, find a properly paid, stable job (which was not the case with the RATP program), start a family, and live in a house with a garden. In the meantime, Islam enabled them to hold on. These young people were not exceptional in being Muslims. On the contrary, they tended to be representative of a majority of young people attempting to navigate the triangle defined above, without either withdrawing into fundamentalism or losing themselves in a modernity for which they feel no attraction.

Similar remarks can be made about the young women. In a book which has been widely discussed, Farhad Khosrokhavar and Françoise Gaspard studied the meaning of the wearing of the Islamic head scarf by young girls.[9] They demonstrated that there is one meaning in particular which should not be underestimated: that the head scarf, in certain cases, corresponds to the subjective affirmation of the young woman wearing it. Thus, the choice to wear the scarf paradoxically affords a young woman a degree of autonomy in relation to her family environment and enables her to assert her personality in the public sphere. It should be added here that Islamization, associated in this way with the construction of the self, is to be found in a variety of social settings, and is not specific to the most deprived. For those who succeed in integrating economically and professionally, Islam offers a way to acquire historical depth and memory, to belong to a community, and (if they come from the most working-class areas and social classes) to maintain a meaningful link with these areas and backgrounds.

These remarks do not constitute a general theory of contemporary Islam in Europe. For many European Muslims Islam remains a question of reproduction, of the subordination of the individual to the group and its law. But the present strength of Islam in Western societies cannot be understood without taking into consideration the fact that the choice to embrace Islam is often prompted by a struggle to articulate personal subjectivity, community identification, and individual participation in modern life. This can be put in another way: for young people of immigrant origin, the construction of self is extremely difficult if one thinks in terms of the classical mechanisms of socialization and individualization. For example, the state educational system does not work in their favor, since they are the first victims of underachievement at school and educational inequalities. And while television and other media contribute considerably to their socialization, it also heightens their feeling that the market values and consumer products they aspire to are inaccessible. This means that for young Muslims in France, the construction of identity involves all sorts of efforts to get around classical mechanisms. Standard notions of individuality are both promised and refused by the dominant values of consumerism and the French Republic. But such notions are not necessarily prohibited, as would be the case in a closed theorization of the "negative individual," as Robert Castel has explained.[10] Instead, they can only be achieved by navigating between the three poles presented here—a process which may at any point be self-canceling. This is why for many Muslims the practice of the religion is itself intermittent or fragmentary. Thus, for example, Ramadan is observed only if one's friends or neighbors also do; people eat pork; and they pray only now and again.

It is important to note that the type of alternative identity construction described here is especially difficult to implement in a country like France. In French society, individualism is associated with the values of the Republic and with a universalism which requires individuals to divest themselves of cultural characteristics when presenting themselves in the public sphere. In this context, there is little room for community formations between the state and the individual. Consequently, people who want to construct themselves through Islam are subject to pressures, contempt, and stigmatization based on a dominant societal model which tells them both that they have a place in the Republic (as long as they do not form a minority), and that they do not have a place because they are different—ethnically, racially, or as a result of their religion.

The above observation leads directly to a discussion of racism. From there I proceed to the question of the relationship between universal values and cultural specificities.

## DIFFERENTIAL RACISM AND ISLAM

Islam in its contemporary form in some ways has to be considered in the light of racism. There are two aspects of this issue which deserve special attention.

Racism has recently been on the rise in Europe. In its present form, it first appeared in the 1960s in Great Britain. It then spread elsewhere, in very general terms from the north to the south. This spread has involved factors which specialists have termed a "new racism";[11] differentialist forms of racism; and neoracism or cultural racism. In general, however, cultural racism, or rather, the cultural approach to racism, has stressed the difference of its victims. As such, it has diverged from classical racism, which claimed to derive a basis in physical science. The idea today seems to be that certain cultural differences between people are insurmountable, and that there is no room for these people in society, since they will never integrate successfully into the dominant culture. According to this view, culturally distinct groups are a threat, to which the only response is exclusion, rejection, expulsion, or—in the last resort—destruction. In contrast to classical racism, which aimed at denigrating the other to facilitate exploitation and therefore inclusion, the cultural approach aims at emphasizing difference to facilitate exclusion.

The new racism—or rather, racism in its renewed meanings—thus takes great interest in the cultural characteristics of its targets, and not only (or primarily or apparently) in their physical characteristics. From this point of view, it is easy to understand how Islam could constitute a choice target. As a religion, it comes from abroad, it is practiced by migrants who are often phenotypically distinct, and it constitutes a cultural characteristic in which it is possible to see a difference which is rapidly described as insurmountable or impossible to integrate.

When the cause for immigration was primarily one of labor, racism primarily contributed to the exploitation of migrant workers, and Islam was not an important characteristic from the point of view of the racists. As already mentioned, its principal utility was to divide workers who believed from those who did not, and so weaken trade union action. Now that immigration has become an issue of settlement, however, and that unemployment, exclusion, and social insecurity have become major social issues, Islam has become much more important. In particular, it has become a basis for a discourse of difference which has sought to exclude still further the immigrants and their descendants. This phenomenon is particularly clear in France, for various reasons. Some of these are definitely due to national history and, in particular, the colonial past. But the most decisive reason seems to originate in the way in which the country thinks of its universality.

## REPUBLIC AND NATION

The above discussion leads to a second issue concerning the connection between present-day racism and Islam. From that point at which Islam alone—or, more frequently, along with other cultural characteristics (belonging to an Arabic culture, national origin, language, etc.)—is perceived as a difference, two types of attitudes often appear which make this difference appear dangerous. (The danger, moreover, is presented as such an integral part of this religion that it becomes naturalized and formulated in terms of race.) The first attitude consists of an appeal to the national identity of the dominant group and an attack on Islam in the name of this identity. Nationalism in this instance—possibly complemented by rigid forms of Christianity, even integrism—then functions as an ideological resource in the service of the war on Islam. This is the most usual and most easily recognizable phenomenon. As such, it has fueled not only extreme-right discourse and political organization, but also infrapolitical forms of violence. But it is equally important to remember that the target of such political action is immigration and immigrants as a whole, rather than Islam and Muslims.

A second attitude, however, consists in appealing to universal values to heighten opposition to cultural characteristics in general, and Islam in particular. Here the assertion is often made that any concession to these characteristics constitutes a threat to human rights and to those universal principles which assert that there are only individuals in the public sphere. Such universalism in itself does not necessarily lead to a fear of cultural difference. But in certain historical economic circumstances, in some countries, or among certain people, universalism may also withdraw into itself and take refuge in abstract principles to wage a merciless battle against certain cultural characteristics. France is an extreme case in Europe in this respect. Since the mid-1980s, public discourse in France has often been characterized by a militant universalism whose most central target, even if it is not always made explicit, is Islam.

It is true that for several centuries French political culture has been particularly hostile to the expression of cultural characteristics in the public sphere. Thus, Jacobinism has often opposed regional movements and their languages. In fact, during the French Revolution, the count of Clermont Tonnerre demanded that the Jews be refused "everything as a nation," and be given "everything as individuals." The 1980s brought a new rise of fear among French people, who have often felt threatened socially and culturally. In this context, in which the institutions of the Republic are themselves in crisis, and have experienced increased difficulty keeping their promise of equality and fraternity, the view has also been spread that an external threat weighs on the Republic and its institutions. In the name of the defense of the universal spirit of human rights and reason, this has led to calls for a form of "republicanism" which is often wishful thinking from an intellectual point of view, and which is often purely repressive in its political implications.

In recent years, the most outstanding example in this respect was the first "head scarf affair." In 1989, the headmaster of a secondary technical school in Creil, a small town in the Parisian region, forbade entry to the school to three young girls wearing Muslim head scarves. This triggered a mobilization by all those who supported, and those who opposed, the decision, inciting intense passions which some compared to the Dreyfus affair. In particular, many intellectuals asked the government not to capitulate, and so to effectively forbid the wearing of the head scarf in the state schools. Among these "republicans," the majority cannot be accused of racism. But this type of position did frequently conceal a real fear of Islam—and, among some people, a hidden hostility which finally found an outlet.

There is no need to dwell on this event other than to recall that it primarily indicates fear. But it is important to see how the rejection of Islam may originate either in a cultural differentialism, which is to some extent racist and buttressed by the idea of the nation, or in an assimilating form of universalism that may crystallize around certain principles and provoke fierce battles against the cultural particularism constituted by Islam. Thus, the nation and the Republic may each in their own way constitute distinct sources for a rejection of Islam, either of which can veer to racism. In practice, these two sources can, moreover, converge to give the rejection even greater force. France is undoubtedly the country in Europe in which universalist sources provide the most fertile ground for the development of an obsessive fear of Islam. And it is clear that France's political culture is less open than that of other countries to dealing politically with such cultural difference. This is why Islam activates certain passions in France which seem to be less intense in other countries.

## DISCUSSION: A DEADLOCK

The above discussion indicates why the discussion on how to deal politically with cultural difference seems to be much more subject to deadlock in France than elsewhere. From the point at which the idea of the nation (rigidified into an anxiety-ridden nationalism) and the idea of the Republic (hardened into republicanism) polarize all discussion, it becomes difficult to introduce other points of view into political, or even intellectual life. Thus, during the first half of the 1990s there was very little space in which to promote the project of intercultural communication. The same went for the idea that democracy could be used to reconcile universal values (personified in France by the idea of the Republic) with cultural characteristics (to which the dominant discourse has widely refused to grant any presumption of legitimacy). Instead of a discussion, therefore, an artificial opposition has most frequently become dominant, one which consists in saying that those who are not for the Republic, hard and fast, are necessarily in favor of unrestrained communitarianism. The latter is inevitably seen as leading to violence (with references being made to the civil war in Lebanon, or to the experience of ex-Yugoslavia). Communitarianism is also accused of fostering a disregard for human rights—and, in particular, rights for women (with references to radical forms of Islam). Finally, it is linked to the disintegration of social cohesion (with references to so-called American-style multiculturalism). In practice, however, cultural conditions today are much different. In particular, whole sections of the French population see the Republic as no longer keeping its promises of emancipation, solidarity, and equality. Today, the Republic would seem to demand of those who find themselves in a minority and excluded—ethnicized and despised for their religion—that they recognize themselves in its abstract universalism. This only reinforces feelings of injustice, radicalness, and the conviction that the republican model is becoming increasingly inaccessible.

In this climate, in France more than elsewhere, it has been possible for Islam to be the subject of all sorts of fantasies, most frequently concerning violence. It is true that France has experienced several episodes of Islamic terrorism. The most serious of these, in the summer of 1995, in all likelihood, however, combined an international dimension, originating in Algeria, and a social dimension, associated with the urban crisis and the problems of transformation to which I have been referring. The figure of Khaled Kelkal, the best-known protagonist of these events, illustrated these processes well. As a young man in the peripheral suburbs of Lyon (Vaulx-en-Velin), he knew delinquency and "hard times." But his discovery of Islam gave him an identity. It was only thereafter that he encountered a radical form of Islam practiced by international activists in Algeria and deviated into terrorist violence.

But while radical, even terrorist, forms of Islam are a reality, they involve very few people. In the main, Islam in France is practiced by people who are anxious to integrate. Thus, it is unrealistic to associate Islam with violence or with delinquency. On the contrary, the delinquent or criminal behavior which may be the doing of young people of immigrant origin has had much more to do with their being young, socially marginal, and living in destructured environments and families with no strong community attachments. Similarly, the growing trend toward urban violence—whether it be the less spectacular lack of "civic behavior," which has been so important in the production of feelings of insecurity in France, or more impressive riots, or "rodeos" (car racing with stolen vehicles)—has nothing to do with any expression of Islam or any other kind of religion. Those who indulge in such actions are not particularly characterized by their practice of Islam. Islam in France is suspected and accused of sustaining hatred and violence, or of providing the bulk of the delinquents. In fact, it often acts as a barrier thereto. Nevertheless, this suspicion has spread, even at the international level, to take the guise of accusations of potential treachery. Thus, during the Gulf crisis and then war, all Muslims—considered an undifferentiated whole to which all Arabs belonged—were considered potential traitors, supporters of Saddam Hussein, and hostile to France.

## ISLAM, RACISM, AND POLITICS IN FRANCE

In some Western European countries, racism has been institutionalized and elevated to the ranks of issues around which political parties are formed. Such institutionalization is, of course, different from the concept of institutional racism, according to which racism is purveyed by institutions, the members of which are not necessarily racist, but which practice color-blind or nonexplicit mechanisms. As I have demonstrated elsewhere, the elementary forms of racism are varied, and it may well be that in one country it is the infrapolitical mode of racism which is predominant (in the form, for example, of violent racial harassment), and in another racism is just as extensive but assumes a political mode.[12]

Contrary to a highly simplified idea, therefore, the institutionalization of racism in France and the rise of the extreme right on the political stage has not necessarily meant that Islam is more rejected or hated than in other countries. In France, racism is strongly institutionalized within a political party, the Front National, which represents as much as 15 percent of the electorate. This party is in power in four local authorities; is represented in various local, regional, and departmental political bodies; and is developing a strategy of centrism in the world of work and community associations. However, this party also claims to represent the *harkis* (those native Algerian backup troops I referred to earlier), and its most racist and xenophobic campaigns, while sometimes deploring the presence of Islam in France, do not make Islam their main issue. Islam rather appears as a possible characteristic of a more general invasion, from which the country has to be protected.

From this point of view, Islam is merely seen as contributing to the weakening of the cultural identity of the nation. It is not at the core of the threat.

By contrast, in Belgium, and more specifically in Flanders, the powerful extreme right is represented by the Vlaams Blok—a nationalist, Flemish, racist, and xenophobic party. This party has actually encouraged the idea of specific institutions for Muslims, a form of differentialism aimed at the recognition of religious difference to prepare for a future in which it will be possible to expel them. But in instances where racism is institutionalized and Islam is concretely rejected, as in France, rejections tend to take place through infrapolitical or localized mechanisms. Thus, in the peripheral suburbs, Islam rarely benefits from decent places of worship, but instead takes shape in cellars and garages more than in mosques worthy of the name. The reason is that local authorities, without necessarily being close to the Front National, have slowed down the opening of mosques and the recognition of Islam. Similarly, in France, it is often noted with regret that the community organizations of the 1960s and 1970s which took charge of the conflictual situations arising from the social and cultural demands of the residents have broken up. Nevertheless, party politicians on both the left and the right, or institutional officials (for example, in the public housing sector), bear witness to a fair degree of color-blindness in the 1980s with regard to the issue of the community organizations setting aside their ethnic and religious bases. Islam frightens people, and this fear does not require the Front National to justify the institutionalized practices of setting apart and nonrecognition.


CONCLUDING NOTE

The above remarks have mainly been based on French experiences, but it would certainly be useful to extend them on a comparative basis to other European countries. There is definitely less rejection of Islam when the political culture is either democratically open to cultural difference, as tends to be the case in Great Britain, or where it is relatively indifferent, as tends to be the case in Italy. In Germany, cultural difference is promoted to heighten the specificity of the dominant group—as has tended to be the case at least with the *ius sanguinis* principle. However, rejection of Islam is developing everywhere, not only as a result of immigration, which is obviously a major input, but also as a result of the very working of the societies in question. It is clear that these societies can no longer be read in the light of evolutionist paradigms. The present period must be considered one in which societies are themselves producing differences which sometimes seem to resist or conflict with instrumental reason. From this point of view, the experience of Europe is certainly not unique—a fact which is, moreover, suggested by the success of Islam in other parts of the world, including the United States.

# NOTES

1. F. Khosrokhavar, *L'islam des jeunes* (Paris: Flammarion, 1997).

2. M. Wieviorka, *Racisme et xénophobie en Europe* (Paris: La Découverte, 1994).

3. G. Kepel, *Les banlieues de l'islam* (Paris: Seuil, 1987).

4. A. Smith, ed., *Ethnicity and Nationalism* (New York: E. J. Brill, 1992).

5. U. Beck, *Risk Society: Towards a New Modernity* (London: Sage, 1992).

6. A. Touraine, *Critique de la modernité* (Paris: Fayard, 1992).

7. Touraine, *Critique de la modernité*. Also see A. Touraine, *Qu'est-ce que la démocratie?* (Paris: Fayard, 1994); and *Pourrons-nous vivre ensemble? Égaux et différents* (Paris: Fayard, 1997).

8. M. Wieviorka et al., *Violence en France* (Paris: Seuil, 1999).

9. F. Gaspard and F. Khosrokhavar, *Le foulard et la République* (Paris: La Découverte, 1995).

10. R. Castel, *Les métamorphoses de la question sociale* (Paris: Fayard, 1995).

11. M. Barker, *The New Racism* (London: Junction Books, 1981).

12. P. A. Taguieff, *La Force du préjugé* (Paris: La Découverte, 1988).

# 8

# The Continental Divide: Islam and Muslim Identities in France and the United States

## Laurence Michalak and Agha Saeed

"There are good men in America, but all are very ignorant of Africa," declared the African-born Lamine Kebe in 1835, after forty years of American slavery in three Southern states. Kebe might have also said, "and very ignorant of Islam in both Africa and America." [1]

The danger resides not in Islam as such, but in the systematic rejection of every expression of Islamic religiosity with an incivility which makes many Muslims feel like "unworthy" citizens of a fortress-like France. [2]

Muslims are a rapidly growing minority in the postindustrial societies of both France and the United States. In both countries there are diverse kinds of Muslims, practicing Islam to different degrees and in different ways and belonging to different ethnic communities. Islam has had a long-standing, multiphenomenal presence in both the United States and France. The Muslim communities in both countries continue to change, both internally and in their relations with larger non-Muslim polities. While the historical, cultural, and legal settings of Muslims in the two countries are very different, we seek to demonstrate that a comparison of Muslim identities in these varied settings suggests overarching patterns of both similarities and differences.

Our concern in this comparison is not so much with Islam as a religious philosophy, but rather with Islam in the context of everyday practice, especially in new environments. We are interested in the interaction of Islam with its French and U.S. environments, which generate different interpretations and understandings of Islam as well as different demands on the part of both Muslims and non-Muslims. We are especially interested in those aspects of Islamic practice which transcend personal piety and have consequences for group identity. Religious—in this case, Muslim—identity is one of multiple competing identities, and it is important to look at how   interacts with other aspects of identity—such as national origin, race, and class. We are concerned here not narrowly and exclusively with Muslims, but with the changing relations between Muslims and non-Muslims, and the views of both Muslims and non-Muslims about the implications of an increasingly visible Islamic presence on the issue of what it means to be a Frenchman or an American, both legally and culturally.

In this chapter we first review the historical development of Islam in the United States, arguing that Islam in America has passed through at least two ethnic phases before reaching its current multicultural conjuncture. In Chapter 7, Michel Wieviorka provides a discussion of Islam in France, so our discussion of the historical development of Islam in that country will be mainly in the context of comparison. Against this background, the main body of this chapter will be a discussion of the patterning of differences and similarities between Islam in the United States and Islam in France. Our conclusion deals with implications for the future, with particular emphasis on patterns of multicultural integration and political participation of Muslims in France and America.

## ISLAM IN THE UNITED STATES AND FRANCE: RACE AND MIGRATION

Although there have been small numbers of Muslims in the United States since before the Civil War, the Muslim population in America increased sharply in the late twentieth century through both immigration and conversion. In 1968 Muslims were only 4 percent of all immigrants, while by 1986 this figure had risen to 10.5 percent.[3] The late twentieth century was also a period of significant conversions to Islam, especially by African Americans.

In 1991 the American Muslim Council estimated that there were more than five million Muslims in the United States. Various estimates of the number of Muslims in the United States at the end of the 1990s range between six to ten million. One of the more systematic projections, from the Center for American Muslim Research and Information (CAMRI), was a population in the year 2000 of more than six and a half million American Muslims, or almost 3 percent of the general population. The ethnic composition of American Muslims was further estimated to be of 29.5 percent African-American and European origin, 33 percent Arab, 29 percent South Asian, 5 percent Turk, 3 percent Iranian, and 0.5 percent other.[4]

Islam in America in the middle and late twentieth century has passed through a series of phases. The early phases were defined by which ethnic group provided leadership and came to be seen as the vanguard of American Muslims. As will be seen, these were not sharply delineated periods, but rather periods of transition from predominantly ethnic Islamic identities to a more multicultural Islamic identity. We do not mean to suggest, however, that Muslims in America as of the new millennium have achieved an ideal Islamic identity that is free of elements of ethnic or national identity, nor even that this is completely desirable.

The first period of significant visibility of Islam in America, roughly from 1930 to 1965, was dominated by African Americans, and especially by the Nation of Islam, an organization founded by Elijah Muhammad during the Depression. After World War II the Nation of Islam grew in importance and in visibility. Americans came to view Islam through the lens of the Nation of Islam, which affirmed a positive Islamic and African-American identity at a time when African Americans were developing an increasing political consciousness. In this period the Nation of Islam was a controversial organization, perceived by many whites as black supremacists, and by many Muslims as heretics and therefore not really Muslims. This was not so much a phase of Islam, however, as of black nationalism adopting Islamic symbols.

In the early 1960s African-American Muslims began to move away from an emphasis on race. The most important example of this was the rejection of black-nationalist Islam by Malcolm X. In his autobiography, Malcolm X wrote of his reappraisal of the "white man":

> In America, "white men" meant specific attitudes and actions toward the black man and toward all other non-white men. But in the Muslim world, I had seen that men with white complexions were more genuinely brotherly than anyone else had ever been.[5]

This first phase in postwar Islam ended in 1965 with the assassination of Malcolm X. After the death of Elijah Muhammad a decade later, the Nation of Islam began to move toward mainstream Islam. Elijah Muhammad's son, Wallace Muhammad, embraced mainstream Islam in 1974. Louis Farrakhan, having initially joined Wallace Muhammad's American Muslim Community, broke ranks and revived the Nation of Islam, which today represents an important minority force among African Americans, but not among American Muslims.

During the 1980s, Islam in America entered a period of transition and reassessment, marked by the emergence of political leadership of Arab groups, and later by the beginnings of multiethnic religious leadership among Muslim groups. The two most prominent organizations during this period were the American-Arab Anti-Discrimination Committee (ADC) and the Islamic Society of North America (ISNA). The ADC was founded by Arab-American Senator James Abourezk in 1980 as an Arab nationalist organization to combat defamation of

Arabs and to defend their civil rights. Since roughly half of all Arab Americans are Muslim, the ADC also became a defender, by extension, of Muslim civil rights.

Early Arab migration to America had been predominantly Christian—primarily from the area that is now Syria and Lebanon—but this migration gradually became more Muslim over the course of the twentieth century. Because much of the discrimination against Arabs was focused against Muslims, and because of the openness of the ADC's Christian Arab leadership to Muslim causes and Muslim politics, the ADC has always been inclusive of Muslims in its orientation. Arab-American intellectual Edward Said captured this spirit during a 1980s interview by Bill Moyers when he said, "I am a Christian by faith and a Muslim by culture"—to which he might easily have added, "I am a Muslim by politics as well."[6] Later in this period the ISNA, a multiethnic umbrella organization, came to represent the future direction of Islam in America; its ethnic composition was mainly Americans of Middle Eastern and South Asian origin, with some African Americans.

During the 1990s and up to the turn of the millennium, Islam in America made important progress in a transition to multiculturalism and internationalism. Religious leadership came to be exercised by two groups—the just-mentioned ISNA and the Islamic Circle of North America (ICNA). ISNA is open to anyone perceived by the Islamic community as a Muslim; ICNA is open to practicing Muslims who are in good standing in Islamic communities. The internationalism period has been one of self-assertion and self-representation, marked by the rise of Muslim political organizations, in which the political leadership of American Muslim communities has shifted, through a complex, interlocked, and overlapping system of transitions, from Arab organizations to multicultural Muslim organizations. This was due in large part to the rising numbers and influence of non-Arab Muslims in the United States. The Arab-American organizations handled this shift with remarkable sophistication and maturity. Most Arab-Americans who joined these newly formed Muslim organizations maintained their memberships in Arab-American organizations as well.

Four other national Muslim political organizations have been prominent in this phase: the Muslim Public Affairs Council (MPAC, founded in 1988); the American Muslim Council (AMC, founded in 1990); the American Muslim Alliance (AMA, founded in 1994); and the Council on American Islamic Relations (CAIR, founded in 1994). In 1998 these four organizations created an umbrella organization, the American Muslim Political Coordination Council (AMPCC), which has been instrumental in developing, in the words of the AMPCC charter, a "unity of purpose and division of labor" among the major Muslim political organizations. According to this agreement, CAIR has focused on civil rights, MPAC on policy development, AMC on lobbying, and AMA on electoral politics. Political leadership of Islam in America today rests primarily in the hands of such multiethnic Muslim organizations.

Against this background, what main differences and similarities emerge in a comparison of Islam in the United States and Islam in France? An important and immediately apparent difference, we would argue, is that the French tend to foreground religious identity in discussions of migration and citizenship, while Americans tend to ignore religion in this context. In France, there has been for at least the past two decades—and at every level from the popular press to academia—a spirited debate on whether and to what extent Muslims can become culturally French. In contrast, in the United States religion is rarely mentioned in debates about migration and national identity. The near absence of religion from American debates about assimilation, integration, multiculturalism, and national identity is all the more remarkable, because statistics indicate that Americans are generally much more religiously observant than the French, who for the most part are nonpracticing Catholics.

One reason for the salience of religion in France is that most non-European immigrants in France are in fact Muslim. This is not the case in the United States, where the sources of migration are more diverse, and where Latino and East Asian immigrants are almost all non-Muslim. Muslims make up a greater proportion of the population in France as compared with the United States. Altogether, 5 percent of French citizens are Muslim (about three million out of sixty million), while only about 2.5 percent of the population of the United States is Muslim (about seven million out of two hundred and seventy-five million).[7] Muslims in France have greater visibility because they are more ethnically concentrated; more than three-quarters of the Muslims in France are Arab-North African in origin.[8]

Another reason for the salience of religion in France is the importance of religion in French history. France has had numerous religious conflicts involving Catholics, Protestants, and Jews. To a considerable extent in French history, religion has been an idiom of conflict, and movements for the separation of church and state have attenuated but not eliminated this conflict. Some French would argue that being French today is a legal matter in which religion is irrelevant. Others would argue that being French has a cultural content which includes religion, so that one must be Catholic to be truly French—from which it follows that Muslims (and Jews as well) cannot be fully French. In the United States, some would argue similarly that a national culture exists which partakes of Christianity. The United States has had episodes of religious conflict and controversy, but in general religion has not figured as prominently in politics as in France.

Perhaps the best illustration of the foregrounding of religion in France is the tendency of the French to lump together people from different parts of the world—North African Arabs, West African blacks, and Turks—referring to them all as "Muslims." Some have suggested that "Muslim" in France has become a code word for "nonwhite." Thus, "Can our country assimilate Muslims?" often really means, "Can our country assimilate nonwhites?" Not all French who emphasize the differences between Christianity and Islam are racists, but some of them certainly are. For example, in his speeches and party rallies Jean Marie Le Pen of the National Front places a strong emphasis on France as a traditionally Catholic country. Le Pen has even pointedly included prayers to Joan of Arc, who helped rid France of foreign occupiers in the Hundred Years War. For him, Muslims are foreign invaders, taking jobs away from the "real" French, and his solution to high rates of unemployment is the expulsion of Muslim foreigners. In cases such as this, "Muslim" is very likely, in fact, a code word for nonwhite. In France one cannot call for the expulsion of nonwhites without being identified as a racist, but one can call for the suppression or reversal of Muslim immigration on economic and or cultural grounds, and people will know what you mean. In the United States, too, there is a racial element in discourse on migration, in that questions are raised with regard to Asian and Latino migration which are not raised about European migration, but Americans do not conflate religion and race.

Another important difference between the French and American settings is that the emergence of a Muslim population in France has been due almost exclusively to immigration. In the United States, although most of the Muslim presence has resulted from the immigration of Muslims, a significant proportion of the Muslim presence—about 30 percent—has been due to conversion to Islam, especially by African Americans. This is not to say that there are no converts to Islam in France. There are some, but not many. Nor is this to suggest that all converts to Islam in the United States are African Americans. However, Islam among African Americans represents a special convergence of religion and race. The history of the Nation of Islam and the American Muslim community in the United States is an ongoing illustration that race and religion can be intertwined in complex ways, even in the case of a nominally universalistic and race-neutral religion such as Islam.

To a certain extent, although not entirely, the topic of Islam in France and the United States relates to debates about migration. Especially in times of economic difficulty, debates about migration in France and in the United States sound strikingly similar. The mainstream of anti-immigration discourse tends to run as follows: "There are too many immigrants in our country; they are a drain on our economy; they take more in social services than they give in labor; and they take away the jobs from the real [Americans French]; therefore we should stop immigration, seek out and deport illegal migrants, and provide incentives to encourage legal migrants to return to their countries of origin." The defense of immigration reply tends to run thus: "Immigrants work for low wages; they do jobs that most [Americans French] would never do; they make our economy strong and competitive; and they provide more to the economy than they take in benefits; therefore we should acknowledge the contributions of immigrants, safeguard their economic and cultural rights, and provide them with social services and access to citizenship."

In both France and the United States, the fact that Muslims are a minority in a largely non-Muslim setting has decoupled the religious and national identities of Muslim immigrants. In other words, someone born in Algeria who has moved to France, or someone born in Pakistan who has moved to the United States, began life as a Muslim because his or her parents were Muslim. In the normal course of events, a person raised in a Muslim country will be socialized into Islamic practice. During Ramadan, for example, this person will most likely fast—not necessarily through conviction, but possibly because everyone else fasts, and because there are negative social consequences for anyone who does not. But when a Muslim emigrates to France or the United States, he or she is no longer under the same external social and moral constraints to observe the rules of Islam. There may be constraints of tradition and family pressure, but generally speaking, in a non-Muslim setting it is easier not to fast during Ramadan, not to pray, and not to observe dietary and other Islamic rules, unless one chooses to do so. This is especially true of succeeding generations born of nominally Islamic parents in non-Islamic settings. Thus, Muslims who practice Islam in France or in the United States do so more as Muslims by choice than as Muslims by birth.

What are the possible behaviors of a nominal Muslim in a non-Islamic setting such as France or the United States? One alternative is to practice Islam, just as anyone born into a religion may become a sincere adherent of that religion, not necessarily through social constraint. A second alternative is to reject Islam—to become an atheist or to convert to another religion—but there are normally strong family and or peer-group constraints against explicit rejection of Islam, and especially against apostasy. A third alternative is to become a nominal but nonpracticing Muslim. One sometimes encounters people who self-identify as Muslims—who say that they believe in God and in Muhammad as His Prophet, and that they believe in doing good and avoiding evil. However, they do not think that the formal obligations of Islam are important—especially those obligations that have nothing to do with how one acts toward other people. Consequently, they do not fast or pray, and they sometimes defend the drinking of alcoholic beverages in moderation.

Imperfect practice is not an unusual phenomenon in any religion. One can be a nominal Muslim, just as one can be a nominal Christian or Jew, though one might not be acknowledged as such by co-religionists who are more religiously observant. In relatively more secularized Islamic countries such as Turkey or Tunisia one sometimes encounters Muslims such as these, who discreetly eat during Ramadan or drink alcohol while taking care to avoid public transgressions of Islam. It is easier to be a nominal Muslim in settings in which Islam is a minority religion and religious and national identity are decoupled. This is an example of what we earlier referred to as environmental factors giving rise to different demands, and of how different ways of dealing with these demands arise in a number of areas, not just in religious practice.

Especially in France, one can encounter "born-again" Muslims—immigrant Muslims who have gone from being nominal Muslims to being Muslims by conviction. This is often true of North African Arabs who migrate to France. An example is a worker from northwestern Tunisia who was interviewed near Marseilles.[9] He had been a nominal Muslim in Tunisia, fasting because of social pressure but not praying. When he arrived in France he abandoned Islamic practice completely. He continued to believe in God and in Muhammad as His Prophet, but he no longer fasted in Ramadan. He drank beer and wine and frequented prostitutes. He worked in a cannery in the Savoie, handling preserved fruit. When he was transferred to the meat section of the cannery he refused to handle pork products, and because of this, he was fired. He joined one of his uncles in a different town in France, gave up wine and prostitutes and began praying five times a day. He found a job in an oil refinery with a good salary and generous health, vacation, and retirement benefits, and he attributes his success to God's intervention in his life. Some have argued that one can be a complete Muslim only in an Islamic country. Yet in a Western environment, confronted with materialistic values and especially with the need to raise children in an ethical manner, a Muslim might rediscover his or her religion and adopt more faithful practices by confronting greater obstacles.

## ISLAM AND IDEOLOGIES OF NATION CONSTRUCTION

The vocabulary of identity is different between the United States and France, making some topics difficult to discuss across respective languages and cultures. For example, the English-language term "ethnicity" has no equivalent in French, since the French term *ethnie* is associated with cultures in the sense of tribes—as used, for example, in reference to African native groups. Nor do the French have the phenomenon of hyphenation to indicate ethnic origin. In the United States it is possible to be Italian-American, but in France there is no such thing as "Italian-French"—even though there are many French people with Italian family names whose families migrated to France not so very long ago. It would seem that you are either French or you are not. Some turns of phrase suggest implicitly that one can be legally or technically, but not really, French. For example, one sometimes hears that such-and-such a person is *Français-Français*, or "French-French," implying that there are other people who are not fully French.

At one time it was fashionable in the United States to document European ancestors who had come to America long ago—preferably on the Mayflower. There are two organizations, called "The Sons of the American Revolution" and "The Daughters of the American Revolution," for people able to trace their American ancestry to colonial times. Such people claimed simply to be

"Americans," without a hyphen, the lack of a marker implying English or other white European ancestry. However, during the latter part of the twentieth century it became a mark of pride for Americans to document their ethnic origins. At the same time, non-European ethnicities and religions were being affirmed. This was epitomized by Alex Haley's best-selling book *Roots* (1976). Haley traced the origins of his family to an eighteenth-century African who was abducted to America as a slave and whose descendants had to struggle for their freedom. In 1977 *Roots* was adapted as a television miniseries and became one of the most widely viewed and discussed television programs of its time. The book *Roots* gave its name to the phenomenon of studying one's genealogy and seeking one's ancestry in the "old country." In the United States today, schoolchildren are often assigned to write about their ethnic roots.

In important ways, Islam in France and the United States can be usefully understood through historic migration processes which involve religion as well as other factors. There has been an Islamic presence in both France and the United States for generations. The flow of Muslim North Africans to France began soon after the conquest of Algeria in 1830, and similarly, many of the African slaves who were involuntarily brought to America were Muslims. However, the origin of most Muslims in France and the United States has largely resulted from migration movements since World War II. Islam in both settings began as a religion predominantly of immigrants and has gradually tended to become an indigenous religion.

France and the United States represent different models for how foreigners become citizens, and one can locate these models along a continuum from assimilation to multiculturalism. In the assimilation model, foreigners are expected to completely give up their cultures of origin and adopt the culture of the country to which they have come. Islam, viewed in this context, is an element of immigrant culture that is imported or left behind, kept or lost, enhanced or diminished, and either maintained unchanged or adapted. To the extent that the immigrant is unable to give up aspects of his or her culture of origin incompatible with the new setting, assimilation is incomplete. Immigrants may retain their culture of origin to a degree, while their children are generally able to assimilate more completely, and may lose their culture of origin completely. The assimilation process may take several generations. In the multicultural model, on the other hand, the nation-state is a framework within which people of different origins share common values that allow the society as a whole to function, but immigrants and their succeeding generations are not expected to shed their cultures of origin. From a multicultural standpoint, cultures of origin are positively valued. Thus, assimilationism suppresses, and multiculturalism promotes, cultures of origin. Both assimilationist and multiculturalist tendencies can and usually do exist within a single country as competing ideologies, but it is possible to locate the dominant ideology of each country along a continuum from assimilationism to multiculturalism.

The dominant ideological model in France is strongly assimilationist; in the United States, however, although there are some who advocate assimilationism to different degrees, the dominant social ideology is relatively multicultural.

Education plays an important role for Muslim immigrants in both France and the United States, and also throws into relief the differences between assimilationism and multiculturalism. For the French, who are generally assimilationist, the educational system takes the children of incompletely assimilated immigrants and completes the assimilation process. Education helps the children of immigrants both to shed their culture of origin and to don their adoptive culture. It perfects their skills in French and teaches them the history, culture, and values of France. To use an overly mechanical metaphor, the educational system is like a sausage machine that takes foreigners, processes them, and makes them into French people. American assimilationists would also agree that this is the proper role of education. For the multiculturalist, on the other hand, education should honor the languages and cultures of origin of immigrants and their children, including their religions, and promote the retention of imported languages and cultures through bilingual education and other programs that promote ethnic pride. The policy of bilingual education generates considerable debate between assimilationists and multiculturalists in the United States. In France, however, there is no such debate. That bilingual education does not exist in France reflects the absence, or at least the extreme weakness, of multiculturalist sentiment in that country.

Language plays markedly different roles in national identity in France and in the United States, in ways that relate indirectly to Islam. In America there is no academy to preside over the purity of the English language; the entry of words into English from other languages does not produce ritual expressions of national pain; and it is common practice to print election ballots in multiple languages—which would be unthinkable in France. For many French, how well one speaks and reads and writes the French language is an index of how civilized one is. Language issues are closely related to bilingual education issues in the assimilationist-multiculturalist debate. For Muslims, and especially for many Arabs in France, Arabic is a holy language, the language of revelation of the Qur'an. However, since there is no bilingual education in France, groups who wish to study Arabic must do so on their own, outside the formal public education system.

The sense in which we use the term *multiculturalism* in this chapter is by no means universal. "Multiculturalism" is an imprecise term which has been used to mean different things at different times. In the United States the term has been associated with cultural studies and curriculum debates in academia, especially regarding the legitimization of ethnic studies: that is, the American debate is about the cultural rights of minority groups who already have citizenship. In Europe, on the other hand, multiculturalism is associated more with migration than with citizenship issues, more with political than with academic issues, and the term is often pejorative, referring to a model which is explicitly rejected. Europeans—especially the French—sometimes criticize multiculturalism as a false issue, arguing that what immigrants need is political rather than cultural rights.

## RECOGNIZING ISLAM IN FRANCE AND THE UNITED STATES

In France there seems to be greater recognition than in the United States that Islam has become or is becoming an indigenous religion. In the first decades after World War II, the French viewed Muslim workers as temporary labor migrants. But as France's Muslim population has changed from unaccompanied males to married couples, and then to families with children born in France, the French have come to recognize that Islam is now a permanent part of the French social landscape. The political right generally deplores this trend while the political left grudgingly accepts it, but French of every political stripe generally recognize that Islam is in France to stay. The debate in France has moved on to the question of assimilation. It has become increasingly apparent that Muslims in France will not assimilate, as, for example, the Italians, Poles, Spanish, and Portuguese have done. The process by which Islam has become rooted in France has been, and continues to be, hotly debated.

No comparable debate has occurred in the United States, where Islam remains relatively invisible and where Muslims still tend to be viewed as foreigners. There are beginnings of recognition of Islam. For example, there is some acknowledgment of Muslim holidays in the newspapers, and the opinions of Muslims in America are occasionally sought regarding political questions—although much of the time this happens when there are terrorist incidents, which tend to be automatically attributed to Muslims. An example of Islam making the news in America came in July 1999, when House Minority Leader Richard Gephart nominated Salam Al-Maryati, executive director of the American Muslim Public Affairs Council in Los Angeles, to the Congressional Commission on Terrorism. Gephart then withdrew the nomination in response to criticism by Jewish supporters of Israel. At the time, Gephart's decision to withdraw the nomination was deplored by a number of newspapers, including *The New York Times* and *The Los Angeles Times*.[10]

In spite of occasional stories about Ramadan and editorials such as the ones just described in the media, the extent to which Muslims are perceived as indigenous Americans and Islam as an American religion remains unclear. A telling incident occurred a few years ago in Stockton, a city in the Central Valley of California. Someone spray-painted "Muslims go home" on the door of a mosque. The police caught the vandals, who turned out to be high school students. The students were required to apologize, undergo sensitivity training, and do community service. The striking thing about this incident, however, is not that intolerance was shown toward Muslims, but that the vandals perceived the Muslims in their community as foreigners. Yet the Muslims in Stockton are not foreigners. They are American citizens. Many have lived in Stockton for a long time, and many were born there. The point is that it is inappropriate to tell them to go home because, in fact, they are already home.

Political leaders in the United States may be slowly catching on to the fact that Islam has become an American religion, but this is a recent phenomenon, and such politicians are part of a vanguard. Not long ago, presidential candidate Walter Mondale refused to accept contributions from Muslims, and in October 2000 Hillary Clinton returned a contribution from a Muslim organization to her senate campaign in New York. At one time, Jesse Jackson was the only presidential candidate who openly accepted and acknowledged the support of Muslims. However, recent years have seen the beginnings of a new political discourse of Abrahamic inclusiveness. In the speeches of Clinton, Dole, Gore, Bush, Buchanan, and others, the expression "churches and synagogues" is gradually being replaced by "churches, synagogues, and mosques." However, this recognition of Islam in the United States is a new phenomenon, and we would argue that Islam is not yet perceived by the general public as an American religion—certainly not to the extent that the French now recognize Islam as a religion rooted in France.

There are scholars in the United States such as Samuel Huntington, Bernard Lewis, and Daniel Pipes who portray Islam as a threat. Their arguments have been analyzed at length by many scholars, but the debate merits at least a brief reference here. Huntington has presented the most sophisticated of these analyses— a "clash of civilizations" schema, a new view of the world to replace the Cold War paradigm that has been rendered outmoded with the fall of the Soviet Union.[11] Huntington has been rebutted by numerous scholars, notably John Esposito and Roy Mottahedeh.[12] Edward Said has been at the forefront of scholars who challenge stereotypes of Islam and provide a framework for critiquing them.[13] A few perceptive American scholars of Islam—notably Yvonne Haddad—have extended their analysis to Muslims in America.[14]

Since his 1993 article in the summer issue of the journal *Foreign Affairs*, Huntington has had a significant impact on the American foreign policy establishment. He may be playing a role in the development of an American foreign policy framework comparable to that of George Kennan in the 1940s, when Kennan wrote a long cable followed by a policy article in a prominent journal, laying down the principles of the Cold War and containment. A possible indication of the impact of Huntington is that, less than six weeks after the publication of his article, the U.S. State Department imposed a one-billion-dollar penalty on China for helping Pakistan with its missile development program.

Scholars such as Huntington and Bernard Lewis write of "Islam *and* the West," as if Islam were a phenomenon to be found only outside the West. Daniel Pipes, on the other hand, writes about "Islam *in* the West." Pipes views with alarm the growing Muslim presence within the United States and Europe. For example, in a recent article he equated dissidence by African American Muslims with subversion and treason. He described many African American Muslims as "self-hating Americans" and wrote of the need "to awaken Americans to this still-incipient but rapidly growing problem." While he recognized that free speech is a protected right in America, but argued that "these Americans are using free speech to influence America malignly; others should use free speech to oppose them." Pipes gave as an example the boxer Cassius Clay, who became a Muslim, adopted the name Muhammad Ali, and refused on religious grounds to go to Vietnam. Many Christians and Jews also refused to go to Vietnam and were praised for their convictions, but for Pipes, Muhammad Ali's actions were akin to treason and attributable to his conversion to Islam.[15] Basically, Pipes' critique amounted to an effort to deny American Muslims their First Amendment rights, which include the rights of protest and dissent.

In the United States, Islam is brought into elite and popular discourse at both the religious and political levels. At the religious level, Islam is too often seen as the religion of an inferior Other and as a threat because of conversions to Islam in America. At the political level, Islam is seen through the prism provided by a number of post-Cold War ideologies. Sami Shama has argued that the two driving forces behind the anti-Muslim campaign in the United States are "the absence of an organized regional or global Islamic voice" and "the ideology vacuum which followed the collapse of the Soviet Union." Shama has suggested that the anti-Muslim campaign appeals to the prejudices of both the learned and the uninformed, and that these appeals are effective because they use "modern, well-developed marketing strategies to sell a negative image of Islam."[16] There has been a shift in mass-media archetypes from a situation in which the enemy is "the Communist," to one in which the enemy is "the terrorist"—increasingly, an Islamic terrorist.

We would argue that France, relative to the United States, has a longer and comparatively more sophisticated tradition of scholarship about Islam, due no doubt to France's intense colonial experience and close geographical linkages to North Africa. French scholarship on Islam, in contrast to that in the United States, is more inclusive of scholars who are themselves Muslim—such as Mohammed Arkoun and Hichem Djait. Also in contrast to the United States, France has numerous scholars who study Islam in France itself—scholars such as Bruno Etienne, Gilles Kepel, Remy Leveau, Catherine De Wenden, and Françoise Gaspard.[17] The ideas of scholars of Islam in France are widely disseminated and intelligently debated on French television and in the media. Hardly a month goes by without a major article relating to Islam in France appearing in the *Nouvel Observateur, Paris Match, l'Express, l'Événement de Jeudi, Le Monde, Le Figaro,* or *Libération.*

## INTRA-MUSLIM RELATIONS AND POLITICAL PARTICIPATION

If Islam is an important element in personal and group identity, then one would expect to see solidarity among Muslims of different ethnic groups and national origins. In France and the United States one would expect to see mosques with mixed congregations that include Arabs, Africans, Turks, Pakistanis, Afghans, and others. To what extent does such interethnic solidarity in fact exist?

In France until recently there has been relatively little cooperation (in some instances, there has even been conflict) among Muslims of different ethnic groups. The largest concentrations of Muslims in France are to be found in the *foyers*—large housing projects for unaccompanied foreign workers who are almost all Muslim. Moustapha Diop has documented friction between North African Arabs and West Africans in the *foyers*. In one incident in Marseille, interethnic violence broke out in a *foyer* which resulted in several deaths. In response to such incidents, the Sonacotra Company, proprietor of the largest chain of *foyers*, began a policy of avoiding the mixing of ethnic groups in their projects.[18] Similarly, many Muslims do not frequent the Mosque of Paris because it is associated with Algerians.[19] However, there are indications that ethnic barriers between Muslims in France are breaking down. Among devout Muslims, the degree to which a Muslim practices his or her faith is increasingly a more important factor for social inclusion than which ethnic group that person is from.

In the United States also, interethnic solidarity among Muslims has been slow to develop but seems to be on the rise. Early mosques in the United States were usually expressions of ethnic Islam. Pakistani American communities built mosques that reflected Pakistani architecture, with Pakistani American *imams* who gave the Friday sermon in Urdu. But ethnic mosques have been giving way to multiethnic mosques. There has been a search for modern architectural forms of the mosque that transcend ethnicity. Bilingualism, when it exists, is one of English and Arabic, even for non-Arabs, because of the special role of the Arabic language in Islam. Generally speaking, Pakistani American Muslims are attempting to promote Urdu among the younger generation, but recognize that the Friday sermon must be in Arabic or in English to accommodate all Muslims. The main issue is perhaps not architecture or language, but rather organizational structure and style of leadership. In this regard, Sulayman S. Nyang has contrasted four styles of leadership—*imam*-led, president-led, group leadership, and hybrid styles which may incorporate elements from different models. Muslims in America are also beginning to marry across ethnic lines, and generational differences are becoming more important than ethnic differences.

In both France and the United States, there are important differences between generations of Muslims. Early Muslim newcomers to France were content with modest rooms in apartment buildings or worker housing projects for holding collective prayers; they prayed discreetly and out of public view. But new generations of Muslims in France want real mosques. They ask, and with good reason: In a country where church and state are separate and religious freedom is guaranteed, if there are churches and cathedrals, why should there not also be mosques? If there can be bells to call people to mass, they argue, then there should also be loudspeakers to call people to prayer. Jocelyne Cesari has described this as a change from the Islam of the catacombs to the demand for "cathedral" mosques.[20]

Among Muslims in France, often the younger generation of *Beurs* (French of North African Arab descent) reproach their elders, the first generation of immigrants to France, for being timid and unassertive. An example is a young man born of Tunisian immigrant parents in Marseilles who was interviewed by Michalak. He asserted that he did not understand how his father could adapt to a country that accepted him only to the extent that he was willing to deny his Arab and Islamic identity. In the United States as well, a new generation of Muslims, many of them doctors and lawyers, is speaking out against defamation and discrimination. Muslim immigrants to the United States in the late nineteenth and early twentieth centuries were relatively uneducated and unskilled and tended to avoid confrontation, but Muslim immigrants in the latter half of the twentieth century, including a high proportion of educated professionals, have tended to be more outspoken.

The complex issue of Muslim integration in both the United States and France has to be analyzed at three levels—ethnicity, religion, and ideology. In the United States, African American and European American Muslims are already integrated in the normal sense of the term. Other groups, however, with further complicating factors of age, gender, class, education, language skills, profession, and length of stay in the United States, are mutually differentiated by virtue of being at different stages of adaptation and assimilation.

The highest level of solidarity is achieved when Muslims of different backgrounds are able to come together and form political organizations to achieve common goals. During the mid-twentieth century in the United States, during a period when the Nation of Islam was the most visible Islamic group in America, many African Americans rejected the American political system and espoused separatism. By the 1990s, however, Muslims in America had come full circle and were advocating active participation in politics. Groups such as the American Muslim Alliance (AMA), the American Muslim Council (AMC), the Council on American-Islamic Relations (CAIR), and the Muslim Public Affairs Council (MPAC) now emphasize the politics of self-empowerment. These groups are engaged in methodical efforts to gain influence in the American political system—to bring Muslims into the mainstream of public affairs, civic discourse, and party politics in all fifty states and each of the 453 congressional districts. For example, the AMA as of the year 2000 has ninety-three chapters in thirty-one states, promoting a positive image of Islam and defending the civil rights of Muslims.

A telling incident took place during the 1996 Clinton-Dole presidential race. Late in the campaign, Bob Dole approached four major Muslim organizations— the AMA, AMC, CAIR, and MPAC—to seek their support. These organizations said they would support Dole on four conditions. Dole would have to take a public stand in support of Muslim civil rights, acknowledge that the United States has a Judeo-Christian-Islamic heritage, declare that if elected he would be willing to negotiate with all Muslim countries, and state his willingness to develop a fair and evenhanded policy toward the Middle East. Dole agreed to these points in a letter published in *The Washington Report on Middle Eastern Affairs*, but he declined to hold a press conference to state these positions. While Dole was taking a special interest in Muslim organizations, the incident suggests that Muslims may acquire political influence in the United States commensurate with their growing numbers as they participate more fully in the political process. This is true as well in France, where French people of Muslim origin are increasingly participating in local, regional, and national politics.

In the November 2000 American presidential election, Muslims proved to be an important constituency. Both George W. Bush and Al Gore made pro-Israeli statements during the election campaign; however, Bush gave indications of greater sensitivity to the domestic concerns of Muslims. In the second televised debate, Bush publicly opposed the secret evidence clause of the Anti-Terrorism and Effective Death Penalty Act of 1995, which had been passed under Clinton and Gore, and which had been used almost exclusively against Muslims. Bush also took a public position against the practice of profiling on highways (where the victims are primarily African Americans) and in airports (where the victims are primarily Arabs and Arab Americans).

As a result, the American Muslim Political Coordination Council (AMPCC) on October 23, 2000, endorsed Bush for president. As we have already mentioned, the AMPCC is the umbrella organization of four major Muslim political organizations in the United States—the AMA, AMC, the CAIR, and the MPAC. Since this was the first major American Muslim endorsement of a candidate for president, it was a significant event. According to AMA and CAIR polls, 71 percent of Muslims in America voted for Bush—a remarkable statistic since African Americans, who constitute over a quarter of Muslims in America, tend to vote Democratic. This suggested that African American Muslims tended to vote differently from the African American mainstream, and that their votes, joined with those of their fellow Muslims, constituted an important voting bloc. According to an AMA poll, 91 percent of the 60,000 Muslim votes in the state of Florida went to Bush for president. Muslims in Florida were particularly sensitive to the issue of secret evidence because an important member of the Muslim community in Tampa, Mazin Al-Najar, had been imprisoned on the basis of the secret evidence law for three and a half years. He was later released between the election and the inauguration.

Of course, one can point in retrospect to many factors which may have affected the outcome of the election. However, it is significant that in the year 2000, American Muslims for the first time attempted to vote as a bloc in a presidential election, achieved a considerable degree of success, and made a difference. American Muslims saw confirmation of their electoral power when, in his inaugural address of January 20, 2001, Bush referred to the importance of "churches, synagogues, and mosques" as providers of social services.

Turning to the case of France, Jocelyne Cesari has described how from the 1970s to the 1990s, the emphasis changed from civil rights demonstrations of the kind formerly organized by the group SOS Racisme to the electoral politics of France Plus, and then from *Beur* politics to Islamic politics.[21] There are now numerous groups in France that mobilize on the basis of Islam and participate fully in French electoral politics. These include revitalized older groups, such as l'Association des Étudiants Islamiques de France (AEIF, founded in 1903), as well as newer groups, such as the Union des Jeunes Musulmans (UJM, founded in 1987) and the Jeunes Musulmans de France (JMF, founded in 1992). Thus, in both France and the United States, Muslims are increasingly participating in politics—not just as voters, but as candidates and as elected representatives.

## CONCLUDING NOTES

This comparison of the dynamics of Islamic identity in France and the United States has yielded a number of similarities and differences. Among other things, it has suggested that the evolution of the ways in which Muslims see themselves and are seen by others, in France and the United States, fits into larger contexts which have to do with respective national ideologies of migration and citizenship. We have argued here that assimilationism tends to dominate in France while the United States tends more toward multiculturalism. In the final analysis, comparing Islam in France and Islam in the United States does not yield absolute similarities and differences, so much as differences of degree arising out of different historical experiences.

In both countries Muslims are increasingly willing to stand up to defend their religious identities. Paradoxically but understandably, they are also increasingly open to reforming their Islamic identities. As Muslims from different cultures of origin experience increasing contact with each other, they are beginning to understand that Islam is a world religion with many different cultural manifestations. Muslims are discovering that some of the things that they had thought were immutable parts of their religion are in fact part of their individual cultures, and should therefore be open to reconsideration and reformulation.

This implies the need for *ijtihad*—the reinterpretation of Islamic religious principles, or what the poet and philosopher Muhammad Iqbal defined as "the reconstruction of religious thought." In less-than-friendly environments, reform sometimes becomes a primary means of resistance, and Islamic reforms are indeed taking place in both France and the United States. As the Muslim communities in France and the United States continue to grow in size and visibility, these changes will undoubtedly have increasingly important repercussions for religious and national identity—not only for Muslims but for non-Muslims as well.


## NOTES

1. A. D. Austin, *African Muslims in Antebellum America: Transatlantic Stories and Spiritual Struggles* (New York: Routledge, 1997), 3.

2. J. Cesari, *Musulmans et republicains: Les jeunes, l'islam et la France* (Paris: Editions Complex, 1998), 151.

3. Y. Haddad, ed., *The Muslims of America* (New York: Oxford University Press, 1991).

4. I. Bayunus and M. Siddique, eds., *A Report of Muslim Population in the United States of America* (New York: Center for American Muslim Research and Information, 1998).

5. Malcolm X, *The Autobiography of Malcolm X* (New York: Grove Press, 1965), 333–34.

6. E. Said, interviewed by B. Moyers in the Public Affairs Television Inc., *The Arabs: Who They Are and Who They Are Not* (New York: Mystic Fire Video, 1991).

7. Bayunus and Siddique, *Report of Muslim Population*.

8. J. Cesari, *Etre musulman en France: Associations, militants et mosquées* (Paris: Karthala, 1994).

9. L. Michalak and M. Diop, "Refuge and Prison: Islam, Ethnicity, and the Adaptation of Space in Worker Housing in France," in B. Metcalf, ed., *Making Muslim Space in North America and Europe* (Berkeley: University of California Press, 1996).

10. *New York Times*, July 9, 1999; and *Los Angeles Times*, July 12, 1999.

11. S. Huntington, "The Clash of Civilizations?" *Foreign Affairs* 72 (Summer 1993); and *The Clash of Civilizations and the Remaking of the World Order* (New York: Simon & Schuster, 1966).

12. J. Esposito, *The Islamic Threat: Myth or Reality?* (New York: Oxford University Press, 1992); and R. Mottahedeh, "The Clash of Civilizations: An Islamicist's Critique," *Harvard Middle Eastern and Islamic Review* 2 (1995).

13. E. Said, *Covering Islam: How the Media and the Experts Determine How We See the Rest of the World* (New York: Pantheon, 1981); and *Culture and Imperialism* (New York: Knopf, 1993).

14. Y. Haddad, *The Muslims of America*.

15. D. Pipes, "Islam in America," *National Review* (February 21, 2000).

16. S. Shama, "The Image Question: Origins, Driving Forces, and Outlook," in P. L.

Lin, ed., *Islam in America: Images and Challenges* (Indianapolis: University of Indianapolis Press, 1991), 63.

17. B. Etienne, *La France et l'Islam* (Paris: Hachette, 1989); G. Kepel, *Les banlieues de l'Islam: Naissance d'une religion en France* (Paris: Éditions du Seuil, 1987); R. Leveau, M. Arkoun, and B. El-Jisr, *L'Islam et les Musulmans dans le Monde* (Beirut: Centre Culturel Hariri), 1993; C. De Wenden, *Les immigrés et la politique: Cent cinquante ans d'évolution* (Paris: Presses de la Fondation national des sciences politiques, 1988); F. Gaspard, C. Servan-Schreiber, and A. Le Gall, *La Fin des Immigrés* (Paris: Éditions du Seuil, 1984); F. Gaspard, *Le Foulard et la République*, (Paris: Découverte, 1995); and A. Goldhammer, *A Small City in France*, trans. F. Gaspard (Cambridge, Mass.: Harvard University Press, 1995).

18. Michalak and Diop, "Refuge and Prison."

19. Kepel, *Les banlieues de l'Islam*.

20. Cesari, *Etre musulman en France*.

21. Cesari, *Musulmans et republicains*.

# 9

# Intellectuals and Euro-Islam

## Renate Holub

The "existential conditions" of ideas have not been of particular relevance to critical theorists for quite some time, though the conditions themselves hold more so than ever. Most dominant among conditions structuring the thought of European intellectuals over the last two hundred years have been the values of secularism.[1] European intellectuals, in their attempts to participate in the forging of modern nation-states, promoted the production of secular intellectual cultures: as a result, intellectual discourses on science, progress, rationality, modernity, and democracy have eclipsed the interest in religious practices and spirituality. Both Marx's dictum of religion as the opium of the people and Freud's psychoanalytic explanation of religion are famous examples of this eclipse. Yet these predominant intellectual-ideological conditions, which promoted the production of an intellectual culture of secularism, have also promoted an indifference to continuities in the organization and social function of religious institutions—and more so, to the role of religion in social and juridical cultures. Hence, the hegemony of secularism in Europe's intellectual cultures has not allowed the acknowledgment of the tension between the claims of secularism and the rootedness of intellectuals in social cultures permeated by the dominance of two major religions, Catholicism and Protestantism. Separation of church and state does not entail a separation between church and society.

## GEOGRAPHIES OF IDEAS

There are also structural conditions that have an impact on structures of thinking. These pertain to the gradual institutionalization of intellectuals in state-dependent universities, academies, and research institutes in the context of increasingly affluent industrial nations. That process has gone hand in hand with their socialization into disciplines governed by the logic of the proliferation of discourses. Even a cursory historical study of Western intellectuals would indicate how their increasing economic dependency on bureaucratic state institutions has separated them from relevant centers of political decision making and power.[2] This independence from political power has been viewed as a guarantor of the intellectual autonomy of intellectuals. Yet such a view underestimates the impact of the intellectuals' economic dependency on institutions.[3] At the same time, the growth of material affluence of the Western industrial nations, coupled with the restless expansion of consumerist ideologies, particularly after World War II, has also affected institutionalized knowledge production. As a result, intermittent claims to the social or political relevance of knowledge production have either receded under the bureaucratized pressure to promote knowledge for knowledge's sake, or they have been left to compete with that promotion. Only the most independent and courageous thinkers have managed to escape this dynamic.

These bureaucratized discursive effects of affluent societies in late modernity have even been noticeable in the social sciences, fields which focus on an analysis and critique of the distribution of power in political and social institutions. Hence, the realms of critical social and political theory have also participated in the proliferation of discourses on power and domination. Alternatively, intellectual workers from within the institutionalized disciplines have tended to select each other as points of reference, rather than choosing to reference the empirical conditions of power and domination within their societies. In the first few decades of this century, when Max Weber and Karl Mannheim began to distinguish between intellectual work and political ideology, they then ideologically prescribed as much of a separation between the two as possible. This process in turn identified an important tendency in the increasingly affluent democratic nation-states.[4] It is a tendency, which has continued, in accelerated form, to this day. It pertains to relegating particular intellectual strata—namely, those who purview and manage the origin and purpose of collective values—into the presumed political neutrality of academies and institutions. By the second half of the twentieth century, those intellectual strata were not only relegated to the academies but also increasingly subjected to the rules, often driven by the market, of intellectual exchange that govern the prestige—or the lack of it—of the discourses of social and political disciplines.

In a very general sense, three of the existential conditions of European thought I have identified thus far—the intellectual-ideological variant, the sociocultural, and the structural variant—also pertain to intellectuals in the United States and other affluent industrial nations that operate primarily within a European intellectual heritage, such as Australia, Canada, and New Zealand. Secularism and the institutionalization of thought are thus part of the intellectual and structural conditions of modernity. Yet there are also existential conditions that are not common to all Western intellectuals. Among these are specific socio-affective conditions, namely, the ways in which various sociocultural environments shape the predominant structure of feeling of various social strata with respect to social and political issues. Intellectual strata are not immune to predominant collective feelings. The socio-affective condition of European intellectuals is particularly apparent in their ambiguous, complex, and contradictory treatment of Europe's most pressing social and political issue: the integration of its immigrants. And finally, the intellectual response to the multiculturalization of Europe is also conditioned by the uneven geographic distribution of the status and prestige of knowledge production. Europe's predominant ideas about multiculturalism accrue to the knowledge producers of Europe's intellectual hegemonies—to the predominant intellectuals of Britain, France and Germany, that is. Here Marx's dictum of the relationship between politico-economic power and predominant ideas still holds, although Italy's marginal status within the European market of ideas (but not on the market of goods) does not quite fit the dictum. Europe's intellectual mandarins (see footnote 1) affect the timing and set the terms of the debates on multiculturalism, such that ideas on the multicultural future of Europe from the periphery gain status only with difficulty. We might call this phenomenon the hegemonic condition of European thought. In this chapter on the changing face of Europe, I reflect on the attitudes—mostly of indifference—of Europe's leading intellectuals with respect to one of Europe's most pressing social and cultural problems: the integration of its immigrants from Muslim majority countries. I hold that significant transformations can only occur with significant changes in the existential conditions of European knowledge production.

## THE "COMMON SENSE" OF INTELLECTUALS

Europe's intellectuals function in a geocultural space which, since the end of World War II, has witnessed the arrival of significant flows of immigrants, asylum-seekers, and refugees. More specifically, intranational migration flows from the south to the north have alternated with flows from the east to the west. International patterns of migration indicate that migrants have not only poured into Europe, but migrants have also left Europe. Historians and demographers of migration are now aware of the extent to which the "national" populations in Europe are the products of complex flows of migration.[5] But the cultural imagination, particularly robust in the powerful economies of Europe, has drawn its own understanding of migration. In it, Europe's emigration experience is today a matter of the distant past, when immigrants, in the course of the nineteenth and early twentieth century, set out for the "classical" immigration countries of the so-called new worlds (the United States, Canada, Brazil, Argentina, Australia, etc.). And in that imagination, Europe has only recently become a geographic host to immigrants. Indeed, the speedy economic reconstruction of Europe's war-torn major industries, desired by U.S. economists for developing markets, required the rapid deployment of cheap labor and demographic imagination. The war had diminished labor supply. Supported by the Marshall Plan, which provided little for poor or small European countries but a lot for the large and the potentially more productive and rich, Europe's industrial heartland energetically embraced its reconstruction.[6] This involved bilateral agreements between the governments of the more industrialized north with the less industrialized south. European regions in which the agricultural sector was prominent were the first to send their young. Hence, immigrants from Portugal, Spain, southern Italy, Greece, and the former Yugoslavia—moved north and west. But there were also migration movements within the nation-states themselves, which were organized along the same principles. Peasants from southern Italy and Sicily became workers in the industrial regions of Italy's north, and fishermen from Germany's north became workers in its industries in the southwest. As Britain, France, Germany, northern Italy, Belgium, the Netherlands, Switzerland, Austria, Luxembourg, and the Scandinavian countries recruited labor from the European south, those nations with significant colonial histories also recruited immigrant workers from their former colonies outside Europe. Britain, France, Belgium, and the Netherlands are cases in point. In these countries many immigrants of the "colonial" variant were not members of, or familiar with, Europe's majority religions. They arrived from Muslim-majority countries. But nation-states without significant colonial histories, such as Germany, also recruited immigrants from Muslim-majority countries. The flow of Turkish migrant workers into Germany is well known to even cursory purveyors of Europe's recent immigration history, but from early on, Germany contracted workers from Morocco and Tunisia as well.[7]

In the context of the above-mentioned bilateral governmental agreements between receiving and sending countries, the governments of Europe's major industrial nations supported the policy of its economic elites in a complex web of geopolitical and geo-economic forces. Europe's most industrialized nations thus offered temporary work, and the right to temporary residence, to "foreign" workers. It was hoped that young, mostly male, workers could be rotated in—and out—of the national labor force, contingent on the exigencies of economic cycles. Furthermore, research on the link between governmental policies and economic reconstruction indicates that in the 1950s political leaders were already reflecting on the social dimensions of immigrant integration.[8] Thus, the French government, for instance, preferred the integration of Catholic "foreign" workers, rather than Muslims, into its labor force, and Spanish and Portuguese workers were particularly welcome.[9] "Catholic" migration into France from southern Italy had already proven expedient in the earlier decades of the twentieth century. By contrast the German government seemed more oblivious to the religious factor in its immigration policies. Its language defined immigrant workers as *Gastarbeiter*, or guest worker, a person who by definition temporarily enters a location from a space of permanence. The term *Gastarbeiter* soon acquired negative connotations of undesired "otherness" in Germany's public spheres. Social-science migration literature now distinguishes between the "colonial" and *Gastarbeiter* variants when documenting post-World War II migration flows into Europe. Statistically, these two were the most significant types of migration in the 1950s and 1960s. Yet the overall profile of immigration into Europe over the last fifty years also includes other variants.

In the early 1970s, when Europe lived through the shock of the oil crisis and a concomitant economic recession, unemployment figures began to rise. Governmental policies went into effect to restrict labor migration in order to protect not only the "national" labor force but also social peace. Policies also encouraged, if not coerced, workers to "repatriate," or return to their homelands. Yet the 1970s also witnessed the institution of family-reunification policies on the basis of which immigrant workers had the right to be joined by their families. When families arrived, or when children were born, immigrants began to form new communities. Eventually, refugees, asylum-seekers, and immigrants from Eastern Europe—among them professionals and intellectuals—changed Europe's initial sociological migrant makeup. Among this fourth variant were again newcomers from Muslim majority countries, such as refugees from Bosnia. And as part of the new competitive game between the economic superpowers, "brain migration," or the recruitment of highly skilled professionals in information-technology fields, as a fifth variant, has now also become a factor in Europe's migration history, particularly since the end of global bipolarity.

Yet the recent transformations in sociological composition do not significantly change three central facts about migrants in Europe. First, immigrant workers substantively participated in the economic reconstruction of the war-torn European industrial nations. Hence, these immigrants, as a cheap and "flexible" low-skilled labor force, played a significant role in the construction of the current global status and power of the European Union.[10] This fact of the immigrant's contribution to Europe's economic productivity is well documented. The second fact, equally well documented, is applicable to all "variants" of Europe's post-World War II immigration history. This pertains to experiences of discrimination, racism, xenophobia, and exclusion on the part of most immigrants.[11] The third factor is more difficult to document. It pertains to the complicity—however unintended—of large parts of Europe's leading intelligentsia in the social, political, and cultural marginalization of Europe's recent immigrants. While right-wing intellectuals have been arrogantly blunt about their feelings, particularly since 1989, the "critical" intellectuals, those of progressive or socialist credentials, had been notably indifferent. I return to this issue in the third part of this chapter.

From the point of view of a North American reader, the facts of immigrant existence in Europe would not seem to differ from immigrant worker existence everywhere else, including the United States.[12] One might argue that the structure of everyday life of low-skilled migrant workers includes many forms of exclusion from the structures of opportunities of the social mainstream of the receiving country. This may not only be so in Europe, where nations such as Germany have difficulties understanding themselves as "immigration countries."[13] Institutionalized patterns of exclusion also exist in the so-called settlement or classical immigration countries—Canada, the United States, and Australia, to name just a few. One might argue further that migrants are, in most countries of the world, subject to ethnic discrimination, which often finds its way into a set of racial categories in formal immigration law or into the more informal social laws of the organization of privilege and status.[14] Yet apart from some very general parallels to the experiences of migrants elsewhere, there also exist significant differences. While all nation-states as far as I know follow a politics of immigration which is contingent on their economic and political priorities, the principles which inform patterns of assimilation and integration are not identical. In the case of Europe, they sharply differ from those of the classical immigration countries. Thus, while the appropriate legislative bodies of the latter, such as the Congress of the United States, regularly review the quotas for immigrant categories to which they wish to issue entry visas, the resulting periodic fluctuations in immigration law do not affect a fundamental principle of their immigration politics.

Historically, this principle has been aimed at economically and politically integrating, as expediently as possible, the desired quantum of newcomers. This philosophy of immigration assumes that, in principle, newcomers, once granted entry, have arrived to stay. It assumes that they will move through their remaining life cycles as integrated and productive members of society, that they have a right to be joined by family members, and that their children will fully integrate with mainstream moral, cultural, political, and national values. Hence, the laws regulating naturalization, or the conferring of citizenship, facilitate, as compared to European naturalization laws, a relatively speedy procedure. Such laws also aim to protect the integrity of family ties. While reasonably speedy political integration of an immigrant into the polity contributes to the maintenance of social cohesion and national unity, institutionalized socialization into the structures of upward mobility, experienced however unevenly by first- and second-generation descendants of most immigrant groups, contributes to the upkeep of national productivity. The predominant politics of immigration of the classical immigration countries thus follow a fairly predictable pattern of economic, political, social, and cultural integration. Surely, the immigration history of almost all those countries includes the legacy of forced cultural assimilation, namely the forfeit of the languages, cultural practices, and values of their place of origin. These forms of cultural discrimination, in the name of cultural homogeneity, evoke uneasy memories to this day. In addition, the patterns of integration and assimilation have by no means been—or are—equally distributed among the arriving immigrant groups. Yet the principle of permanent settlement informs the immigration politics of the classical immigration countries. It affirms that those individuals who have been accorded immigrant status have arrived to stay. Hence, they not only have economic rights (the right to work), but also political rights (the right to citizenship). Citizenship can thus be acquired by immigrants in a reasonable time period. Furthermore, future children of immigrants are, by virtue of *ius solis*, citizens by birthright.

In the wake of the multiculturalism debates in the United States and Canada over the last two to three decades, leading intellectuals have engaged in discussions on the unevenness of the pattern of integration and assimilation of immigrant groups. Widespread interest among researchers in the social sciences and the humanities into experiences of exclusion based on ethnicity—the question of minorities—has produced significant knowledge not only about the pain and suffering of many ethnic groups due to marginalization and discrimination, but also about racial discrimination. The conceptualization of the policies of affirmative action has expressly recognized institutionalized patterns of racial and ethnic discrimination—as well as gender discrimination. Ensuing debates among political philosophers, legal scholars, and social theorists, again particularly in the United States and Canada, has helped to clarify distinctions between political, social, and cultural rights, their relation to the concept of citizenship, and the nature of the concept of citizenship itself.[15] No doubt, conceptual breakthroughs in the fields of feminist research on sexism and in research conducted by members of minority groups on race, racialization, and racism have been enabling factors on these debates, for feminist theorists and race theorists have insisted on the study of the effects of cultural and symbolic underprivilege on consciousness and the unconscious alike.[16]

In other words, what the multicultural debates have highlighted is the fact that the relatively expedient process of acquiring citizenship in the United States and Canada, or the right to equal political rights, and some social rights, has not necessarily conferred equal access to cultural and symbolic rights. Cultural and symbolic spaces are inclusive and exclusive, just as cultural and symbolic needs are included and excluded. These multicultural debates have continued in the northern part of the American continent to this day, and they are unequaled, in the West, in terms of their sophistication and depth with respect to the complexity of rights in a multinational and multicultural constitutional democracy. While the intellectual leaders of these debates differ in terms of their understanding of the relations between liberalism, constitutionality, and multiculturality, none of them has ever, to my knowledge, proposed a principle whereby the right to cultural rights or cultural pluralism is either separable from the right to political rights, or contingent on political diversity or the uneven distribution of political rights.

While the political principle of the right to citizenship of immigrants has not been an issue in North America, in the multicultural debates in Europe it has often taken center stage. The nonquestioning of equal access to political rights in the North American debates is a reflection not only of the social fact of nations, the citizenry of which always contains a significant contingent of immigrants turned citizens, but it is also a reflection of the degree to which the critical intellectuals of a nation, namely those who manage the historical organization of collective values and ideas with a sincere eye to social justice, have internalized the principle of equal access to citizenship. To make use of Gramscian concepts in this context, North American critical intellectuals "spontaneously produce consent" to the hegemonic status of the principle of equal access to political rights for all members of its polity. The hegemonic status of this principle pervades the intellectual strata in the settlement countries. Conceptions of collective identities and collective action, forged in the interstices of civil society and reproduced in the discourses of public spheres, principally do not contradict the hegemony of this political principle. In its most essential feature, it accords the immigrant the right to coexist in the polity. It is "natural" to interact with immigrants; that he or she occupies common political national boundaries "makes sense." It would be against "common sense," to again use a Gramscian term, to think or feel otherwise.

It is this type of common sense, embedded in the collective structures of thinking and feeling of critical intellectuals with classical immigration countries, that is to a large degree absent in Europe. The degree is measurable. For one, the Eurobarometer Opinion Poll no. 47.1, first presented at the Closing Conference of the European Year against Racism, states that a EU-wide survey carried out in the spring of 1997 shows a worrying level of racism and xenophobia in member states, with nearly 33 percent of those interviewed openly describing themselves as "quite racist" or "very racist."[17] What is significant here is not the fact of racism itself, but that in Europe it is linked to xenophobia, to the rejection of the idea that immigrants and refugees, while residing in the European Union, have an intrinsic right to continue to live in the European Union. The report concludes that "many of the declared racists were in fact xenophobic; as the 'minorities' who were the target of racist feeling in each country varied, according to its colonial and migration history and the recent arrival of refugees."[18] It should be noted that the rejection of the idea of permanent residence of immigrants in the European Union pertains in particular to immigrant groups from outside Europe.

Most immigrants from non-EU countries are not only from Muslim-majority countries, but many of them practice their religion in a variety of forms. Indeed, 43 percent of those interviewed said that "legally established immigrants from outside the European Union should be sent to their country of origin if they are unemployed,"[19] and almost half of those interviewed said their country would "be better off" without their presence.[20] I am obviously not suggesting here that racism exists primarily in the immigration countries of the new Europe and not in "older" immigration countries, such as the United States, Canada, Brazil, and so on. The racial aspects of the access to privilege and status or the social marginalization of groups on the basis of race or color constitutes a worldwide pernicious phenomenon, the sociopsychological function and reproduction of which has not yet been fully understood.[21] What I am suggesting is that while in the United States over the last fifty years or so the sociopsychological collective production of a negative "otherness" with respect to most immigrants has decelerated, in Europe it has not. And while there exist marked variations in the EU states with respect to the degree of the links between racism and xenophobia—not all negative stereotyping of immigrants is motivated by racism, as surveys indicate[22]—all of the European public spheres over the last fifty years or so have been the sites of ambiguities, ambivalence, negative stereotyping, aggression, and even violence with respect to immigrant populations. Indeed, the aggression against immigrants in general, but against immigrants from Muslim-majority countries in particular, has increased since the early 1990s.

When the Directorate of Social Affairs of the European Commission launched the "European Year against Racism" in 1997, it then responded not only to the escalation of violence against immigrants. It also responded to the insight that Europe's "common sense," produced in the discourses of its civil societies, could only be wrested from the considerable degree of legitimacy it provided to xenophobic behavior by attempting to systematically participate in the transformation of the discourses and practices of its civil and political societies with respect to immigrants.[23] The European Union (however supranational) must be concerned with social peace, civic virtues, and political unity. That its political leadership systematically engaged in such activities also points to the fact that Europe's intellectual elites have remained largely indifferent to the concerns of immigrants. I take that to be a serious matter, because of the status and prestige that accrues to the work of Europe's mandarins on a global scale, and in particular among the intellectuals of the global "south."

## THE "TREASON OF THE *CLERCS*"

By 1970 to 1975, the minority populations of Belgium constituted 8.5 percent of the population, 7.9 percent in France, 6.6 percent in West Germany, 7.8 percent in Great Britain, 2.6 percent in the Netherlands, 5 percent in Sweden, and 16 percent in Switzerland.[24] Such figures usually exclude those immigrants who have been naturalized, or who have had easy access to citizenship due to their status as members of a former colony. This factor is particularly relevant in Great Britain and in France. With the increase of foreign populations into Europe, negative reactions against them on the part of the "national" populations increased as well. Since xenophobic behavior, particularly among young citizens of working-class background, is not unrelated to rising unemployment figures, the increase in violent transgressions against immigrants is not only contingent on the increase in the number of immigrants. However, fluctuations in the patterns of violence against immigrants do not annul the fact of xenophobic violence.[25]

By 1990, the foreign resident population was 9.1 percent of the total population in Belgium, 6.4 percent in France, 8.2 percent in Germany, 4.6 percent in the Netherlands, and 3.3 percent in Great Britain. Again, these figures do not reflect the number of naturalized citizens in France and Britain, nor do they reflect the "subjects" from the former colonies who "naturally" turned into citizens. In addition, since the 1990s, Italy, Spain, Portugal, and Greece have also increasingly become immigrant-recipient countries. Official statistics show a figure of more than one million for Italy alone, in spite of the immigration policies at the EU level to restrict immigration from non-European countries. The so-called new immigration countries in Europe's south also experience xenophobia and racism.[26] Among the total population of newcomers to Europe, by 1997 there were more than two million Muslims in Germany (out of a foreign or foreign-born population of more than seven million, or 9 percent of total population), two and a half million in France (out of a foreign or foreign-born population of three and a half million, or 6.3 percent of its total population), and about one million in the United Kingdom (out of a foreign or foreign-born population of about two million, or 3.6 percent of its total population).[27] And two and a half million Muslims were citizens of the former Yugoslavia. Overall in the European Union today, the average percent of foreign or foreign-born populations who participate in the labor force is roughly just under 10 percent of the population, a similar figure that obtains for the United States.[28] As early as the early 1970s, writers from within immigrant populations, whom I designate as "organic intellectuals" in my topology of intellectuals, indicated their resistance to xenophobia and racism by recording their experiences of discrimination, exclusion, and "otherness" in literary pieces, in poetry and plays. This phenomenon continues to this day, such that cultural critics have adopted the term *minority cultures* when considering recent developments in literature, music, and art in Europe. Bilingual literary productions in Turkish and German have gained recognition in Germany's public spheres, and so has the bilingual Arab-French "Rai Music," produced by its youth cultures in France.

Yet "minority" cultures, in the broader sense, have emerged in many sectors of Europe's civil societies. New immigrant communities have become increasingly visible.[29] Organizations have been formed, on the local, regional, and national level, in order to systematically articulate claims to spaces in the larger community.

These have pertained, in the case of Muslim immigrants, to claims to spaces in the juridical, educational, and denominational areas, to family law, religious education, and the establishments of mosques and cemeteries. While these claims emerged first in Britain in the 1960s, they were increasingly also present in the rest of the European countries by the 1970s and the 1980s.[30] Negative reactions to these claims by both the European media, what I call the "middle-strata intelligentsias," and the public, as measured by opinion polls, have indicated that the nature of the claims, based on a very general philosophical framework of Islam, has activated a series of tensions between nations, religions, and states, recalling the claims to legitimacy of one denomination over and above other denominations. These tensions have not been resolved to the extent to which secular intellectual cultures had assumed for many decades.

The demands for public space which religiously identified organizations have put forth have met with many difficulties, particularly where Muslim-identified organizations have been concerned. But more important are the debates which have surrounded particular events in this context, such as the well-known veil affair in France, the Rushdie affair in Britain, and the cross affair in Germany. These debates in Europe's public spheres have enacted the struggles over space, or more precisely, over the symbolic content of public space. Immigrants to Europe, particularly those from Muslim-majority countries, have moved into a spatial environment the symbols of which are not simply related to secular traditions, such as those of the revolutions or struggles that once led to the creation of today's modern democratic liberal nation-states. Immigrants have also moved into spatio-cultural, temporal, and symbolic environments that transmit traditions that are older, more persistent, and more difficult to grasp— on purely conceptual levels. I am referring to the spatio-cultural, temporal, and symbolic environments marked by Europe's majority religions, such as the marking of physical space by the presence of cathedrals, churches, and church towers all over the European landscape, the marking of collective-national time on the basis of a myriad of religious holidays, and the extensive presence of Christian iconology and symbols in Europe's hegemonic artistic, musicological, and literary space. To my knowledge, no major studies have measured the collective psychology of symbolic space and time in relation to newcomers in contemporary Europe, particularly in relation to newcomers who make their own independent claims to access to the symbols of space and time. But this does not exclude its measurability.[31] When young citizens in Germany plan and execute arson attacks on the spaces immigrants occupy, one cannot simply assume that all that is at stake here are competitive claims over economic and material spaces.[32] These attacks have ramifications for the perception of symbolic and spiritual spaces as well. Anthropological and ethnographic studies will no doubt help to clarify these relations in Europe in the future.

Ten years ago, when newspapers, weekly journals, and television commentaries began to report regularly on transgressions against members of the immigrant population everywhere in Europe, none of the leading intellectuals of Europe's dominant cultures expressed much interest in the immigrant question. Even a cursory analysis of the content of the concerns of the critical intellectual cultures of Europe until 1990 suggests that European intellectuals either conversed with each other about the state of "Marxism," or of "modernity," or they focused on "national" issues important to their particular nation-state. In fact, there has been a quite clear trajectory on which the intellectuals have moved. In the 1960s, under the impact of the powerful social movements and working-class struggles seeking social justice, most mandarins theorized about Marx. All the mandarins wrote books on or against Marx, historical materialism, or both.[33] In the 1980s, the intellectual leaders of Italy, Britain, France, and Germany—to stay again with Europe's most prestigious cultural powers—theoretically fought the retreat of the left in their respective societies. As always in competitive dialogue with each other, whether directly or indirectly, Giddens, Habermas, Touraine, and Bobbio—to name some of the central first-order actors—set out to define the extent and limits of Marxism. The emphasis now lay on the project of "modernity"—the mission and goals of a modern liberal democracy, that is. All of the mandarins wrote books on "modernity."[34] By the early 1990s, Bobbio was still able to distinguish between a left and a right, while Giddens, in the name of a third way, had abandoned a desire for that distinction.[35] Habermas defended his theoretical terrain in Germany against the influence of Niklas Luhmann's system theory. Since in the context of that theory, substantive political action and collective decision making were increasingly problematized, Habermas insisted, in the promotion of his theory of communicative action, on the possibility of substantive collective action despite modern society's increasing differentiation.

While Habermas acknowledged a world of constraining systems, he also still envisioned a sphere of freedom in which citizens, empowered by their communicative ethics, were able to actualize their political and social rights. Dialogic communication thus became the vehicle for the civilized organization of citizens' demands. In this sense, Habermas attempted to uphold a democratic liberation project.[36] Touraine, who for some time saw significant progressive political energies in the plurality of social movements in the context of a particular nation-state, was one of the first among the European mandarins to abandon the concept of the modern nation-state. Hence, he abandoned a belief in the possibilities of its survival, while Giddens did not. As Touraine began to reflect on the possible form of new political subjects beyond the nation-state, Bobbio and Habermas reiterated their promotion of the principles of their respective constitutional states.[37] In both cases, they continued to educate the intellectual strata of their respective societies in the relation that obtains between constitutions and the rights and obligations of citizens. In this sense, both Habermas and Bobbio responded to intellectual pressures in political and constitutional theory—such as the revival of Carl Schmitt's theories in Germany and those of Gianfranco Miglio in Italy—which intermittently called into question the elements that guarantee the constitutionality of the modern constitutions.

These intellectual survivals in right-wing political theory, to which Bobbio and Habermas took a stand, legitimated right-wing political movements in the early 1990s in both Italy and Germany. While both phenomena, right-wing movements and their theoretical legitimization by intellectuals, were also occurring in France, it should be pointed out that it was not in France, but in Germany and Italy, that such revivals occurred in the context of social cultures which had, despite their anchorage in a democratic constitution, witnessed an unceremonious historical overthrow of their constitutions by Nazism and Fascism. Hence, "modernity" signaled for the German and Italian mandarins above all a safeguarding of their democratic constitutions in the form of a nation-state.

Yet whether the key concepts of the debates from the 1950s to 1990s centered on "Marxism" or "modernity," these debates had something essential in common. They tended to focus on "national" problems. Although Marxism, in principle a globally oriented theory, informed the most significant intellectual and emotional experiences of Europe's post-World War II intellectual generations, the predominant intellectual interests of Europe's intellectuals were more local and national, rather than global in perspective. In addition, whether in the discourses on Marxism or modernity, discourses on the "national" were based on a particularly exclusionary conception of the "national."

As attacks on immigrants, asylum-seekers, and refugees constituted the subject matter of innumerable media reports, the conceptual and normative instruments of Marxist or modernist analyses by Europe's intellectuals on the whole applied not to the immigrant others, but to their "own" others. Exclusion, discrimination, and social injustice were concepts that were exclusively applicable to the working class of their respective nation-states. When there was "otherness," it was national otherness to be brought, in the interests of national solidarity, to the national table. Even in Great Britain and in France, where from early on immigrants or "organic intellectuals" had begun to formulate their own version of the "immigrant question," the meetings of the sociological associations throughout the 1970s and 1980s rarely focused on immigrant-related issues.[38] In Germany, as late as 1996, the sociological association operated with a concept of "difference" derived from Niklas Luhmann's understanding of differentiating modern societies. It had little to do with "immigrant" difference. Similarly, the hegemonic publishing houses stuck to their themes of Marxism and modernity, or the "crisis of Marxism" or the "crisis of modernity," respectively. Those researchers who documented xenophobia and racism in relation to the immigrant question were relegated to less prestigious or even marginal publishers. In addition, an empirical analysis, from 1960 to 1990, of the key concepts and content in some of the most important intellectual journals in France—for instance, *Les Temps Modernes, Tel Quel or l'Esprit*—indicated that only about 2 percent or less of all articles dealt with Muslim issues, that is, with issues pertinent to the majority of its immigrant population.[39] Similarly, an analysis of major British intellectual journals for the same period, such as *New Left Review*, also indicated a low profile with respect to interest in issues pertinent to its largest immigrant group.[40] National issues simply did not apply to immigrants. Moreover, a study of the major trends of the intellectual journals in Italy in the period from 1944 to 1990 equally documented the interest of its intellectuals in "national" issues.[41] These pertained most centrally to the social and cultural integration of its working class into the projects of either Marxism or modernity.

Until the 1990s, Europe's intellectuals were also preoccupied with their own recent past. With regular intervals, the facts of the Holocaust, Nazism, and Fascism commanded the agenda of national debates, particularly on the Continent. The *Historikerstreit* in the 1980s in Germany, or the debates in France about the extent of France's complicity with Hitler's regime, are cases in point. Italian intellectuals had the tendency to deploy their aesthetic-artistic talents to address the same historical issues. The principal focus on the "national otherness" of Europe's critical intellectuals, whether adopting Marxist or modernist terms, is also apparent on the whole in the work of the leading feminists. In other words, while democracy, equality, and justice, for feminists as for critical intellectuals in general, constituted concepts central to their life projects, these concepts, in relation to the immigrant question, remained largely mute. Thus, from the point of view of hegemonic intellectual cultures, the state of the nation-state, as a social and cultural construct, was beyond express reflection. As a result, there was no need to conceptualize and theorize the question of national identity or national loyalty. The intellectuals knew who and where they were. Since bankers and military and economic elites had actually crafted the economic, political, and military institutions of the new supranational Europe that emerged after World War II, its intellectual elites were left to craft social and political issues within the boundaries of national cultures. However imaginary, these concepts of national community remained the most powerful common denominator among intellectuals in post-World War II Europe.


## THE MANDARINS AND THEIR "OTHER"

The exclusionary enchantment of Europe's elites with their national projects came abruptly to an end in 1989. With the fall of the Berlin Wall, German unification, the end of state socialism, and the establishment of the European Union, Europe's intellectuals scrambled to determine their identity, sovereignty, and loyalty in a rapidly evolving new polity. The "Question of Europe" emerged.[42] What is most fascinating is that all of a sudden the leading intellectuals engaged in wondering who they were, where they had come from, and where they were going; hence, they engaged in a geographic question of sorts. Surely there is no comparison with the thousands of studies on Europe's economy and institutions which have appeared during the same time period. Yet with the exception of feminists—who were principally kept out of the debates—Gellner, Dahrendorf, Lash, and Gadamer to Vattimo, Derrida, Ricoeur, and Morin all seemed to question the basis, origin, and future of their identity.[43] Thus, at a moment in which "organic intellectuals," by their increasing presence, pressured national intellectuals into reflecting on ways of integrating otherness into their national polities and cultures, the political and economic elites of Europe's new union pressured the intellectual elites to supranational forms of loyalty and sovereignty.[44] From the periphery of Europe's hegemonic cultures, Norbert Bilbeny has offered a fabulous resumé of the European quest for identity.[45] Questioning what informs the unifying principles of European identity led Europe's intellectuals to seek their roots in the *demos* of the Greeks—in Greek political theory on the one hand, and in the *nomos* of Rome, or Roman law, on the other hand. It was in the context of the debates on the relationship between *demos* and *nomos* that Europe's intellectuals began to conceptually reflect on the "others," or "ethnos," among them. For what they found in their common political and juridical traditions was the priority of the enforceability of laws, democratically established in constitutional form and procedure, over the nonenforceability of customs, beliefs, traditions, and conventions. Hence, the principle of the group or "ethnos" in political theory had to submit to the principles of demos and nomos, which identified the individual, and not the group, as the bearer of rights and the participant in his or her own legislation. As a result, the concept of "cultural identity" was closely linked to "citizenship," a right which was contingent on citizenship laws which excluded many "immigrants."

I am quite certain that no irony was intended, but the elites' perception of their common European rootedness in Roman law is a bit perplexing. Rome's *Lex Peregrinus* protected newcomers as persons, it is true, but not as citizens, and hence there were limits to that protection, quite similar to the legal status of many immigrants in Europe's nation-states today.[46] Moreover, Roman law, apart from excluding "things," such as slaves, from its protection, almost always functioned in a state, whether republican or imperial, in which the separation of religion and politics, or church and state, was nonexistent.[47] In this sense Roman law came closer to Islamic law than to modern secular law, as an observer from far away, a former judge of India's high court, pointed out in his reflections on secularism.[48] So, in effect, what the modern *peregrinus* has in common with his her Roman counterparts is the right to private property—indeed, a significant element that ties secular law to Roman law.

The critical debate on the essentials of what it means to be European today is among the most spectacular events in recent European intellectual history. In spite of the increasingly constraining impact of institutionalized discursive practices on modes of thought and expression, Europe's intellectual elites have recently brilliantly displayed the range of their historical knowledge in Europe's millennial traditions in juridical, political, and ethical theory. Yet the debate on the essentials of "Europeanness" has focused, with a few exceptions, primarily on political and juridical institutions, thereby bypassing the religious dimension of European cultures. Thus when, by the mid-1990s, two of Europe's greatest mandarins, Alain Touraine and Jurgen Habermas, stepped up to the "Question of Europe," they did so by upholding these intellectual conditions. Religion as a concept was clearly not part of the analytical apparatus. Yet the "Question of Europe" is inseparable, it seems to me, from the "Question of Non-Europe," particularly given the geographic position of Europe's territory and its borders to the south and southeast with societies governed by Muslim majorities. Political Islam, or fundamentalism, is a concept which is semantically expandable, without necessary justification, to immigrant groups in Europe marked by the terminology of "Muslim" and "Islam"—notwithstanding the actual indifference of many members of these groups to their cultural or religious background. Even reputable weekly magazines such as *Der Spiegel* in Germany or *L'Express* in France had, by the middle of the 1990s, grafted negative stereotyping onto its immigrants from Muslim majority countries, depicting them as the nonintegrable "other."

Touraine and Habermas, respectively, entered the debate on "otherness" with their *Die Einbeziehung des anderen* and *Pourrons-nous vivre ensemble? Egaux et Différents.*[49] They did so at a moment when globalization had begun to exert conceptual and moral pressure. There were some limits to the free flow of capital, goods, and services. Some global regions participated in the control of the organization of the flows, while others were excluded from participation. And it is from those regions that immigrants, asylum-seekers, political refugees—and in particular, economic refugees—increasingly knock at the doors of, or simply try to enter, if clandestinely, Europe. As Europe became a "we," reminding itself of common juridical and political roots, non-European others increasingly constituted the "others." Indeed, the concept of "otherness" is central to both authors. If Habermas is more direct about the centrality of this concept, Touraine is a bit more indirect. Yet in both cases, ontological difference governs. In Touraine's case, "togetherness" as a concept presupposes its opposite, namely "nontogetherness" or "separation," and his subtitle reflects the antagonism of the conceptual pair: *Egaux et Différents*. However, whereas Touraine's "other" already lives in the same space of a "we," Habermas's "other" is still in need of being *einbezogen*, or of being pulled into a space. It is unclear to what extent their express interest in otherness by the mid-1990s is related to an unrelenting crafting of a negative and excluded otherness onto Muslims, Islam, and immigrants from Muslim-majority countries in the mass media. Nor is it clear to what extent their interests were sparked by the increasing participation of "organic intellectuals" in the debates on citizenship, identity, and immigration—a participation which has increasingly forged the terms of the debate.[50] Habermas, in his discussion of otherness, expressly takes as a point of reference the North American debate on multiculturalism—namely, on the relation of citizenship, group recognition, and rights. In particular, he chooses Charles Taylor's contribution to the multiculturalism debate, in which he supported the struggle for recognition of group rights in the context of Canadian demographic and ethnic realities.[51] By doing so, Habermas has also accepted the terms of that debate, which is a debate about citizens, expanded citizenship, and rights, and not about noncitizens and rights.

There is an indifference, in the North American debate, with respect to noncitizens. Given the naturalization politics of classical immigration countries which I discuss earlier in this chapter, this indifference to the status of noncitizens on the part of political and social theorists makes sense in the North American context. However, in the German context, it becomes quite problematic, for the most pressing political issues for immigrants and their descendants in Germany pertain to the social and cultural difficulties they experience on a daily basis due to their difficulty of obtaining German citizenship. Although the European Court of Justice has been able to begin the process of overturning cases ruled in German courts on immigrant issues, the fact still remains that immigrants to Germany, who have legally resided there and worked for fifteen years, can only obtain German citizenship by forfeiting their original citizenship. Dual citizenship is not possible for a person whose mother or father is not German. Moreover, the children of immigrants, though born in Germany, do not become Germans by birthright, by virtue of *ius solis*, as in Britain or France. If one of their parents has resided in Germany legally and as a working person, for eight years, the child is a German citizen, but he or she is also a citizen, by descent (or the principle of *ius sanguinis*), of the country of his or her father and mother. Hence, within five years of his or her eighteenth birthday, by the age of twenty-three, the young person must declare his or her decision with respect to forfeiting or retaining the citizenship they hold in a foreign country. If they choose to retain the citizenship of the country of origin of their parents, they lose their German citizenship. Failure to declare also equals loss of German citizenship. In comparison to Spain, France, Greece, Italy, and Britain—to name just a few European states—it takes much longer in Germany for European and non-European immigrants to obtain citizenship. It is therefore somewhat surprising that Habermas bypassed the political reality of immigrants and their descendants in Germany by turning the "others" of his discourse into citizens.

There is a possibility that one can read Habermas's treatise on the "inclusion of the other" as a moral call for granting citizenship to its immigrants, particularly since throughout the 1990s the Social Democrats in Germany repeatedly organized the passing of legislation which would overhaul German citizenship laws dating back, in spirit, to the early nineteenth century. A German reader, particularly a citizen, might interpret it that way. In his argument, Habermas pointed to the priority of political rights in a constitutional nation-state over and above other types of rights. Hence, the right to political agency ultimately enables the exercise of social and cultural rights. But it seems to me that Habermas is much more concerned with participating in a discourse with his North American colleagues about the concept of active citizenry and the essence of modern liberal constitutions than with the rights of the "others." It should be pointed out here that Habermas's argument against the recognition of group rights, on which the multicultural debates in North America has hinged, is a particularly sensitive issue in the German context, since there is a clear precedent in German citizenship laws to distinguish between two types of citizens: the *Staatsbuerger*, and the *Staatsangehoerige*. In fact, differences in citizenship status were among the first legal conditions that Hitler activated in his persecution of Jews.

Throughout his career as mandarin intellectual Habermas has demonstrated a consistent critical conscience with respect to Germany's Nazism. His intellectual project has been deeply marked by that critical conscience, and so have been the concepts he upholds in his education of the intellectual elites. Indeed, "active citizenry" is key in his understanding of the life and survival of modern liberal constitutional democracies. By contrast, a "passive citizenry," a citizenry that merely votes, defies the modern liberal constitutional project. Hence, recognizing in the constitution the rights of groups for special treatment—as supporters of multicultural citizenship such as Taylor upholds—contradicts, according to Habermas, the essence of modern liberal constitutions which are based on the internal connection between the individual rights of private persons and the public autonomy of the citizens who participate in making the laws. The citizen, as the individual bearer of private rights, meets in dialogic communication with other citizens. Against the background of a set of ethical norms, to which they consent, citizens as individuals will participate together in proposing the rules that manage the access to the distribution of common resources. In this model, the ethics to which an active citizenry adheres in principle can change with the composition of the citizenry. Yet while the norms may change with the cultural composition of the citizens, the principle that enables change—namely, the essence of citizenship—in the individual as bearer of rights (inalienable) of person, does not change. Civil society is civil in modernity precisely by safeguarding the nexus between the rights of the individual to actively participate—in communicative action with others—in the shaping of enforceable ethical norms: laws, that is. Yet access to the rights of the individual and their enforceability are ultimately guaranteed, but also conditioned, by citizenship. And this is what many of Germany's "others" do not have.

Habermas's political theory has always focused on actors that get their strength from, as they give their strength to, the political system. As they transform the state, they support it. As such he intransigently upholds the modern constitutional polity. Hence, the advice he has for his readers is to seek membership in it. Touraine, to the contrary, has always been—without disregarding educational and juridical systems—much more interested in the political force that can accrue to social and cultural movements. After all, the student movement in France did substantively challenge the political system. And, moreover, cultural identity has become a major political force in many global regions, notably in those that border on Europe's south. Thus, in contradistinction to Habermas, Touraine critiques the modern state. In fact, he accuses the political elites of his republic of not sufficiently recognizing the disintegration of its economic, political, social, and cultural spheres. How can one speak of the integration and assimilation of immigrants into a culture that is disintegrating, he wonders, thereby no doubt responding, among other things, to the assimilationist positions in the French debates on citizenship?[52] Indeed, according to him, the democratic ideal itself has declined. "How are we to avoid the conclusion that the democratic idea no longer mobilizes hopes and demands, that it has been reduced to the defense of institutional safeguards, and that it relies on the influence of consumers, rather than the will of citizens?" he provocatively asks.[53]

Touraine's analysis of demodernization triggered by the crisis of modernity impacts his treatment of the "other." Indeed, demodernization promises a solution for "others" and "nonothers" alike. The solution consists in the "personal project," in the production of oneself as a "subject." Against this background, Touraine has argued that a person can only become a subject by recognizing the "other" as such. Where Habermas sees a citizen and a state, even a supranational state, such as Europe, Touraine sees a multitude of individuals whose lives are transformed—on personal and collective levels—by global forces which transcend the citizen and the state. Both the "nonother" and the "other" have two things in common in Touraine's depiction of the current *condition humaine*: first, they are sitting in the same global boat, and, second, they both command the power to live in that boat with a measure of authenticity and dignity. They can both build a personal life project. They are authors, and not recipients, of subjectivity. This new condition of demodernization brings with it responsibility, but also freedom. For Touraine, grasping the social, cultural, and economic dissolution of the processes of demodernization, rather than resisting them in the name of an outdated political vocabulary, is a condition for participating in the crafting of new relations. This includes the relation to the "other." The "other" is, like everyone else, part of and participant in this process of transformation. Globalization excludes no one, including resistance to it.

If Habermas has been driven to extend his notion of civil society beyond Europe to the entire globe, Touraine, too, offers a global vision: the subject creates his or her personal freedom next to struggles for collective freedom everywhere.

Ultimately, though, there is still a dependency on institutional support in order to produce the new subject. One needs to educate the educator. The new subject will emerge from the new schools, where children learn from each other to recognize cultural difference. These schools will improve the chances of the individual to become "subjects of their existence."[54] These subjects, by constructing their personal life project, will become the political actors of the future. If the principal political actors were citizens and workers in the age of modernity, in the age of demodernization the principal actors are individuals or groups who "strive to reconcile private cultural experience with involvement in the world of instrumental action."[55] For Touraine, these actors already exist. Young people, women, immigrants, members of minorities, and defenders of the environment all belong in the category of this new acting subject.

Since Touraine, in contradistinction to Habermas, is more in tune with the social forces of politics, he does recognize the religious-cultural dimension in the struggle over collective resources. Touraine, too, takes recourse to a notion of communicative action in negotiating this struggle. However, democratic communication in the epoch of demodernization can only be intercultural communication, particularly since "in a world of intense cultural exchanges, there can be no democracy unless we recognize the diversity of cultures and the relations of domination that exist between them."[56] Intercultural communication can only occur, according to Touraine, if subjects escape their "communitarian" communities. By critiquing communitarianism, as a practice and theory, Touraine does explicitly address the presence of religious ideologies and identities in France. Such identities do not only pertain to immigrants. In this sense Touraine acknowledges a social reality which Habermas ignores. By primarily engaging with North American theorists, Habermas has also adopted the terms of the noncommunitarian wing of these theorists when dealing with the concept of citizenship in relation to identity. Accordingly, a citizen's multiple identities may include religious affiliations, but none of these identities can impact his or her rights to the rights of citizenship. In the North American debate, the discourse on the plurality of identities operates with a symmetrical ascription: a person's identity may consist in being a woman, a Catholic, a Hispanic, and a mother at one and the same time. What this ascription obscures is the extraordinary weight any of these identities may carry at the expense of the remaining ones in the perception and judgment of the world.

The recent electoral events in the United States speak to the fact not only that such plurality of identities can give way to singularity under certain conditions—in that the religious identity of many voters carried the day—but also that citizenship and identity, neatly separated by Habermas, can converge. It is there, as compared to Habermas, that Touraine makes an important concession to the presence of religion in the states undergoing demodernization. As such, it is also a recognition of the religious, symbolic, and affective environments of the recipient countries within which immigrants by little choice move. The personal life project, as Touraine would have it, is to leave the communitarian behind. In this vision the question of religion is put to rest. However, in a region such as Europe—the constitutions of which almost all principally acknowledge the Christian religion, and half of whose populations define themselves as religious— is such an intellectual gesture reasonable? If it is the task of intellectuals to bring some order to public opinion, as Touraine has written, then it is surely the task of the mandarins to bring some order to the public opinion of intellectuals. Bypassing the question of religion in Europe without examining the spiritual dimensions of its secularism merely reproduces the fact that northern intellectuals can still ignore the contingencies of their intellectual production: namely the location of their nation-states, however disappearing, in the geopolitical space of economic power and domination. This is what southern intellectuals cannot afford to do.

## NOTES

1. For working purposes in the context of this paper only, I mean by "European" the nation-states which now form the European Union. *Intellectuals* I define, along Gramscian lines, as that social group which manages the organization of the history of predominant ideas and values and which reflects on the conceptions and ethical norms that capture the present and the future of their respective societies. Important intellectual historians sometimes use the term *mandarins* or *clercs*, when referring to leading intellectuals.

2. Heidegger's attempt to become the "national philosopher" after Hitler's takeover is a significant reminder of his awareness of the directive functions the mandarins assumed in the formation of nation-states.

3. M. Sabour, "Between Patronage and Autonomy: The Position of Intellectuals in Modern Society," in P. K. Lawrence and M. Doebler, eds., *Knowledge and Power: The Changing Role of European Intellectuals* (Aldershot, U.K.: Avebury, 1996).

4. M. Weber, "Politics as a Vocation" and "Science as a Vocation," in H. H. Gerth and C. W. Mills, eds. and trans., *From Max Weber: Essays in Sociology* (New York: Oxford University Press, 1946, c 1922); and K. Mannheim, *Ideology and Utopia*, trans. L. Wirth (London: Kegan Paul, 1946, c 1926).

5. B. Stora, *Aide-Memoire de l'immigration Algerienne: 1922–1962,* (Paris: L'Harmattan, 1992); K. Bade, *Auswanderer-Wanderarbeiter-Gastarbeiter: Bevölkerung, Arbeitsmarkt und Wanderung in Deutschland seit der Mitte des 19. Jahrhunderts,* 2 vols. (Ostfildern: Scripta Mercaturae, 1984); P. Weil, *La France et ses etrangers. L'aventure d'une politique de l'immigration: 1938–1991* (Paris: Calmann-Levy, 1991); R. Brubaker, *Citizenship and Nationhood in France and Germany* (Cambridge, Mass.: Harvard University Press, 1992); L. Cavalli-Sforza, P. Menozzi, and A. Piazza, *The History and Geography of Human Genes* (Princeton, N.J.: Princeton University Press, 1994); and M. Bacci, *The Population of Europe: A History*, trans. C. de Nardi-Ipsen and C. Ipsen (Malden, Mass.: Blackwell, 1999).

6. M. Chatterji, H. Jager, and A. Rima, eds., *The Economics of International Security: Essays in Honour of Jan Tinbergen* (New York: St. Martin's, 1994). West Germany (1.4 billion) thus received less than Italy (1.5 billion), half as much as France (2.7 billion), which in turn fell almost half a billion short of Britain (3.2 billion).

7. S. Castles and M. Miller, *The Age of Migration: International Population Movements in the Modern World* (New York: Guilford Press, 1993).

8. J. Hollifield, *Immigrants, Markets, and States: The Political Economy of Postwar Europe* (Cambridge, Mass.: Harvard University Press, 1992).

9. For an introduction to the history of immigration into France over the last few hundred years, see R. Brubaker, *Citizenship and Nationhood in France and Germany* (Cambridge, Mass.: Harvard University Press, 1992); and G. Noiriel, *The French Melting Pot: Immigration, Citzenship, and National Identity,* trans. G. de Laforcade (Minneapolis: University of Minnesota Press, 1996).

10. G. Steinmann and R. Ulrich, eds., *The Economic Consequences of Immigration to Germany* (Heidelberg, Ger.: Physica-Verlag, 1994); and K. Zimmermann, ed., *The Economics of Migration* (Aldershot, U.K.: Edward Edgar, 1998). For a general introduction into the patterns of migration and labor markets, see the Organisation for Economic Cooperation and Development, *Trends in International Migration: SOPEMI 1999 Edition,* 1999, http: www.oecd.org els migration pubs.htm

11. The literature on the migrant experience in Europe follows the evolutionary pattern of "minority" literatures. The first stage consists of literary expressions, such as poetry, plays, and novels. In the second stage, "organic intellectuals" emerge to seize the terms and content of social-science literature and critical studies from the point of view of immigrants, mostly severely critiquing the marginalization of the minorities. This second stage may be called the "victimology" stage of minority studies. In the third stage, "organic intellectuals" offer more differentiated views of the immigrants. T. Ben Jelloun's *La fiancee de l'eau; suivi de, Entretien avec Monsieur Said Hammadi, ouvrier algerien* (Actes Sud Theatre populaire de Lorraine, 1984) is a good example of the first stage. For France, see W. Woodhull, *Transfigurations of the Maghreb: Feminism, Decolonization, and Literatures* (Minneapolis: University of Minnesota Press, 1993). For Italy, see P. Verdicchio, *Bound by Distance: Rethinking Nationalism through the Italian Diaspora* (Madison, N.J.: Fairleigh Dickinson University Press, 1997). For Germany, see A. Seyhan, *Writing Outside the Nation* (Princeton, N.J.: Princeton University Press, 2001). For the third stage, see the work of T. Modood: in particular, T. Modood and P. Werbner, eds., *Debating Cultural Hybridity: Multi-cultural Identities and the Politics of Anti-racism* (Atlantic Highlands, N.J.: Zed Books, 1997) and *The Politics of Multiculturalism in the New Europe: Racism, Identity, and Community* (London: Zed Books, 1997). For social-science studies by nonimmigrants, which mostly evolved in the 1990s, see K. Bade and M. Weiner, *Migration Past, Migration Future: Germany and the United States* (Providence, R.I.: Berghahn Books, 1997); K. Bade, *Migration, Ethnizitat, Konflikt* (Osnabruck: Universitatsverlag Rasch, 1996); A. Hargreaves, *Immigration, "Race," and Ethnicity in Contemporary France* (London: Routledge, 1995); M. Ghirelli, *Immigrati Brava*

*Gente: La societa italiana tra razzismo e accoglienza* (Milan: Spelling and Kupfer, 1993); V. Bolognari and C. Sirna, eds., *Razzismo e Frantumazione Etnica: Politche sociali e interventi educativi: Atti del Convegno tenuto a Messina nei giorni 25–27 marzo 1993* (Rome: Herder, 1993); G. Benton and F. Pieke, eds., *The Chinese in Europe* (New York: St. Martin's, 1998); *Tackling Racism and Xenophobia: Practical Action at the Local Level* (Strasbourg: Publishing and Documentation Service, Council of Europe, 1995); G. Ford, *Report Drawn up on Behalf of the Committee of Inquiry into Racism and Xenophobia on the Findings of the Committee of Inquiry* (Luxembourg: Office for Official Publications of the European Communities, 1991); R. King, ed., *Mass Migrations in Europe: The Legacy and the Future* (London: Belhaven, 1993); U. Knight and W. Kowalsky, *Deutschland nur den Deutschen? die Auslanderfrage in Deutscheland, Frankreich und der U.S.A.* (Erlangen: Straube, 1991); M. Read and A. Simpson, *Against a Rising Tide: Racism, Europe and 1992* (Nottingham, U.K.: Spokesman for Nottingham Racial Equality Council and European Labour Forum, 1991); and D. Schnapper, *L'Europe des immigres: Essai sur les politiques d'immigration* (Paris: Editions Francois Bourin, 1992).

12. For a powerful historical description of immigrant experience in the United States see R. Takaki, *A Different Mirror: A History of Multicultural America* (Boston: Little Brown and Company, 1993).

13. R. Hedwig, "Die Dynamik der Einwanderung im Nichteinwanderungsland Deutschland," in H. Fassmann and R. Muenz, eds., *Migration in Europa: Historische Entwicklung, aktuelle Trends, politische Reaktionen* (Frankfurt: Campus, 1996).

14. Immigration law in Australia restricted the reception of Asian immigrants. In the United States, immigration categories define newcomers in ethnic terms. Irish and Italians, for instance, used to be defined as black people. See T. Allen, *The Invention of the White Race: Racial Oppression and Social Control* (London: Verso, 1994). And in Brazil, which consists of many variants of ethnic groups, including many groups of African origin—and therefore, of black people—the intellectual and political elite consists mostly of people of white origin.

15. G. Shafir, ed., *The Citizenship Debates: A Reader* (Minneapolis: University of Minnesota Press, 1998).

16. Leading North American intellectuals such as Charles Taylor in Canada and Michael Walzer in the United States have helped frame these debates. Frantz Fanon's pioneering work on the moral dimensions of the symbolic colonization of the unconscious with respect to race has been an important point of reference among race theorists. Feminist research on gender-based distribution of power and domination has also begun to touch upon the central role of the unconscious in the reproduction of inequalities and discrimination. The group of feminist philosophers called "Diotima" of the University of Verona, Italy, produced, under the impact of the work of Luce Irigaray, important insights in this respect in the 1980s. I think, however, that only collaborative research efforts among the groups most affected by racism and sexism will be able to advance this project in significant ways. This will have to include analysts and researchers from the so-called underdeveloped and developing world.

17. *Report on Racism and Xenophobia in Europe* (Brussels: European Commission, Directorate General V, 1997).

18. *Report on Racism and Xenophobia in Europe*, 1.

19. *Report on Racism and Xenophobia in Europe*, 7.

20. *Report on Racism and Xenophobia in Europe*, 7.

21. *Report on Racism and Xenophobia in Europe*, 7.

22. *Report on Racism and Xenophobia in Europe*, 7.

23. *Tackling Racism and Xenophobia: Practical Action at the Local Level* (Strasbourg: Council of Europe, 1995); and D. Dadsi, *Specificities and Universality: Problems of Identities: Report of the Seminar Held in Klingenthal (France), 23–25, June 1994* (Strasbourg: Council of Europe, 1995).

24. Castles and Miller, *The Age of Migration*.

25. S. Virdee, *Racial Violence and Harassment* (London: Policy Studies Institute, 1995); and R. Witte, *Racist Violence and the State: A Comparative Analysis of Britain, France and the Netherlands* (London: Longman, 1996).

26. V. Bolognari and C. Sirna, eds., *Razzismo e Frantumazione Etnica: Politche sociali e interventi educativi: Atti del Convegno tenuto a Messina nei giorni 25–27 marzo 1993* (Rome: Herder, 1995).

27. J. Nielson, *Towards a European Islam* (New York: St. Martin's, 1999); S. Vertovec and C. Peach, eds., *Islam In Europe: The Politics of Religion and Community* (New York: St. Martin's, 1997); G. Nonneman, T. Niblock, and B. Szajkowski, eds., *Muslim Communities in the New Europe* (Berkshire, U.K.: Ithaca Press, 1996); T. Gerholm and Y. Lithman, eds., *The New Islamic Presence in Western Europe* (New York: Mansell Publishing, 1988).

28. OECD, *Trends in International Migration*.

29. J. Rex, D. Joly, and C. Wilpert, eds., *Immigrant Associations in Europe* (Aldershot, U.K.: Gower, 1987); K. Liebkind, ed., *New Identities in Europe: Immigrant Ancestry and the Ethnic Identity of Youth* (Aldershot, U.K.: Gower, 1989); S. Castles, H. Booth, and T. Wallace, *Here for Good: Western Europe's New Ethnic Minorities* (London: Pluto Press, 1984); and R. Barot, ed., *Religion and Ethnicity: Minorities and Social Change in the Metropolis* (Kampen, the Netherlands: Kok Pharos Publishing, 1993).

30. B. Metcalf, ed., *Making Muslim Space in North America and Europe* (Berkeley: University of California Press, 1996).

31. Michel Laguerre has engaged in research on minoritized space and time, but not in Europe. See his *Minoritized Space: An Inquiry into the Spatial Order of Things* (Berkeley: University of California Press, 1999). Postcolonial explorations of space, particularly as they pertain to Third World cinema, have also begun to examine the realm of the symbolic for counterhegemonic purposes.

32. The most vicious attacks occurred on November 23, 1993, when three residents of Turkish descent were burned to death in a Nazi firebombing in Moelln in northern Germany. A few months later, ten people, including five children, died in a fire at a residence for Asian and African immigrants in the north German city of Lubeck.

33. A. Giddens, *Power, Property and the State: A Contemporary Critique of Historical Materialism* (Berkeley: University of California Press, 1981); A. Touraine, M. Wieviorka, F. Dubet, *The*

*Worker's Movement*, trans. I. Patterson (New York: Cambridge University Press, 1987); and J. Habermas, *Zur Rekonstruktion des Historischen Materialismus* (Frankfurt: Suhrkamp, 1976).

34. N. Bobbio, *Liberalismo e Democrazia* (Milan: F. Angeli, 1986); A. Touraine, *Critique de la Modernite* (Paris: Faynard, 1992); A. Giddens, *The Constitution of Society: Outline of the Theory of Structuration* (Berkeley: University of California Press, 1984); J. Habermas, *Der Philosophische Diskurs der Moderne,* 2 vols. (Frankfurt: Suhrkamp, 1985); and G. Vattimo, *The End of Modernity: Nihilism and Hermeneutics in Postmodern Culture* (Baltimore, Md.: Johns Hopkins University Press, 1988).

35. N. Bobbio, *Destra e sinistra: ragioni e significati di una distinzione politica* (Rome: Donzelli, 1994); and A. Giddens, *Beyond Left and Right: The Future of Radical Politics* (Stanford, Calif: Stanford University Press, 1994).

36. For Habermas, see his theory of communicative action in *Justification and Application: Remarks on Discourse Ethics* (Cambridge, Mass.: MIT Press, 1993); and for Touraine's theory about the return of the actor, see *Return of the Actor: An Essay in Sociology* (Minneapolis: University of Minnesota Press, 1988).

37. N. Bobbio, *The Age of Rights* (Oxford: Polity Press, 1996); and for Habermas, see an entire series of works on Germany, such as *A Berlin Republic: Writings on Germany* (Lincoln: University of Nebraska Press, 1997).

38. On the other hand, it was in the United Kingdom that the first important journals on race and migration emerged. The first publication of the *The Journal of the Institute of Race Relations* dates back to 1958—changing its name to *Race and Class* in October of 1974. The journal *Immigrants and Minorities* began its publications in March of 1982.

39. Kavita Ann of the University of California, Berkeley, assisted me in the compilation of this data for France.

40. Philip Smith of the University of California, Berkeley, assisted me in the compilation of this data on Britain.

41. R. Holub, "Italian Cultures: 1950–2000," in *Cambridge History of Literary Criticism* 9 (Cambridge, U.K.: Cambridge University Press, 2000).

42. D. Smith and S. Wright, eds., *Whose Europe?: The Turn Towards Democracy* (Boston: Blackwell, 2000); F. Anthias and N. Yuval-Davis, eds., *Racialized Boundaries: Race, Nation, Gender, Colour and Class and the Anti-Racist Struggle* (New York: Routledge, 1992); M. Guibernau and J. Rex, eds., *The Ethnicity Reader: Nationalism, Multiculturalism and Migration* (Cambridge: Polity Press, 1997); P. Gowan and P. Anderson, eds., *The Question of Europe* (London: Verso, 1997); and T. Ash, *In Europe's Name: Germany and the Divided Continent* (Random House: New York, 1993).

43. I cite here selectively, though the high "national" status of the publishing houses involved is interesting. E. Gellner, *Conditions of Liberty: Civil Society and Its Rivals* (New York: Allen Lane Penguin Press, 1994); H. G. Gadamer, *Das Erbe Europas: Beitrage* (Frankfurt: Suhrkamp, 1989); P. Ricoeur, *Soi-meme comme un autre* (Paris: Seuil, 1990); and E. Morin, *Penser l'Europe* (Paris: Gallimard, 1987).

44. While some of the "organic intellectuals" directly address "religious otherness" in their work, many of them do so more indirectly. However, they all participate in the proj-

ect of enlightening a European public on aspects of "religious otherness." See M. S. Abdullah, *Was will der Islam in Deutschland* (Guetersloh: G. Mohn, 1993); M. Arkoun, *Rethinking Islam: Common Questions, Uncommon Answers*, trans. R. Lee (Boulder, Colo.: Westview, 1994); A. Hourani, *Islam in European Thought* (Cambridge, U.K.: Cambridge University Press, 1991); B. Tibi, *The Challenge of Fundamentalism: Political Islam and the New World Disorder* (Berkeley: University of California Press, 1998); S. K. Jayyusi, ed., *The Legacy of Muslim Spain*, 2 vols. (New York: E. J. Brill, 1994); and T. Modood, ed. *Church, State, and Religious Minorities* (London: Policy Studies Institute, 1997).

45. N. Bilbeny, *Europa despues de Sarajevo: Claves eticas y politicas de la Ciudadania Europea* (Barcelona: Destino, 1996). I would like to thank N. Bilbeny here for many enlightening discussions.

46. Recently, the European Court of Justice has overturned cases against immigrants which had been tried under national legislation. For press releases, annual reports, and reports of proceedings in the period of 1996–2000, see http: www.curia, eu.int enpei index.htm. I am indebted to Christine R. Guluzian of the University of California, Berkeley, for providing me with information on the most important decision of the European Court of Justice.

47. Giambattista Vico's *Scienza nuova* (1644), a major text in the area of constitutional history, found, as a Catholic intellectual in a Europe before the French Revolution, the links between the Roman state and religion quite appealing.

48. M. H. Beg, *Impact of Secularism on Life and Law: The Third Motilal Nehru Memorial Lectures* (New Delhi, India: People's Publishing House, 1985).

49. J. Habermas, *Die Einbeziehung des anderen Studien zur politischen Theorie* (Frankfurt: Suhrkamp, 1996); and A. Touraine, *Pourrons-nous vivre ensemble? Egaux et Differents* (Paris: Fayard, 1997).

50. I am thinking of Tariq Modood's and Bassam Tibi's work. Both authors are included in this volume.

51. C. Taylor, "Multiculturalism and 'The Politics of Recognition': An essay," in A. Guttmann, ed., *Multiculturalism and the Politics of Recognition* (Princeton, N.J.: Princeton University Press, 1992).

52. D. Schnapper, *La France de l'integration: Sociologie de la nation en 1990* (Paris: Gallimard, 1991).

53. A. Touraine, *Pourrons-nous vivre ensemble? Egaux et Differents* (Paris: Fayard, 1997), 238.

54. Touraine, *Pourrons-nous vivre ensemble?* 266.

55. Touraine, *Pourrons-nous vivre ensemble?* 266.

56. Touraine, *Pourrons-nous vivre ensemble?* 266.

# SELECTED BIBLIOGRAPHY

AlSayyad, Nezar, ed. *Hybrid Urbanism: On the Identity Discourse and the Built Environment.* Westport, Conn.: Praeger, 2001.

Arkoun, Mohammed. *Rethinking Islam. Common Questions, Uncommon Answers.* Translated and edited by Robert D. Lee. Boulder, Colo.: Westview, 1994.

Barbieri, William A. *Ethics of Citizenship: Immigration and Group Rights in Germany.* Durham, N.C.: Duke University Press, 1998.

Castells, Manuel. *End of Millennium.* Malden, Mass.: Blackwell, 1998.

———. *The Power of Identity.* Oxford, U.K.: Blackwell, 1997.

———. *The Rise of the Network Society.* Oxford, U.K.: Blackwell, 1996.

Castles, Stephen, Heather Booth, and Tina Wallace. *Here for Good: Western Europe's New Ethnic Minorities.* London: Pluto Press, 1987.

Cesarani, David, and Mary Fulbrook, eds. *Citizenship, Nationality and Migration in Europe.* London: Routledge, 1996.

Cohen, Robin. *Frontiers of Identity: The British and the Others.* London: Longman, 1994.

Delanty, Gerard. *Inventing Europe: Idea, Identity, Reality.* London: Macmillan, 1995.

Favell, Adrian. *Philosophies of Integration: Immigration and the Idea of Citizenship in France and Britain.* London: Macmillan, 1998.

Goddard, Victoria A., Joseph R. Llobera, and Chris Shore, eds. *The Anthropology of Europe: Identity and Boundaries in Conflict.* Oxford, U.K.: Berg Publishers, 1994.

Gowan, Peter and Perry Anderson, eds. *The Question of Europe.* London: Verso, 1997.

Hadjimichalis, Costis and David Sadler, eds. *Europe at the Margins.* Chichester, U.K.: Wiley, 1995.

Hall, Stuart, David Held, and Tony McGrew, eds. *Modernity and Its Future.* Cambridge, U.K.: Polity Press, 1992.

Hobsbawm, Eric, and Terrence Ranger, eds. *The Invention of Tradition.* Cambridge, U.K.: Cambridge University Press, 1983.

Hourani, Albert. *Islam in European Thought.* Cambridge, U.K.: Cambridge University Press, 1991.

Ireland, Patrick R. *The Policy Challenge of Ethnic Diversity: Immigrant Politics in France and Switzerland.* Cambridge, Mass.: Harvard University Press, 1994.

Jacobson, David. *Rights Across Borders: Immigration and the Decline of Citizenship.* Baltimore, Md.: Johns Hopkins University Press, 1996.

Kepel, Gilles. *Allah in the West.* Stanford, Calif.: Stanford University Press, 1997.

Khosrokhavar, Farhad. *L'islam des jeunes.* Paris: Flammarion, 1997.

King, Russell, ed. *Mass Migrations in Europe: The Legacy and the Future.* London: Belhaven, 1993.

Lewis, Philip. *Islam in Britain: Religion, Politics, and Identity among British Muslims.* London: I. B. Tauris, 1994.

Liebkind, Karmela, ed. *New Identities in Europe: Immigrant Ancestry and the Ethnic Identity of Youth.* Aldershot, U.K.: Gower, 1989.

Metcalf, Barbara, ed. *Making Muslim Space in North America and Europe.* Berkeley: University of California Press, 1996.

Modood, Tariq, ed. *Church, State, and Religious Minorities.* London: Policy Studies Institute, 1997.

Modood, Tariq, and Pnina Werbner, eds. *The Politics of Multiculturalism in the New Europe: Racism, Identity and Community.* London: Zed Books, 1997.

Noiriel, Gérard. *The French Melting Pot: Immigration, Citizenship, and National Identity.* Translated by Geoffrey de Laforcade. Minneapolis: University of Minnesota Press, 1996.

Ohmae, Kenichi. *The Borderless World.* New York: Harpers, 1990.

Read, Melvyn, and Alan Simpson. *Against a Rising Tide: Racism, Europe and 1992.* Nottingham, U.K.: Spokesman for Nottingham Racial Equality Council and European Labour Forum, 1991.

Rex, John, Daniele Joly, and Czarina Wilpert, eds. *Immigrant Associations in Europe.* Aldershot, U.K.: Gower, 1987.

Salins, Peter D. *Assimilation American Style.* New York: Basic, 1997.

Schnapper, Dominique. *L'Europe des immigres: Essai sur les politiques d'immigration.* Paris: Editions Francois Bourin, 1992.

Seyhan, Azade. *Writing Outside the Nation.* Princeton, N.J.: Princeton University Press, 2001.

Shadid, W. A. R., and P. S. Van Koningsveld, eds. *Muslims in the Margin: Political Responses to the Presence of Islam in Western Europe.* Kampen, the Netherlands: Kok Pharos Publishing House, 1996.

———. eds. *Political Participation and Identities of Muslims in Non-Muslim States.* Kampen, the Netherlands: Kok Pharos Publishing House, 1997.

Smith, Anthony D. *Nations and Nationalism in a Global Era.* Cambridge, U.K.: Polity Press, 1995.

Sorensen, Jens Magleby. *The Exclusive European Citizenship: The Case for Refugees and Immigrants in the European Union.* Avebury-Ashgate, U.K.: Aldershot, 1996.

Soysal, Yaseman Nuhoglu. *The Limits of Citizenship: Migrants and Postnational Membership in Europe.* Chicago: University of Chicago Press, 1994.

Tibi, Bassam. *The Challenge of Fundamentalism: Political Islam and the New World Disorder.* Berkeley: University of California Press, 1998.

Touraine, Alain. *Critique de la modernité.* Paris: Fayard, 1992.

Turner, Bryan S. *Orientalism, Postmodernism and Globalism.* London: Routledge, 1994.

Wieviorka, Michel. *Racisme et xénophobie en Europe.* Paris: La Découverte, 1994.

# INDEX

75, 79, 80, 85, 88, 95, 97, 135, 152, 153,
156, 161, 177; intellectuals, 25; labor,
34; leaders, 12; migrants migration,
19, 20, 32, 33, 35, 36, 37, 38, 39, 41, 45,
46, 47, 48, 85, 87, 132, 133; minority, 1,
45; population, 2, 84, 148, 152, 157;
scholar, 18, 31; secular, 10, 13, 19, 23,
24, 37, 46, 47, 48, 78, 100, 102, 106,
122, 126, 177; societies, 12, 22, 78, 92,
100, 102, 103, 105; women, 11
Muslim Brotherhood, 78, 104
Mustafa, Hala, 22, 23

Nagel, Tilman, 19, 38, 50n27
nation-state, 20, 21, 54, 55, 58, 59, 61, 62,
63, 65, 69, 71, 73, 74, 75, 76, 81, 85, 87,
88, 117, 155, 178, 179, 180, 184
nationalism nationalist, 3, 15, 21, 24, 53, 58,
62, 63, 65, 69, 72, 73, 75, 76, 79, 87,
101, 102, 103, 115, 116, 118, 119, 120,
126, 135, 140, 142, 144, 149
native, 2, 33, 36, 63, 143, 154
NATO, 2, 73, 82
Nazism, 179, 180, 184
neoliberalism, 70
network, 4, 21, 22, 39, 58, 69, 70, 72, 75, 76,
77, 78, 79, 80, 81, 84, 85, 86, 87, 132
Nietzsche, 117
Non-Aligned Movement (NAM), 94
non-Muslims, 11, 13, 45, 77, 148, 164
noncommunitarian, 186
nonwhite, 25, 79, 85, 115, 118, 119, 120, 127,
129n16, 151, 152

oppressed, 93, 119, 121
oppression, 13, 102, 103, 120, 121
Orientalist, 5, 19, 38
Orientalizing, 15, 16
Orientals, 15
orthodox, 42, 47, 56, 117
other others, vii, 20, 28, 54, 57, 120, 179,
181, 182, 183, 184, 185
Ottomans, 78, 104

Pakistan Pakistani, 12, 24, 33, 37, 54, 63, 113,
114, 119, 120, 122, 123, 153, 158, 160
Palestine Palestinians, 23, 93, 98, 99, 103,
105, 106, 121
pan-Arabism, 92
Pipes, Daniel, 158, 159
postcolonial, 19, 23, 92, 190n31

postcolonialism, 15
postindustrial, 10, 63, 86, 92, 136, 147
postnational, 20, 59, 60, 61, 62, 65, 81, 87,
88
prejudice 42, 59, 127, 159
Prophet Mohammed, 77

Qur'an, 43, 156

race, 20, 24, 25, 114, 115, 118, 123, 127, 140,
148, 149, 152, 173, 175, 189n16, 191n38
racial, 5, 18, 72, 80, 85, 86, 95, 113, 114, 115,
116, 120, 123, 126, 127, 129n28, 135,
139, 143, 152, 172, 173, 175
racism, 24, 31, 39, 41, 42, 97, 113, 118, 119,
123, 127, 136, 137, 139, 140, 141, 143,
144, 171, 173, 174, 175, 176, 179,
189n16
racist, 32, 127, 132, 134, 140, 141, 143, 144,
152, 174
Ramadan, 139, 153, 154, 157
refugees, 82, 113, 169, 171, 174, 179, 182
religion, 10, 11, 16, 20, 22, 23, 24, 25, 26, 34,
37, 43, 45, 47, 54, 55, 56, 57, 64, 75, 77,
85, 91, 92, 93, 103, 104, 107, 121, 122,
123, 124, 125, 126, 127, 131, 133, 134,
135, 136, 137, 139, 140, 142, 143, 151,
152, 153, 154, 155, 156, 157, 158, 159,
161, 163, 164, 167, 170, 174, 177, 181,
182, 186, 187, 192n47
representation, 84, 99, 117, 124, 126
residents, 19, 20, 33, 35, 36, 55, 62, 64, 73,
74, 79, 81, 84, 85, 87, 95, 144, 190n32
revolution, 3, 56, 70, 102, 134, 141, 154, 177,
192
Rex, John, 60
right-wing, 24, 26, 46, 73, 75, 95, 121, 126,
171, 179
Rushdie, Salman, 54, 60, 113, 114, 125, 126,
177
Russia, 54, 55

school, 3, 5, 12, 13, 14, 18, 53, 60, 83, 86, 122,
124, 125, 129n25, 138, 141, 157, 186
sectarian, 24, 33, 37, 78, 84, 102, 103, 136
secular, 10, 13, 18, 23, 24, 37, 46, 47, 48, 78,
80, 100, 102, 104, 106, 122, 126, 167,
177, 181
secularism, 10, 12, 19, 23, 24, 63, 93, 98,
107, 125, 129n33, 167, 168, 181, 187
Serbia, 22, 96, 97

Shadid, 83
sharia, 78
Sikh, 14, 54, 113, 114, 118, 122, 123
Smith, Anthony, 57, 136
social, 2, 3, 4, 5, 16, 17, 18, 19, 20, 21, 22, 23,
    25, 32, 33, 34, 36, 37, 39, 48, 56, 57, 60,
    61, 62, 63, 70, 71, 72, 73, 77, 81, 82, 83,
    84, 86, 91, 92, 95, 100, 101, 102, 103,
    104, 107, 114, 116, 117, 120, 124, 132,
    133, 134, 135, 136, 137, 138, 140, 142, 144,
    152, 153, 154, 156, 157, 160, 163, 167,
    168, 169, 170, 171, 172, 173, 174, 175,
    178, 179, 180, 183, 184, 185, 186, 187n1
Socialist, 3, 10, 13, 80, 102, 116, 172
South Asia South Asian, 18, 23, 24, 33, 36,
    80, 85, 113, 118, 121, 129n16, 148, 150
sovereignty, 1, 74, 76, 181
Soviet Union, 95, 99, 105, 158, 159
Soysal, Yasemin, 59, 60, 61, 64, 81, 88
space, 4, 15, 27, 28, 61, 69, 70, 76, 77, 82,
    117, 119, 120, 121, 127, 137, 142, 169,
    171, 173, 176, 177, 182, 187, 190n31
Spain, 1, 2, 3, 46, 54, 57, 58, 84, 170, 176, 183
synagogue, 158, 163

terrorism terrorist, 2, 24, 43, 132, 134, 136,
    142, 157, 159, 162
Third World, 6, 32, 91, 190n31
Tibi, Bassam, 19, 20, 25, 83
tolerance, 19, 22, 31, 32, 37, 38, 43, 44, 48,
    87, 97, 107
Touraine, Alain, 136, 137, 178, 182, 185, 186,
    187
tradition traditional, 5, 9, 10, 12, 13, 14, 16,
    18, 24, 25, 26, 27, 34, 41, 43, 44, 45, 56,
    57, 58, 59, 75, 80, 82, 85, 86, 91, 97,
    100, 101, 104, 107, 119, 126, 133, 134,
    135, 136, 152, 153, 159, 177, 181, 182
transnational, vii, 20, 21, 55, 58, 59, 61, 62,
    65, 70, 72, 76, 77, 78, 79, 81, 84, 85

Tunisia, 12, 54, 80, 92, 94, 103, 153, 154, 161,
    170
Turkey Turkish, 1, 2, 9, 10, 11, 13, 14, 15, 16,
    17, 34, 36, 37, 59, 60, 80, 82, 88, 93,
    94, 95, 98, 107, 153, 170, 176, 190n32
Turner, Bryan, 79, 104
twentieth century, 15, 17, 25, 61, 78, 79, 100,
    104, 148, 150, 155, 161, 168, 170, 171

umma, 21, 76, 78, 79, 121
unemployed unemployment, 12, 35, 63, 71,
    83, 95, 101, 134, 135, 140, 152, 171, 175,
    176
United Kingdom, 3, 9, 12, 33, 36, 95, 115,
    118, 123, 176, 191n38
United Nations (UN), 96, 97, 105
United States, 4, 5, 23, 25, 26, 49, 60, 61,
    62, 70, 71, 72, 93, 95, 96, 98, 99, 102,
    105, 106, 113, 114, 125, 144, 147, 148,
    150, 151, 152, 153, 154, 155, 156, 157,
    158, 159, 160, 161, 162, 163, 164, 168,
    170, 172, 173, 175, 176, 186, 189n16

van Koningsveld, 83
violence, 1, 2, 37, 75, 95, 97, 103, 133, 140,
    142, 143, 160, 175, 176

Wallace, William, 62
Weber, Max, 91, 168
welfare, 35, 59, 61, 62, 70, 72, 74, 81, 132
Wittgenstein, 117
World War II, 26, 33, 54, 149, 155, 157, 168,
    169, 171, 179, 180

xenophobia xenophobic, 19, 35, 38, 73, 75,
    82, 132, 134, 143, 144, 171, 174, 175,
    176, 179

Yugoslavia, 1, 75, 82, 96, 142, 170, 176

# CONTRIBUTORS

**NEZAR ALSAYYAD** is Professor of Architecture and Planning and Chair of the Center for Middle Eastern Studies at the University of California at Berkeley.

**MANUEL CASTELLS** is Professor of Sociology and City and Regional Planning and past Chair of the Center for Western European Studies at the University of California at Berkeley.

**RENATE HOLUB** is Adjunct Professor in the Interdisciplinary Studies and International and Area Studies Teaching Program at the University of California at Berkeley.

**KRISHAN KUMAR** is Professor of Sociology at the University of Virginia at Charlottesville.

**PAUL LUBECK** is Professor of Sociology at Merrill College of the University of California at Santa Cruz.

**LAURENCE MICHALAK** is Vice Chair of the Center for Middle Eastern Studies and Lecturer at the University of California at Berkeley.

**TARIQ MODOOD** is Professor of Sociology, Politics, and Public Policy at the University of Bristol, U.K.

**HALA MUSTAFA** is Director of Research at the Center for Political and Strategic Studies of the Al Ahram Foundation in Cairo, Egypt.

**AGHA SAEED** is Lecturer in Speech Communications at California State University at Hayward.

**BASSAM TIBI** is the Georgia Augusta Professor of International Relations at the University of Göttingen, Germany.

**MICHEL WIEVIORKA** is Directeur d'Etudes, Centre d'Analyse et d'Intervention Sociologiques of the Ecoles des Hautes Etudes en Sciences Sociales in Paris, France.